O Infante Dom Henrique (Prince Henry "The Navigator")

"The noble spirit of this Prince was ever urging him both to begin and to carry out great deeds. . . . He had also a wish to know the land that lay beyond the Isles of Canary and that Cape called Bojador, for that up to his time, neither by writings, nor by the memory of man, was known with any certainty the nature of the land beyond that Cape . . . . It seemed to him that if he or some other lord did not endeavor to gain that knowledge, no mariners or merchants would ever dare to attempt it, for it is clear that none of them ever trouble themselves to sail to a place where there is not a sure and certain hope of profit."

From *Crónica do descobrimento e conquista da Guiné*
by Gomes Eanes de Zurara
Bibliothèque Nationale, Paris (Item 30).

PORTUGAL BRAZIL

The Age of Atlantic Discoveries

Essays by
Luís de Albuquerque
Charles R. Boxer
Francisco Leite de Faria
Max Justo Guedes
Francis M. Rogers
Wilcomb E. Washburn

A Note to the Reader
from
Fernando Collor, President of Brazil
and
Mario Soares, President of Portugal

Forewords by
Iza Chateaubriand Sessler
Timothy S. Healy

Editors
Max Justo Guedes
Gerald Lombardi

Bertrand Editora
Franco Maria Ricci
Brazilian Cultural Foundation

This book accompanies the exhibition
Portugal-Brazil: the Age of Atlantic Discoveries.

The New York Public Library
June 2 – September 1, 1990

and a poster exhibition to be circulated throughout the Americas with the cooperation
of the Organization of American States, the Federation of State Humanities Councils,
and the National Association of the Partners of the Americas, Inc.

Project Director
Iza Chateaubriand Sessler

Project Administrator
Gerald Lombardi

Project Assistance
Rosanna Hirsch, David Wirtz

Registrar
Albina De Meio

Chief Curators:

Brazil: Max Justo Guedes
Portugal: António Estácio dos Reis
United States: Wilcomb E. Washburn
with the assistance of Francisco Contente Domingues

The Brazilian Cultural Foundation expresses its gratitude for the generous
assistance and cooperation of

José Sarney, *former President of Brazil*
Roberto Abreu Sodré, *former Minister of External Relations of Brazil*
Admiral Henrique Sabóia, *former Minister of the Navy of Brazil*
Eurico de Melo, *former Minister of Defence of Portugal*
Maria Teresa Gouveia, *former Secretary of State for Culture of Portugal*
Admiral António de Sousa Leitão, *former Chief of Naval Operations of Portugal*
Eduardo Henrique Serra Brandão, *former Commissioner-General*
for the Commemoration of Portuguese Discoveries
Claiborne Pell, *United States Senator, Rhode Island;*
Chair, Subcommittee on Education, Arts & Humanities
Angier Biddle Duke, *Chancellor, Southampton College*
Vartan Gregorian, *former President, The New York Public Library*
Diantha Schull, *former Director of Exhibitions, The New York Public Library*

Catalogue
Design: Franco Maria Ricci, Laura Casalis
Editors: Silvia Fois, Karen Lenardi, Ruth Sullivan
Translations: Richard Crum, Gerald Lombardi, Francis M. Rogers
Chronology and bibliography: Francisco Contente Domingues
Colour Separations: Fotoincisioni Bassoli, *Milan*
Printed in Italy in April 1990 by Arti Grafiche Federico Motta, *Arese*

© 1990
Bertrand Editora, Rua Anchieta 29, Lisbon
Franco Maria Ricci, Via Montecuccoli 32, Milan
The Brazilian Cultural Foundation, 100 Park Avenue, New York

ISBN 972-25-0504-1

Table of Contents

Honorary Commissions

National Curatorial Commission

BRAZIL

President
Roberto Luiz Assumpção de Araújo
former Ambassador in New Delhi

Chief Curator
Max Justo Guedes
*Director, General Documentation Service;
Director, Naval and Oceanographic
Museum, Brazilian Navy, Rio de Janeiro*

Isa Adonias
*former Director, Map Room of the
Ministry of External Relations,
Palácio Itamaraty, Rio de Janeiro*

Lygia da Fonseca Fernandes da Cunha
*Chief of the Special Reference Division,
Biblioteca Nacional, Rio de Janeiro*

**Celina do Amaral Peixoto Moreira
Franco**
*Director, National Archives, Rio de
Janeiro*

João Marino
São Paulo

José Antônio Gonsalves de Mello Neto
*President, Archeological, Historical, and
Geographical Institute of Pernambuco*

José Mindlin
São Paulo

Lauro Barbosa da Silva Moreira
*former Cultural Attaché, Brazilian
Embassy, Washington D.C.*

António Luiz Porto e Albuquerque
*former Deputy Director, National
Historical Museum, Rio de Janeiro*

PORTUGAL

President
Ruy de Brito e Cunha
*former Ambassador in Islamabad;
Commission for the Commemoration
of Portuguese Discoveries*

Chief Curator
António Estácio dos Reis,
*Navy Central Library; Commission for
the Commemoration of Portuguese
Discoveries*

Luís de Albuquerque
*Professor of Mathematics Emeritus,
University of Coimbra;
President of the Scientific Council of the
Commission for the Commemoration
of Portuguese Discoveries*

Francisco Leite de Faria
Portuguese Academy of History

Inácio Guerreiro
*Deputy Director, National Archives of
Torre do Tombo, Lisbon*

Maria Helena Mendes Pinto
National Museum of Ancient Art, Lisbon

João Gonçalves
National Library, Lisbon

Lourdes Simões de Carvalho
*International Relations, Secretariat of
State for Culture*

UNITED STATES

President
Sérgio Corrêa da Costa
*former Ambassador of Brazil in
Washington; Professor of History,
University of South Carolina;
Member, Brazilian Academy of Letters*

Chief Curator
Wilcomb E. Washburn
*Director, Office of American Studies,
Smithsonian Institution, Washington DC*

Charles R. Boxer
*Professor of Portuguese Emeritus,
University of London*

Charles T. Cullen
*President and Chief Librarian, The
Newberry Library, Chicago*

Norman Fiering
*Director, The John Carter Brown
Library at Brown University,
Providence RI*

Richard Kugler
*Senior Curator, Old Dartmouth
Historical Society, New Bedford MA*

Kenneth Maxwell
*Director, The Camões Center, Research
Institute on International Change,
Columbia University in the City of New
York*

Francis M. Rogers *(d. 1989)*
*Nancy Clark Smith Professor of the
Language and Literature of Portugal
Emeritus, Harvard University*

Carleton Sprague Smith
*Professor of History Emeritus, New York
University*

Carol Urness
*Head Librarian, James Ford Bell
Library, University of Minnesota;
President, Society for the History of
The Discoveries*

Maria Luisa Lopez-Vidriero
*Director, Special Reference Division,
Biblioteca Nacional, Madrid*

Douglas Wheeler
*Department of History, University of
New Hampshire; Co-Founder and Chair,
International Conference Group on
Portugal*

The Brazilian Cultural Foundation, Inc.

Sponsors

Major support for this project has been provided by

The National Endowment for the Humanities
Washington, D.C., a federal agency

and by an indemnity from
The Federal Council on the Arts and Humanities

and by
Comissão Nacional para as Comemorações dos Descobrimentos Portugueses

Fundação Calouste Gulbenkian

Fundação Luso-Americana para o Desenvolvimento

Fundação Oriente

Ministry of External Relations, Consulate General of Brazil in New York

VITAE – Apoio à Cultura, Educação e Promoção Social

Support for this project was also provided by the following institutions and individuals:

American Portuguese Society
Francisco Norton de Matos

Banco Real
Humberto Carvalho

Banco Português do Atlântico
Alfonso Finocchiario

Banco Econômico
José Roberto David de Azevedo

Banco Itaú
Luiz Aurélio Serra

Banco do Brasil
Joaquim Ferreira Amaro

Bertrand Editora, Ltda.
Antero Braga

British Airways

Citibank
David H. Barnes

Companhia de Seguros Bonança

Coopers & Lybrand
Frederick Heerde

Eluma North America
Luiz Eduardo Campello

IBM Corporation
Robeli Libero

Iberia Airlines of Spain

Jean Manzon Produções Cinematográficas Ltda.
Jean Manzon

Latin American Marketing Ltd.
Albert Bildner

Manhattan Equities
Cid V. Keller

Morgan Guaranty Trust Company of New York
Gonzalo de las Heras

Oppenheimer Wolff & Donnelly
W. Hubert Plummer

Petróleo Brasileiro – Petrobrás
Gerson Nogueira Braune

Philip Morris International
Marc S. Goldberg

Pinheiro Neto – Advogados

Quantum Chemical Corporation
John Salisbury

Republic National Bank
Ness Pinto

Rio Doce America
Vitor Hallack

Soeicom, S.A.
Luiz Champalimaud

TAP-Transportes Aéreos Portugueses

VARIG Brazilian Airlines

XEROX Corporation
David Myerscough

Manuel Boullosa

Alma Braun

António Champalimaud

Joseph Cullman 3rd

Iza Chateaubriand Sessler

A Note to the Reader

from
Fernando Collor, President of Brazil

It is with great pleasure that I, in the prestigious company of His Excellency Mario Soares, President of the Republic of Portugal, have accepted the Brazilian Cultural Foundation's invitation to contribute with some opening words for the catalogue of the exhibition, Portugal-Brazil: The Age of Atlantic Discoveries.

This initiative, taken by close friends of Brazil and Portugal, has generated much interest in my country, and I am sure that it will achieve the highest success in its task of acquainting the North American public with an important aspect of Brazilian history.

Brazil's nationhood begins with the very discovery of our land by Portuguese navigators and their determined efforts to settle the land, mixing their blood and their culture with those of the indigenous peoples they encountered and, soon afterward, incorporating other ethnic groups into the harmonious blend that constitutes the Brazil of today.

This exhibition has the merit of anticipating by ten years the opening event of the quincentennial celebration of the epic of the discovery of Brazil.

This dramatic moment was marked by three essential characteristics: the audacity of the venture; the utilization of the most advanced technology of the day; and the sense of freedom of those who not only dared to search for new lands, but also created the means to do so, and eventually discovered more, perhaps, than they had imagined in their dreams of adventure.

As we invoke the memory of the navigators, we give special emphasis to such characteristics. We believe these qualities were present throughout the evolution of Brazil, and that today more than ever they must continue to guide us in the construction of our future as a country, and as a member of the international community.

The navigators set out in search of the new and the unknown. Brazil today, with great effort and sacrifice, seeks full development, and widespread access to the benefits of progress. We therefore know what we wont to achieve, we are aware of the difficulties and obstacles along our path, and we shall attain our goals in the same spirit with which our Portuguese ancestors defied the immensity of the Atlantic.

Above all, the celebration of the Portuguese discoveries is a tribute to universal understanding among men, to the greater understanding among peoples who, until then, had lived far apart.

For Brazil and Portugal, it is a time to celebrate five hundred years of fraternal unity, which constitute a basis for the achievement, in the twenty-first century, of the visions of those who discovered the New World.

A Note to the Reader

from
Mario Soares, President of Portugal

We are commemorating the quincentenary of an extraordinary adventure which radically transformed the world and human destiny, and, it could be argued, laid the foundation of our modern culture and world-view. This amazing undertaking was conceived, planned and realized by our ancestors.

The Portuguese discoveries are not only the most important event in Portuguese history, but also highly significant for having launched the modern era in world history. It is a rare occurrence indeed when the free will of a people redirects a nation's history along new paths, thereby redirecting the history of humankind.

The modern, democratic, European and generous Portugal, to which we aspire, arises from the experience of the discoveries. In peace and in freedom, Portugal rises to the pressing challenges of scientific and technical innovation, reform of society and the State, modernization of economic and social life and cultural renewal. We place trust in the spirit of inquiry, in liberty, in our youth and in the intelligence of our people. We know that democracy is the way of the future, and that there is no other course.

With the decline of the age of imperialism, Portugal found its place as a full member of the European Community. But the country also knows that the sea is one of its most profound raisons d'être, that the sea unifies and does not divide, that by forging fraternal bonds with people across the seas the Portuguese fulfill a perennial calling. The new Portugal therefore takes its place in Europe as a nation whose historical destiny was to show Europe the way across the sea.

As the millennium draws to a close we celebrate with legitimate pride, but without clinging to the past, the Great Portuguese Discoveries: Bartolomeu Dias and the rounding of the Cape of Good Hope (1487-1488); Vasco da Gama and the discovery of the maritime route to India (1498); and Pedro Álvares Cabral and the discovery of Brazil (1500). We commemorate this extraordinary human endeavour in the same enterprising and universal spirit that gave it incentive and inspiration.

We face the future as members of humanity in these momentous times of space travel and new scientific and technological discoveries which, we hope, will bring renewed happiness to all humankind. We join with the Portuguese communities worldwide, in Brazil and the African nations where the most wonderful seed of the discoveries – the language of Camões, Machado de Assis, and Pessoa – is flourishing, and with all countries that recognize and honour the Portuguese presence in all corners of the globe, in making the final years of the century an occasion for paying an eloquent and living tribute to our humanist, free and fraternal tradition as Portuguese.

Preface
by
Iza Chateaubriand Sessler

With this book, published in conjunction with the exhibition Portugal-Brazil: The Age of Atlantic Discoveries, *world-renowned twentieth century Luso-Brazilian scholars pay homage to the spirit of adventure that, in the fifteenth century, made the entire world known to itself for the first time. This project is the culmination of a five-year effort led by The Brazilian Cultural Foundation and realized through the cooperation of the Brazilian, Portuguese and the United States governments, many foundations, private organizations and corporations, as well as scholars and curators from leading libraries and museums in several countries.*

The mission of The Brazilian Cultural Foundation is to strengthen relationships between the people of Brazil and the United States, and to foster a better understanding of the heritage and culture of Brazil.
Portugal-Brazil: The Age of Atlantic Discoveries *is a dramatic fulfillment of that mission.*
The Foundation is proud that its efforts will help to acquaint the American people with crucial events in the histories of Brazil and Portugal.

Hundreds of people deserve to be thanked for making this work possible; on behalf of the Board of Directors of The Brazilian Cultural Foundation, I thank you all.
Together, we have produced a memorable tribute to the intellectual curiosity and feats of daring that led to the great sea-borne discoveries of five centuries ago.

Foreword

by
Timothy S. Healy
President, The New York Public Library

It is with great pleasure that the New York Public Library hosts the exhibition "Portugal-Brazil: The Age of Atlantic Discoveries" in the Gottesman Exhibition Hall of the Central Research Library.
The exhibition and its accompanying catalogue document the exploratory expeditions and settlement authorized by the government of Portugal in the fifteenth and sixteenth centuries, as well as the encounters between the peoples of South America and Europe. Reflecting the Library's central mission to be a resource for public education, open to all without restriction, the theme and the scope of this exhibition present an unusual opportunity for the Library to participate in increasing public knowledge about the contributions of both European and native American peoples in shaping the culture and heritage of the New World.
The breadth of the Library's collections renders it a most appropriate home to "Portugal-Brazil: The Age of Atlantic Discoveries." I am particularly proud that more than thirty items on display have been selected from the Library's collection of incunabula and sixteenth and seventeenth-century books.
As an international project, "Portugal-Brazil: The Age of Atlantic Discoveries" strongly relied on the cooperation of many scholars and institutions both in the Americas and in Europe. The Library wishes to join the sponsor, the Brazilian Cultural Foundation, in expressing its deep gratitude to these institutions for lending their treasures, most often viewed exclusively by the scholarly community, in order to share them with a broad audience.
Together with the Brazilian Cultural Foundation, the Library is grateful for the generous grant from the National Endowment for the Humanities, a federal agency, and the support of an indemnity from the Federal Council on the Arts and Humanities.
Many individuals and institutions were responsible for the development of this project. In particular, the Library wishes to thank Iza Chateaubriand Sessler, President of the Brazilian Cultural Foundation, for coordinating all aspects of the project.
The project was ably served by an international group of dedicated scholars and curators, who deserve the highest praise for their contributions, evident both in the exhibition and in the catalogue.
Finally, I wish to pay tribute to the staffs of the libraries and cultural institutions who have worked with the Brazilian Cultural Foundation to realize this exhibition. Their efforts will enable Americans to understand the multi-cultural legacy of the discoveries in the Americas and their impact on the world.

On the Origins of the Exhibition

by
Wilcomb E. Washburn

September 1986: Harvard University's 350th anniversary. At a dinner table in Quincy House I found myself seated next to Mr. Albert Bildner, a vice president of the Brazilian Cultural Foundation, Inc., of New York. Mr. Bildner asked me about scholars in the field of Portuguese and Brazilian history, particularly those concerned with the early history of Portuguese overseas expansion. In 1986 Americans had already begun to organize celebrations and commemorations of Columbus' epic voyage of 1492 and Spain's subsequent settlement of vast areas of what would become Latin America. But the role – even the existence – of the Portuguese during, and before, the same period was virtually ignored in these plans. I was delighted to supply Mr. Bildner with the names of several specialists. An exhibition was soon planned as the principal focus of the project. In a series of meetings in New York, Rio de Janeiro, and Lisbon, Curatorial Commissions were formed in each country made up of individuals who could most effectively bring the authority and scholarship of their countries to bear on the project. Support from the National Endowment for the Humanities was deemed a "must" in order to persuade private sources of the viability of the idea. Our application was successful, support came from other sources, and the Curatorial Commissions began to plan in detail the organization of the exhibit. Having found myself installed as Chief Curator of the American Commission, I prepared a draft outline of objects for the proposed exhibition. At each successive meeting, the draft outline was criticized and new suggestions made. When the list reached what seemed to be a near final product, representatives of each national Commission met in New York and pared down the list to what was believed to be the number of items that were vital to the exhibition, and the like. All such efforts were handled with skill by the staffs of the Brazilian Cultural Foundation and New York Public Library. The three-month exhibition at the New York Public Library was not the only thing that fell to the responsibility of the national Curatorial Commissions. All agreed that the exhibition should be supplemented by (and have an after-life through) a scholarly catalogue in book form and the creation of travelling exhibitions of photographic reproductions of many of the objects. It is our hope that this will help to promote in the United States knowledge of the history of Portugal, Brazil and the other Portuguese speaking countries that share the Atlantic basin with the descendants of Spanish, English and French explorers and settlers.

Portugal-Brazil:
the Age of Atlantic Discoveries

by Luís de Albuquerque
and
Max Justo Guedes

Between the beginning of the eleventh century and the end of the thirteenth, there occurred within Europe – or more accurately, within Christendom – a series of political, technological, cultural, social and economic transformations so overwhelming in their nature that they put an end to the Middle Ages and gave birth to the Renaissance and the Modern Age.

These transformations brought into being new practices and necessities unknown until then. They forcibly opened for Europe a network of long-distance commercial relationships, with subtropical Africa and especially with Asia. Along the routes that were opening up at that time, leading to Persia, to India and to farthest East Asia, the city of Alexandria and the ports of Syria and Byzantium gained special relevance as nearly-obligatory stopping-points.

It didn't take long for destabilizing elements to arise, taking shape as successive waves, not just in opposition to the pressure of European expansion, but equally expansionist themselves. While at first it was the Arabs in the seventh and eighth centuries, lastly – with enormous strength, came the Ottoman Turks.

If the Christian campaigns to open new pathways by force (i.e., the Crusades) enjoyed only partial and temporary success, having lost their momentum, it could be said that much more successful was the non-militaristic path of commercial activity, originating in the enormous dynamism of new urban concentrations forming in Italy, Flanders, Burgundy, France, Catalonia and Aragon. Cities like Genoa, Venice, Amalfi and Pisa quickly expanded their maritime power and, aided by great organizations of credit and by letters of exchange, assumed command of Mediterranean commerce. Genoa, aside from its interests in the Levant, turned in the other direction as well, towards the Strait of Gibraltar. As early as 1162, ships had passed beyond this strait and goods from the Atlantic coast of Northwest Africa were being sold at the other end of the Mediterranean and in the Black Sea. In 1191, we find the Genoese established in Ceuta: they even had an accredited consul-general there.

It is perfectly believable that, as a chronicle states, two Genoese brothers named Vivaldi set out into the Atlantic in 1291. By the same token, we cannot doubt that the Canary Islands had been reached by Lanzarotto Malocello in the first half of the fourteenth century.

Also in the mid-thirteenth century, Europeans went in search of direct contact with China and its Mongol Khan, Kublai. Along land routes initially opened the Venetian merchants Nicolau and Mateus Polo made a first trip there in 1261-1269. It was after going there a second time, with their nephew Marco in tow, that upon their return to their homeland in 1295, Marco would dictate his adventures, composing his famous Il Milione. Alongside Rubruck's Itinerarium and the Historia Mongolarum, Marco Polo's

19

story is one of the first reflections in medieval geography of the personal experiences of European travellers to the Far East.

Then, in 1453, the Ottoman Sultan Mehmed II, "the Conqueror," put an end to the better part of these established commercial links by capturing Constantinople.

Let us turn our gaze, then, back toward the extreme western end of Europe, to the Iberian peninsula, as Europeans themselves had to do when the eastern gate to Asia was shut against them. There, the energy of Christianity was fully engaged in the Reconquest of the land from the Moors, in veritable crusades against Islam. But commerce was flourishing as well, even with the enemy himself.

By fits and starts, beginning around 1095, a new kingdom called Portugal was coming into being. On these nearly 90,000 square kilometers — a huge terrace facing the unknown Atlantic — there arose a people tempered by more than a century and a half of struggle, but possessed also of a strong commercial spirit and an inclination to maritime activity, nurtured by the existence of an expansive shoreline and sheltering ports. Fishing and coastwise merchant shipping provided incentive for people to engage in naval construction and in commerce with those in other lands. At first, this commerce was with the countries to the north, helped along by a series of marriages between princesses and princes. A no less important factor for the foreign marketing of Portuguese products was the Crusades. Flemings, French, Germans, Danes, English and Frisians, aboard the fleets carrying them to the Levant, would stop in Lisbon. Some took part in the struggle there against the Moors; if they remained, they might be richly rewarded with high office for the services they had rendered, and thus strengthen the links between Portugal and their homelands.

It is in this context that we reach the end of the thirteenth century and the reign of King Dom Dinis (1279-1325). Soon after ascending the throne, this monarch extended to the mariners of Lagos and Tavira, extremely active in the Moorish period, the privileges enjoyed by those of Lisbon. The logical consequence was that new commercial options opened up, oriented towards the Mediterranean and North Africa, towards the Maghreb; and this is in fact what happened.

Other important factors enter into the picture: for one, the founding of the Order of Christ. This organization's fundamental role was to lead the struggle against the Moors. For another, Dom Dinis' contract with the Genoese Manuel Pessagno, to serve as admiral of the royal galleys. He was to have always at his disposal twenty men well-acquainted with the sea, to be masters aboard those ships. Evidently, this is how the king gave his royal fleet a much-needed push, putting at its head the excellent mariners of Genoa, skilled in the latest nautical techniques. With Pessagno, the defense of the Lusitanian coast was guaranteed and, what seems just as likely, Portugal now might carry the war to the Moors' own homeland, Africa. Since the admiral was allowed by contract to dedicate himself to maritime commerce so long as it did not prejudice his service to the king, it is easy to imagine the benefits this would bring to the commerce already taking place in Portugal, now favoured with an experienced Genoese hand.

Stimulated by successive monarchs (especially Dom Afonso IV and Dom Fernando, the last of his dynasty), who were personally interested in maritime affairs and commerce, Portuguese merchants expanded their field of action uninterruptedly; important in this were the feitorias or trading posts such as the one established in Flanders. Portuguese commercial agents also occupied a very prominent position, which required Portuguese-built ships and their Portuguese crew members to carry them far and wide. The recognized talent for sailing that Portuguese natives had, and the kingdom's maritime power, were not affected by dynastic problems after the death of Dom Fernando. Dom João, the Master of Aviz and bastard son of the deceased monarch, ascended the throne in 1385. If war with Castile distracted the nation's attention, then a peace treaty with its eternal Iberian rival in 1411, in combination with the other factors mentioned above, made it possible for Portugal to open a new theater of maritime activity, namely the Atlantic. Portuguese interest already existed there, as demonstrated by Dom Afonso IV's complaint when the Pope made Don Luis de la Cerda the Prince of the Canary Islands. As the fifteenth century progressed, a good part of the rivalry between Portugal and Castile would take place on the vast ocean. Previously it had consisted only of Portugal's struggles to maintain independence in the face of its adversary, which sought to expand at every opportunity, aided by indisputable military and naval power and by its own aggressive pursuit of commerce. Castile, too, was in search of new markets for its goods.

For the first great move in this new direction, the conquest of Ceuta, Portugal's Dom João I made careful preparations. He was aided by his three oldest sons: Dom Duarte, who inherited the throne, Dom Pedro and Dom Henrique, who in time would become the Grand Master of the Order of Christ and use its wealth to give a major impetus to Portuguese maritime expansion. In 1415, using all the resources available to the nation, they conducted an overwhelming amphibious operation that captured Ceuta. This was the first European stronghold on the African continent, and the first milestone along the road to expansion.

The exhibition, Portugal-Brazil: The Age of Atlantic Discoveries, looks at the first phase of this journey, the conquest of the Atlantic. This led in turn to the discovery of the sea route to India and to direct contact between Europe and the peoples of the Orient. Portuguese were the first Europeans to arrive in their ships. In the exhibition, we show the extraordinary advances that had to be made in the art of sailing, leading in successive stages to the development of astronomical navigation; and the advances in naval construction which led to the development of vessels – the caravel, the nau and the Portuguese galleon – which were better adapted to new and difficult conditions encountered on the high seas.

Since the inevitable consequence of Portuguese voyages was contact between cultures, we give ample evidence of this, including those cultures of Africa that were previously unknown to Europeans, but paying special attention to the Indians of Brazil, looking at what transpired between the Europeans and the Indians they found living there already, and looking at the ways that the Portuguese slowly found to consolidate their control over this vast territory and its original inhabitants.

As would be expected, contact with peoples whose cultures were entirely different from those of Europe provoked intense curiosity in the Old World. The press lost no time in broadly and rapidly disseminating information about these contacts. A selection of important works containing literary echoes of the Portuguese discoveries is presented in a section of the exhibition and catalogue, giving evidence of the enormous impact they caused among Europeans of the period.

Section I

Luís de Albuquerque
The Art
of Astronomical Navigation
Introduction by
Wilcomb E. Washburn

The Portuguese dared to engage the great oceanic sea. They entered it fearlessly. They discovered new islands, new lands, new seas, new peoples, and what is more important, new heavens and new stars. And they so conquered fear that neither the great heat of the torrid zone nor the excessive cold of the extreme south, of which the ancient writers were wont to warn us, could hold them back . . . .
Now it is clear that these discoveries . . . were not achieved through guesswork; our seamen set off well trained and provided with instruments and rules of astronomy and geometry.

From Pedro Nunes, Tratado da Esphera, *1537. (Item 9)*

The science of navigation in the fifteenth century was developed to its highest level by the Portuguese. Yet individuals from many nations played important roles in its development and, thus, contributed to the evolution of the art of conquering the oceanic barrier surrounding the European peninsula. Portugal was fortunate in being able to call upon learned men from throughout the Mediterranean world to support its interest in exploring the islands in the Atlantic and moving its flag down the coast of Africa. Prince Henry, "the Navigator" (1394-1460), third son of King John I, sent out many of these expeditions. Although he was not himself a navigator, his activities on Portugal's rocky outpost at Cape St. Vincent form an appropriate symbol of Portugal's determination to transform the sea from a barrier into a pathway. Combined with technical advances in ship design, nautical instruments and cartography, the development of the science of celestial navigation provided Portugal with a reputation that attracted both book-bound theorists and blue-water sailors to this small Iberian country on the eve of the great discoveries that made Europe a dominant force in world affairs.

W.E.W.

The art of navigation originated in classical antiquity. Its subsequent development was very slow, however. To be strictly accurate, it is only for the medieval period that we possess concrete data concerning its evolution, and even then merely for the later years.

Specifically, we know that at the end of the thirteenth century the mariner's compass was used aboard ship *(Item 13)*. In those days it was but a needle of magnetized steel soaked in olive oil and set afloat in a receptacle with water!

Around the same time or a little later, the chart or map specially drawn for navigation made its appearance. In the nineteenth century it came to be called a "portolan chart" *(Item 1)*, an appropriate name because it was simply a graphic translation of the *portolani* or "sailing directions" of the epoch. Today somewhat less than twenty are known, but in the early days they must have numbered in the tens or hundreds in order to satisfy the demands of the Mediterranean pilots.

Compass Navigation in the Mediterranean
It was precisely in the Mediterranean area (Majorca and Italy) that the art of navigation saw the light of day

1. Portolan Chart.
c.1325. Perrinus Vesconte

The earliest European nautical charts were the so-called "portolan charts", a graphic form of the sailing instructions designed to assist mariners in getting from port to port. This example by the Italian Perrinus Vesconte is undoubtedly one of the oldest still in existence. The limits of European knowledge are evident: accuracy wanes and detail becomes sparse as one proceeds away from Europe. Soon, voyages of discovery spearheaded by the Portuguese Crown would radically widen these limits.

Anonymous Lender
(Page 33)

2. Tablas de Madrid.
Portuguese Almanacs of Madrid.
14th c. Anonymous

The Portuguese Almanacs of Madrid *were drafted in Coimbra, according to a note on one of their pages. Besides astrological and calendrical charts and astronomical tables, they also contain the so-called "sun rules" which might have been used later by mariners, but scholars can neither confirm nor deny that this work helped lead to the development of later navigational tables.*

Biblioteca Nacional, Madrid
(Below)

3. Almanach Perpetuum.
Perpetual Almanac.
1496. Abraham ben Solomon Zacuto

The known solar declination tables used by Portuguese pilots were initially taken from this work of Abraão (Abraham) Zacuto, who fled to Portugal when the Jews were expelled from Spain, and after a brief stay in Portugal was again forced to flee under similar circumstances. Such tables provided information by which navigators could compute latitude, after using an astrolabe or cross-staff to measure the altitude of the sun at high noon. In this particular copy, an enterprising astronomer apparently sought to expand the utility of the tables by inserting his own calculations.

The New York Public Library
(Page 27)

2

and flourished in this form, that is, with sailing directions, mariner's compasses, and charts, and also with dead reckoning of distances. These latter came to be very close to the true ones, thanks to the experience the mariners accumulated in making their calculations.

The sailing directions had their antecedents in the *peripli* of antiquity, of which a small number of specimens have come down to us. The compasses and the marine charts, on the other hand, were novelties introduced into medieval navigation, although it is not known exactly how or by whom.

What is certain is that the use of the compass for sailing purposes, if not in fact its invention, has frequently been attributed to a navigator of Amalfi, Flavio Gioia by name. This attribution is even registered in a Portuguese book of the beginning of the seventeenth century written by the Jesuit Father Francisco da Costa. However, the Italian navigator's supposed innovation still lacks confirmation from a suitable source.

As for the portolan chart, we have sure indications that it was in use only in the second half or end of the thirteenth century, but we haven't the least idea of the navigator who first prepared one. All that can be said with certainty is that the oldest known chart of this type dates from the end of the thirteenth century (or from the first years of the following century), is in a rather deteriorated state, and is labelled by historians the "Pisan Chart", because its maker's name is unknown but it was found in that Italian city.

During the fourteenth and fifteenth centuries the art of navigation was practiced by

Mediterranan pilots with the above elements as a basis. To them we can add:
1) the rules for the so-called "establishment of the port" (that is, the time of high water at a given place on the coast), of which we know at least two examples, one expressed graphically and the other by a set of explanatory rules;
2) the *toleta de marteloio* or elementary traverse board, which was used to lead a pilot back to the direct course if he had wandered from it; and
3) perhaps also a set of rules, the so-called *Regimento* or "Regiment", to determine the time at night by observing the constellation Ursa Minor, or else just the North Star, that is, Polaris.

If we understand, as we suppose it should be understood, that navigation can only be called celestial or astronomical when the determination of at least one of the geographical coordinates is carried out by means of celestial observations, it is clear that "Mediterranean" sailing cannot be categorized as astronomical navigation.

Practiced in accordance with compass courses – the phenomenon of magnetic variation was as yet unknown – and aided by a knowledge of distances whose values depended upon the capacity of the pilot to calculate them (even though, as was said above, the distances came to be very close to true ones), navigation at that time, as reflected on the portolan charts, became a compromise between rules and means. All was precise because the one agreed with the other, although the portolan chart, which was the mirror of the means employed, ended up being deformed in the eyes of those who demanded that it be "real" (in relation to latitudes, for example) instead of being simply a product of the way in which one navigated.

In the sixteenth century, various astronomers, among them Pedro Nunes *(Item 9)*, were to note that the Portolan chart was "erroneous". Nunes points out that it presented deformations in the Mediterranean, locating various places in latitudes that differed two or more degrees from their true values. That was true. The fact, though, is that it was not reasonable to put latitude measurements on a chart that had been drawn without the designer's paying attention to such measurements, above all when, in the use to which the chart was put (namely, navigation), that terrestrial coordinate was not measured and had no meaning *(Pages 38-39)*. For this reason, and also because magnetic variation had changed very little with time in the Mediterranean until the eighteenth century, both the portolan chart and the navigational art that underlay it continued to be used and practiced for more than three centuries, without sailing being in the least affected!

Coastwise Navigation off West Africa

In 1434, when the Portuguese began their reconnaissance of the African coast south of Cape Bojador, navigators could use with certainty only the methods already outlined. It is beyond doubt that magnetic compasses were already employed aboard Portuguese vessels – references to this fact exist. But it is extremely doubtful that the portolan chart was extensively employed by them, and unthinkable that navigational charts were being drawn in Portugal at that time. The writings of contemporaries that are above suspicion – in particular those of Duarte Pacheco Pereira *(Item 4)* – show that, when the Portuguese realized it was necessary to produce charts for navigational purposes, a Majorcan cartographer, James by name, was contracted by Prince Henry ("the Navigator") to come to Portugal in order to pass on his knowledge and create a school. He was the son of the Jewish cartographer Abraham Cresques, author of the celebrated Catalonian planisphere drawn in 1375 and now in the National Library of Paris *(Pages 34-35)*. Today, doubt has been cast on the participation of James of Majorca in Portuguese navigational affairs. But regardless of who was responsible for introducing this art into Portugal, the Belgian scholar Charles Verlinden recently showed, on the basis of a careful reading of Gomes Eanes de Zurara's *Crónica na qual som scriptos todollos feitos notavees que se passarom na conquista de Guiné* (Chronicle of Guinea) *(Item 30)*, that navigational charts began to be drawn in Portugal about 1445. This beginning is an indication of inevitable change, although the technique of drawing such maps did not immediately undergo any alteration whatsoever. But change did come, because the traditional portolan chart was no longer useful. As Zurara says, it had to be expanded to show the outlines of the African coast beyond Cape Bojador as had been seen by the explorers with their own eyes *(Items 24, 25)*, and not in an arbitrary manner like the fill-ins found on fourteenth-century charts.

4. Esmeraldo de Situ Orbis.
1505-1508. Duarte Pacheco Pereira

This work was not published until the end of the 19th century; however, it was in circulation in manuscript form in the 16th century and we know that it was highly regarded. The book is essentially a book of sailing directions written in a personal style with the author's addenda on cosmography, navigational astronomy, anthropology and geography.

Duarte Pacheco Pereira was a navigator, military man and commander of the Fortress of São Jorge da Mina, a Portuguese outpost in West Africa. In the discharge of this last duty he had serious disagreements with Dom João III, who eventually had him imprisoned.

Biblioteca Pública e Arquivo Distrital de Évora, Portugal
(Page 28)

3

5. Seguese ho regimento da declinaçam do sol pera per ella saber ho mareãte em qual parte esta se aquem ou dalem da linea equinocial. Com ho regimento da estrella do norte.
The Following is the Regiment of the Declination of the Sun in order for the Mariner to know in what part he is, on this or that side of the Equator. With the Regiment of the North Star.
c.1516. Anonymous

This is the world's first printed nautical guide. Although undated, it is considered to have been published in 1516 in Lisbon. The copy exhibited here is the world's only known copy of the second edition. It contains the Portuguese translation of an early Treatise on the Sphere, and navigational miscellany. It is an elementary book, but the information it contains was adequate for a pilot's normal needs.

Biblioteca Pública e Arquivo Distrital de Évora, Portugal
(Pages 30, 31)

4

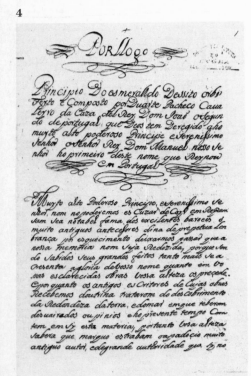

Successive expansions of the cartographic depiction of the world's coastlines as actually observed, rather than as imagined, would continue until the beginning of the seventeenth century, when the depiction of Australia completed the picture. These maps reflect the rapid evolution that the art of navigation experienced in the Age of Maritime Discoveries.

High-Seas Navigation and the Need for Fixes

Sailing south of the Canary Islands did not present the difficulties that many historians exaggeratedly insist upon, and we know that as early as the thirteenth century a few vessels risked going beyond that limit. Nevertheless, it was only in 1434, at the order of Dom Henrique, Prince of Portugal, that a navigator from the Algarve named Gil Eanes rounded Cape Bojador and endeavoured to reconnoitre a portion of the coastline that lay as far as he could see to the south. The following year he repeated the voyage and went still farther south. Others followed in his wake. The whole world was being opened up to satisfy the curiosity of Europeans.

We needn't discuss the reasons that motivated such voyages, for that does not concern us here. What is of interest, however, is to note that the navigators involved in this pioneering experience eventually found themselves confronted by a set of geophysical conditions that greatly complicated the task of returning to their kingdom. In short, winds and currents in that part of the Atlantic generally stood in opposition to a direct return route.

The navigators began to recognize the existence of Atlantic currents and wind systems; these were the first steps toward a geophysics of the great ocean masses. In more practical terms, the navigators adopted the practice of frequently changing course, what came to be known in nautical language as "tacking". As a result, it became necessary to select or design a vessel that, by its construction and its type of sails, could adapt easily to such manoeuvres and still be appropriate for the exploration of bays, inlets and rivers that such voyages entailed. The caravels satisfied these requirements *(Item 15)*. Finally (and this is most significant for the repercussions it had on navigation), navigators learned they could most rapidly reach home port by a seemingly lengthy route that skirted the physical forces opposing a direct return. This route was an enormous semicircle trending westward in the Atlantic, that could carry vessels to the latitude of Lagos or Lisbon without great difficulties, whence they would sail eastward more or less along that parallel to their destination.

This clever nautical manoeuvre, which was executed for centuries and carried the navigators close to the Azores (and, in the sixteenth and seventeenth centuries, they eventually made stops on one of the islands of that archipelago), is called by modern historiographers the *volta do largo* (return from the high seas). In the Age of Discoveries it was known as the *volta da Guiné* (return from Guinea) or *volta da Mina* (return from the Mine), because it was from the Guinea coast or the fortress of São Jorge da Mina in today's Ghana that the vessels departed to begin their tack in an arc to the northwest and thence eastward

to the coast of Portugal.
For the first time in the history of the voyages of Western peoples, vessels isolated themselves at sea for several weeks, or as long as two months. In the maritime voyages of preceding centuries, in the Mediterranean and around the Iberian peninsula to the ports of the English Channel and the North Sea, one navigated close to shore. As a general rule, it was not difficult to sail within constant sight of land in order to establish the vessel's position. But now, on this manoeuvre out to sea, between water and sky, the comforting sight of land no longer existed. Just as in the Mediterranean, so in the Atlantic, pilots would have their compasses, would possess their charts, would use soundings, would estimate the distance made good. In the Mediterranean, however, this latter procedure was confirmed by the observation of what the Portuguese of old called *conhecenças* ("familiarities", or hints that aided the navigator). In the case of a lengthy passage on the high seas, it became much more of a gamble. It became imperative to make checks on the old procedure and eventually to confirm it by other means. To put the matter differently, it became convenient, during a long voyage without any reference from shore, to know the vessel's approximate position, if not at all times then at least once a day. The solutions adopted may be viewed as having developed in a series of phases.

First Phase: Latitude-Difference by Comparison of Meridian Altitudes

In the first phase, the problem was satisfactorily solved by recourse to meridian altitudes of celestial bodies (Polaris and other well-known stars, and eventually the sun, albeit with certain precautions). All that was needed was to compare those altitudes, taken anywhere at sea by means of quadrants, and eventually also astrolabes *(Item 12)* and, still later, cross-staffs *(Item 14)*, with the meridian altitudes that the same body exhibited in Lisbon or in any other place that the pilot might take as a reference. The difference between the two values of the astronomical coordinate gave the value of an arc of the meridian calculated between the parallels of latitude of the two places being compared and, accordingly, also the number of leagues that the vessel had to go in a north-south or south-north direction in order to reach the parallel of the port or place of destination.
In connection with this method, a degree of latitude was first estimated by Portuguese navigators at 16 2/3 leagues and later at 17 1/2 leagues.
A simple multiplication, of the value of the arc by the estimated number of leagues per degree, determined the vessel's distance from its destination. Carrying out this operation at that time, however, was not simple, and therefore the products were furnished by tables prepared in advance. This method was probably just an adaptation of a procedure that, for slightly different purposes, John of Holywood (Joannes de Sacrobosco) foresaw in his *Treatise on the Sphere* in the thirteenth century.

6. Book of Francisco Rodrigues.
(annexed to the Digest of the Orient *of Tomé Pires). 1513? Francisco Rodrigues*

The so-called Book of Francisco Rodrigues, *known with certainty to have been compiled before 1520, is a small yet complex text: it contains abbreviated sailing directions, astronomical navigation guidelines, including a unique solar declination table (with numbers on one page consistently off by 10° due to a copyist's error). Appended to this book are many nautical charts of Oriental lands, presumed to be copies of drawings by local pilots, probably Malayan.*

Bibliothèque de l'Assemblée Nationale, Paris (Below)

6

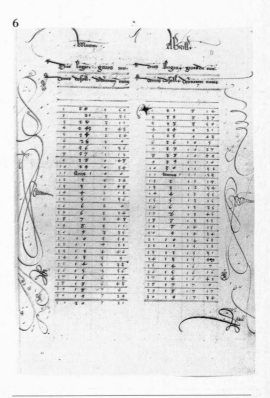

5

Seguese ho regimento da declinaçam do sol pera per ella saber homareãte em q̃tal parte esta. s. aquem ou dalem da linea equinocial. Com ho regimento da estrella do norte.

GERMAM GALHAR·DꝰE

ℭRactado da Spera do

mūdo tirada de latim em lingoagē portugues
Com hūa carta que huũ grāde doutor Alemani man
dou a elRey de Portugall dom Joam ho segundo.

1. Portolan Chart.
c.1325. Perrinus Vesconte

Anonymous Lender
(Page 33)

Catalan Atlas.
1375. Abraham Cresques

One of the treasures of early cartography, this map of the world is on twelve panels that fold like a screen. Combining ecclesiastical assumptions (such as the approximately central position of Jerusalem) and navigational data derived from portolan charts of the Mediterranean, the map also incorporates data on central Asia from the travel narratives of the thirteenth century. Depicted on its westernmost panel are six islands in the Atlantic, perhaps representing the Azores.

Abraham Cresques, described as a "master of maps of the world" and a compass-maker, and his son Jehuda, were members of a predominantly Jewish group of chartmakers and cartographers on the island of Majorca.

Bibliothèque Nationale, Paris
(Pages 34-35)

World Map.
1459. Fra Mauro
(Detail)

This map, the original of which is in the Biblioteca Marciana in Venice, has been called the "summit of Church cartography". Prepared by a monk in the Camaldulian monastery on the island of Murano near Venice, the map is a copy of one commissioned by Afonso V, King of Portugal. The map shows the influence of Marco Polo's narratives, portolan charts, Ptolemy's Geography, Arab cartography, and the Portuguese voyages down the African coast. It projects an open sea route around Africa to Asia, which is consistent with Arab cartography but in contrast to the beliefs of some European cartographers. The map is oriented with North at the bottom and South at the top.

Biblioteca Marciana, Venice.
(Pages 36-37)

Portolan Chart.
1492. Jorge de Aguiar
Manuscript map on vellum.

Aguiar was a Portuguese cartographer; this work is the oldest signed and dated Portuguese portolan chart known to us: the legend "Jorge Daguiar made me in Lisbon in the year 1492" is located at the border of the parchment. As a "working chart" that was made to be laid on a table and walked around, its toponymy and legends are oriented to be read from various angles.

Designed for mariners, the map leaves the interior of the European and African continents virtually blank, and pays attention only to coastal cities and landmarks. The detail inside the African continent is a portion of the West African coastline that did not fit within the borders of the vellum sheet; it shows Portuguese settlements (note the Portuguese flags) at "Serra Leoa" (Sierra Leone) and Elmina. It also shows the Canaries, Azores, Cape Verde and Madeira archipelagoes, early Atlantic outposts found by Iberian navigators.

Beinecke Rare Book and Manuscript Library, Yale University
(Pages 38-39)

10. Livro da Marinharia.
Book of Seamanship.
16th c. Andre Pires

Bibliothèque Nationale, Paris
(Pages 40-41)

12. Portuguese Astrolabe.
1555.

Dundee Art Galleries and Museums
(Page 42)

13. Magnetic Compass.
1711. José da Costa Miranda

Whipple Museum of the History of Science, University of Cambridge
(Page 43)

20. Livro das traças de Carpintaria.
Book of Carpentry Drawings.
1616. Manuel Fernandes

Biblioteca da Ajuda, Lisbon
(Pages 44-45, 46-47)

18. Livro da Fabrica das Naos.
Book of Shipbuilding.
1570. Fernando Oliveira

Biblioteca Nacional, Lisbon
(Page 48)

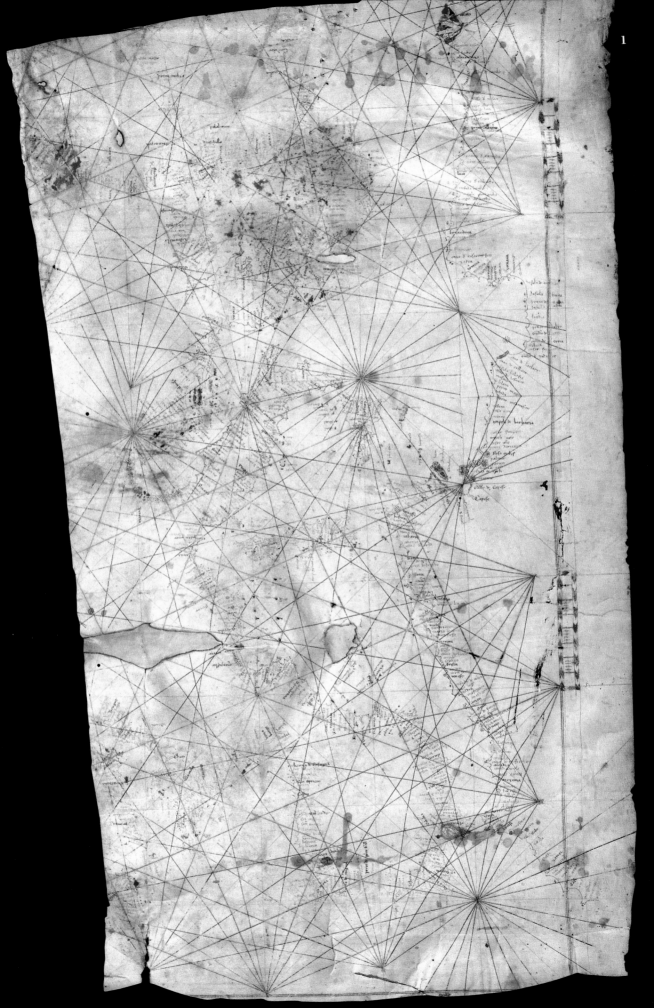

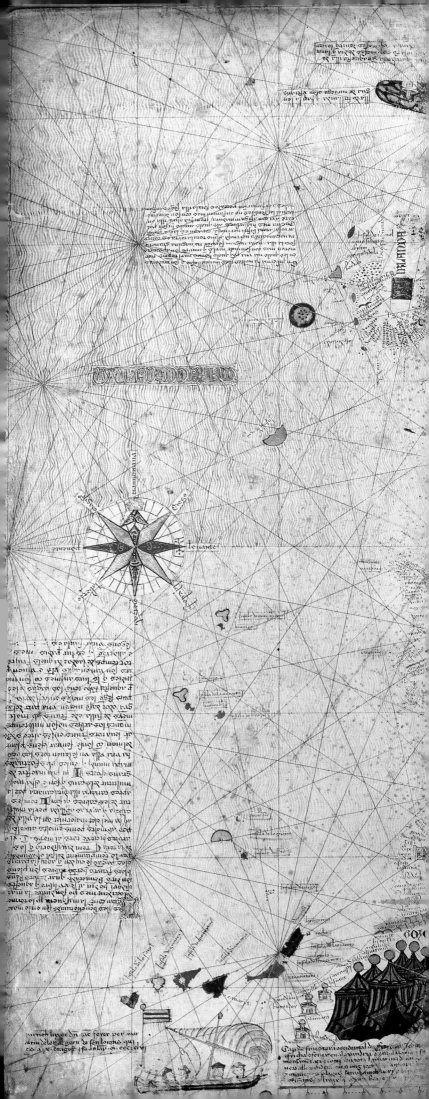

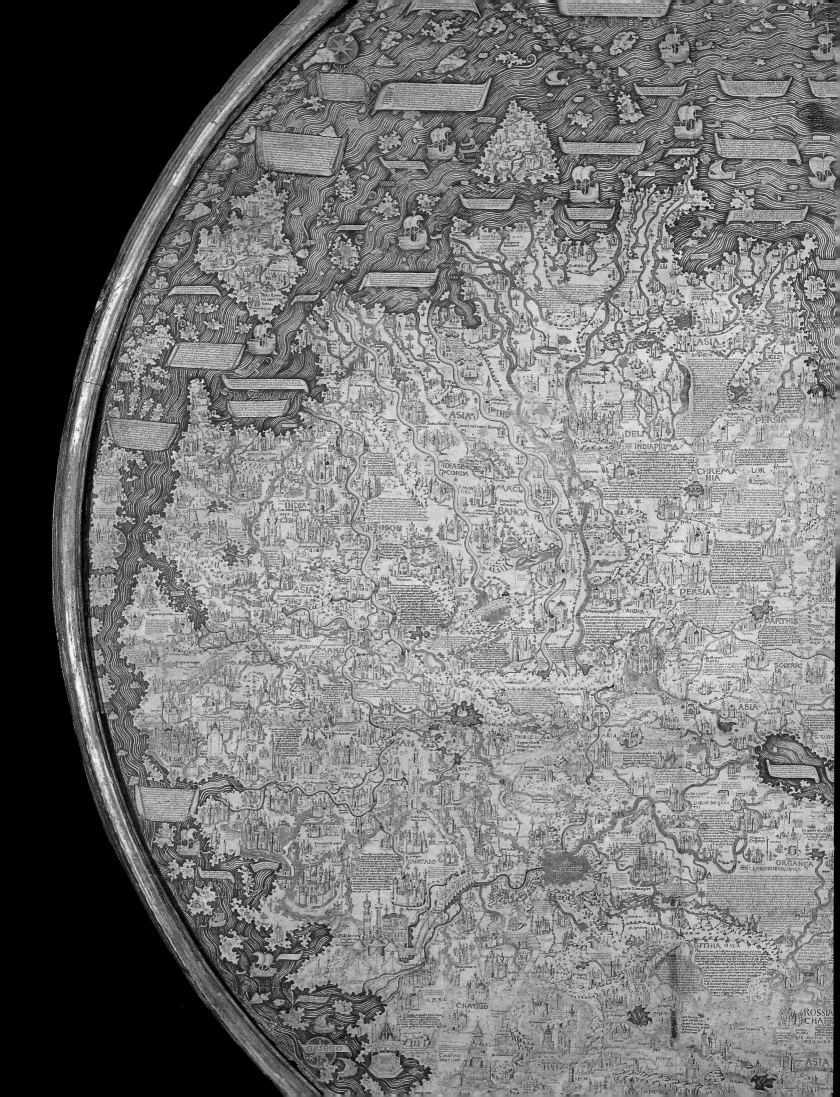

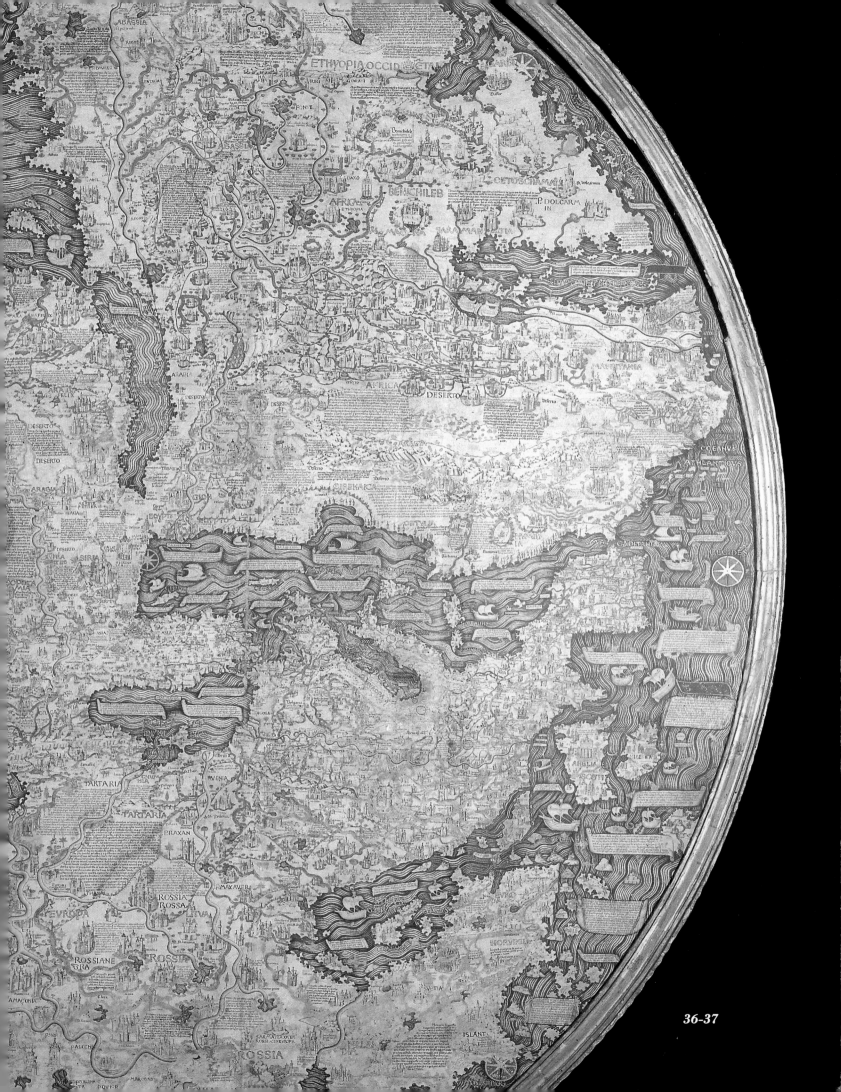

36-37

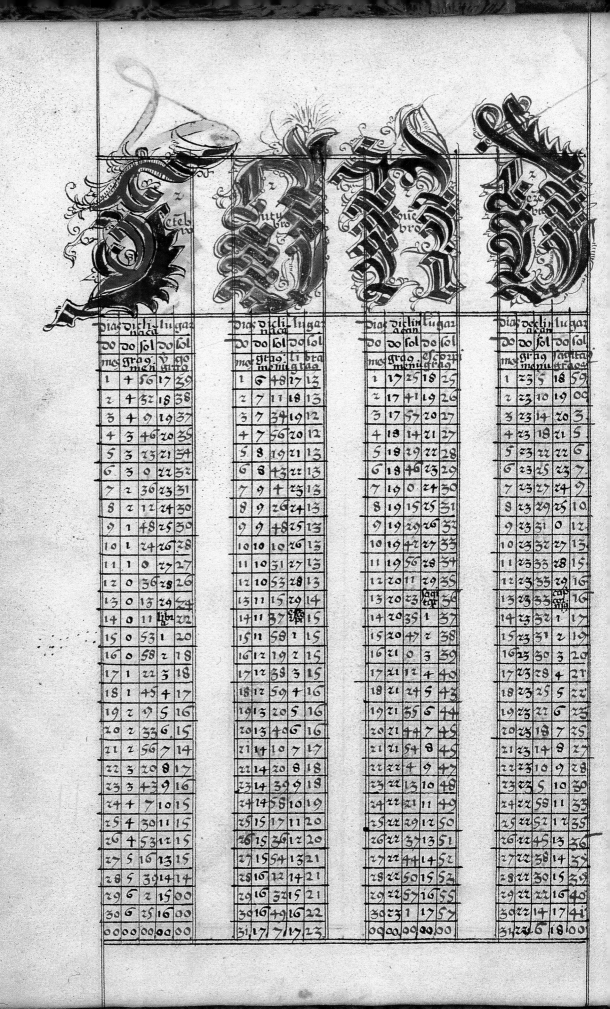

Setembro — Virgo

Dias do mes	declinacão do sol graos menutos		lugar do sol Virgo graos	
1	+	56	17	39
2	4	32	18	38
3	4	9	19	37
4	3	46	20	35
5	3	23	21	34
6	3	0	22	32
7	2	36	23	31
8	2	12	24	30
9	1	48	25	30
10	1	24	26	28
11	1	0	27	27
12	0	36	28	26
13	0	13	29	24
14	0	11	libra	22
15	0	53	1	20
16	0	58	2	18
17	1	?	3	18
18	1	45	4	17
19	2	9	5	16
20	2	33	6	15
21	2	56	7	14
22	3	20	8	17
23	3	43	9	16
24	4	7	10	15
25	4	30	11	15
26	4	53	12	15
27	5	16	13	15
28	5	39	14	14
29	6	2	15	00
30	6	25	16	00
0	00	00	00	00

Outubro — Libra

Dias do mes	declinacão do sol graos menutos		lugar do sol libra graos	
1	6	48	17	13
2	7	11	18	13
3	7	34	19	12
4	7	56	20	12
5	8	19	21	13
6	8	43	22	13
7	9	4	23	13
8	9	26	24	13
9	9	48	25	13
10	10	10	26	13
11	10	31	27	13
12	10	53	28	13
13	11	15	29	14
14	11	37	scorpi 0	15
15	11	58	1	15
16	12	19	2	15
17	12	38	3	15
18	12	59	4	16
19	13	20	5	16
20	13	40	6	16
21	14	10	7	17
22	14	20	8	18
23	14	39	9	18
24	14	58	10	19
25	15	17	11	20
26	15	36	12	20
27	15	54	13	21
28	16	12	14	21
29	16	32	15	21
30	16	49	16	22
31	17	7	17	23

Novembro — Escorpio

Dias do mes	declinacão do sol graos menutos		lugar do sol Escorpi graos	
1	17	25	18	25
2	17	41	19	26
3	17	57	20	27
4	18	14	21	27
5	18	29	22	28
6	18	46	23	29
7	19	0	24	30
8	19	15	25	31
9	19	29	26	32
10	19	42	27	33
11	19	56	28	34
12	20	11	29	35
13	20	23	sagitar 0	36
14	20	35	1	37
15	20	47	2	38
16	21	0	3	39
17	21	12	4	40
18	21	24	5	43
19	21	35	6	44
20	21	44	7	45
21	21	54	8	45
22	22	4	9	47
23	22	13	10	48
24	22	21	11	49
25	22	29	12	50
26	22	37	13	51
27	22	44	14	52
28	22	50	15	53
29	22	57	16	55
30	23	1	17	57
0	00	00	00	00

Dezembro — Sagitario

Dias do mes	declinacão do sol graos menutos		lugar do sol Sagitar graos	
1	23	5	18	59
2	23	10	19	00
3	23	14	20	3
4	23	18	21	5
5	23	22	22	6
6	23	25	23	7
7	23	27	24	9
8	23	29	25	11
9	23	31	0	12
10	23	32	27	13
11	23	33	28	15
12	23	33	29	16
13	23	33	capricor 0	16
14	23	32	1	17
15	23	31	2	19
16	23	30	3	20
17	23	28	4	21
18	23	25	5	22
19	23	22	6	23
20	23	18	7	25
21	23	14	8	27
22	23	10	9	28
23	23	5	10	30
24	22	59	11	33
25	22	52	12	35
26	22	45	13	36
27	22	38	14	37
28	22	30	15	39
29	22	22	16	40
30	22	14	17	41
31	22	6	18	00

Janeiro

dia do mes	declinaçam do sol (grao, menu)	lugar do sol (graos)
1	21 57	20 44
2	21 48	21 45
3	21 39	22 46
4	21 28	23 48
5	21 18	24 49
6	21 6	25 50
7	20 55	26 52
8	20 43	27 53
9	20 31	28 54
10	20 19	29 56
11	20 5	acario 57
12	19 55	1 58
13	19 37	2 0
14	19 24	3 1
15	19 10	4 2
16	18 56	5 3
17	18 39	6 4
18	18 20	7 5
19	18 4	8 6
20	17 50	9 7
21	17 32	10 8
22	17 15	12 9
23	16 58	13 10
24	16 40	14 11
25	16 22	15 12
26	16 4	16 13
27	15 46	17 14
28	15 28	18 15
29	15 9	19 16
30	14 48	20 17
31	14 29	21 18

Fevereiro

dia do mes	declinaçam do sol (grao, menu)	lugar do sol (graos)
1	14 10	22 15
2	13 50	23 15
3	13 30	24 16
4	13 10	25 17
5	12 50	26 17
6	12 29	27 18
7	12 9	28 18
8	11 48	29 18
9	11 27	pisces 19
10	11 5	1 19
11	10 44	2 19
12	10 22	3 19
13	10 0	4 19
14	9 38	5 19
15	9 16	7 19
16	8 54	8 20
17	8 32	9 20
18	8 9	10 20
19	7 45	11 20
20	7 22	12 20
21	6 58	13 20
22	6 36	14 20
23	6 13	15 19
24	5 50	16 19
25	5 27	17 19
26	5 2	18 18
27	4 40	19 18
28	4 15	18
00	00 00	00 00
00	00 00	00 00
00	00 00	00 00

Março

dias do mes	declinaçam do sol (grao, menu)	lugar do sol (graos)
1	3 54	20 52
2	3 30	21 31
3	3 6	22 31
4	2 44	23 30
5	2 19	24 30
6	1 56	25 29
7	1 30	26 28
8	1 6	27 28
9	0 42	28 27
10	0 19	29 26
11	0 5	aries 26
12	0 29	1 25
13	0 52	2 24
14	1 16	3 23
15	1 40	3 22
16	2 4	4 21
17	2 27	5 21
18	2 51	6 20
19	3 14	7 20
20	3 37	8 19
21	4 0	9 18
22	4 24	10 17
23	4 47	11 16
24	5 10	12 14
25	5 33	13 12
26	5 54	14 10
27	6 17	15 8
28	6 39	16 6
29	7 2	17 5
30	7 25	18 3
31	7 48	19 1

Abril

dias do mes	declinaçam do sol (grao, menu)	lugar do sol (graos)
1	8 8	20 59
2	8 32	21 58
3	8 53	22 56
4	9 13	23 54
5	9 35	24 53
6	9 57	25 51
7	10 19	26 49
8	10 39	27 47
9	11 0	28 46
10	11 21	29 44
11	11 42	tauro 42
12	12 3	1 40
13	12 23	2 38
14	12 42	3 36
15	13 1	4 34
16	13 22	5 31
17	13 40	6 29
18	13 58	7 27
19	14 17	8 25
20	14 36	9 23
21	14 55	9 21
22	15 14	10 17
23	15 32	11 14
24	15 50	12 11
25	16 6	13 9
26	16 24	14 6
27	16 41	15 3
28	16 56	16 2
29	17 22	17 0
30	17 39	18 59
00	00 00	00 00

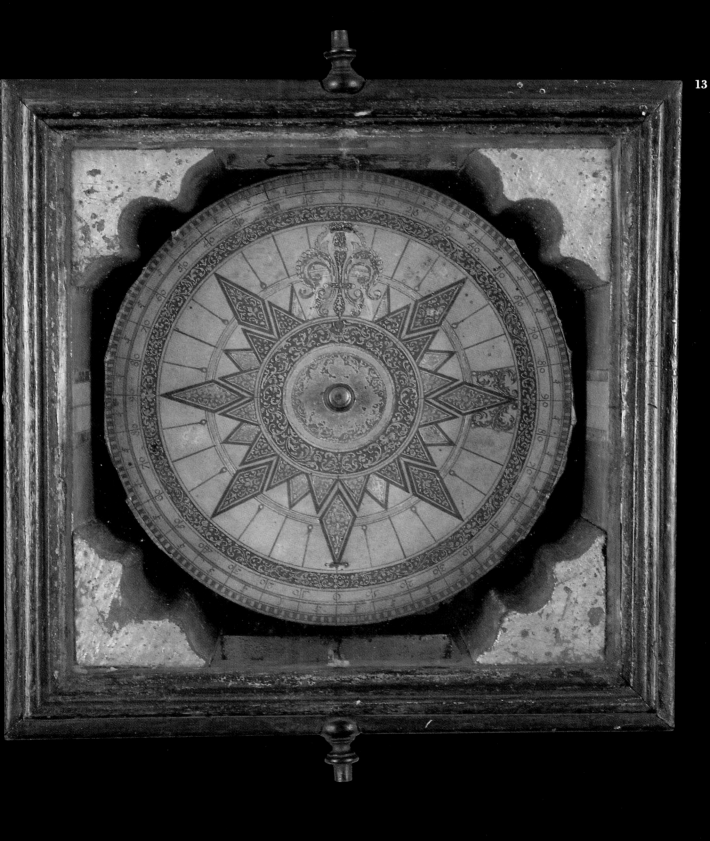

13

Este he o modello da segunda Cuberta Desta Carauella cõ todas suas larguras e medidas como se vera no Regimento

este he o modello do leme desta Caraueulla

Este he o modello da carauella acabada

este he o pitipe da medida desta carauella

3   6   9

Pitipe de

E ſte he o modello da primeira Cuberta.

eſta traça ſe moſtra

18 21 2✝ 2ɔ

Este he o modello da terceira cuberta deste Galeaõ.

ESTE HE O MOD

de quinhen

de comprido

O DO GALEAM

nelladas, tem
adria desquadria

pal: por que quanto a altura, ate aly he a ordinaria,
ẽ proporcionauel de que falamos: ẽ se lhe ĩprs tere,
nao seja munto: ẽ quanto aa largura, tambẽ aly
he a mayor: ẽ da ẽ pa todalas partes recolhe, assy
pa bayxo como para cima, ẽ para os cabos de popa
ẽ proa: como se logo veraa: E para se entenderem
o q dixe facilmente lho mostro na figura seguinte.

¶ Figura da quilha, altura,
largura da nao, medidas
per rumos, ẽ palmos.

Conues.

palmos. 48. Largura   da boca. 8. rumos.

Altura da nao. 6. rumos.

Rumos,   Largura do fudo. 3.   ẽ palmos.

Longura da quilha. 18. rumos.

Second Phase: Latitude-Difference by Comparison of ex-Meridian Altitudes of Polaris

A second phase in this transformation of the navigational art, and one of short duration, came about as a result of three factors:
1) the preference of navigators for observing Polaris,
2) the fact that, in its motion around the north pole, this star described at that time a circle corresponding to a polar distance of 3°30'; and
3) the fact that the heavenly body was not always observable, either because the sky was cloudy or because one of its two meridian transits took place during daylight hours, when stars are not visible. Thus, navigators were compelled to select, in addition to the two meridian passages, six additional positions of the star in its apparent daily circle and to register for any of the usual reference places the values of the eight altitudes observed at those points. The eight numbers probably would have been provided in "Regiments", though only a single copy of such a set of rules has come down to us. Nevertheless, we do have various copies of a diagram that was equivalent to a Regiment. It is in the form of a circular crown (what the sailors called a *roda* or wheel). At the end of each radius pointing to the direction at which the star was seen, it contains in written form the altitude that would have been observed at the place for which the wheel was constructed.

All these so-called "Polaris Wheels" or "Wheels of Altitudes" that we know of take Lisbon as their point of reference, but they could have been constructed for other places frequented by navigators. In an archaic passage inserted in the 1563 edition of the *Reportório dos Tempos*, an early nautical almanac translated by Valentim Fernandes and published by him for the first time in 1518, one may infer the existence of a reference to a wheel for the port of Funchal on Madeira.

Now, concerning the first phase mentioned previously, we have indications that it was applied at sea – the contemporary authority Diogo Gomes, for example, alludes to its use. We also know for a fact that meridian altitudes of Polaris in various places were written on the very scale of the quadrant used to make the observation. But we have no evidence of the practical use of "Polaris Wheels". Nevertheless, we find them reproduced at least five times in nautical texts, four of them datable to the first quarter of the sixteenth century; moreover, the fact that such wheels were in use during the next (third) phase of the evolution of latitude-measurement, as will be discussed, seems to indicate that they were frequently used and very well accepted by pilots.

Third Phase: Latitude from Polaris' Altitude and Time of Night

The next step was certainly decisive for the modernization of navigation, for it implied a leap forward to the self-contained determination of latitudes aboard ship. Recourse to the use of Polaris Wheels during the second phase must have facilitated this decisive advance. Let us consider the Wheel of Altitudes reproduced by Valentim Fernandes in his 1518 edition of the *Reportório dos Tempos*, and let us bear in mind that the latitude of Lisbon was then calculated as 39° N.

7. Tratado da Sphœra.
Treatise on the Globe.
1536? João de Castro

Dom João de Castro (1500-1548), a military man and navigator, wrote three major works on navigation, containing his observations of magnetic declination (which led him to the discovery of the "magnetic deviation" phenomenon), hydrographic surveys of the ports he visited, analysis of the movement of the sun, implementations of suggestions made by Pedro Nunes, etc.

The work shown here is a commentary to the Treatise on the Sphere, *by John of Holywood (Sacrobosco), the most famous cosmographer of the Middle Ages. This is the only known copy.*

Biblioteca Nacional, Madrid (Below)

7

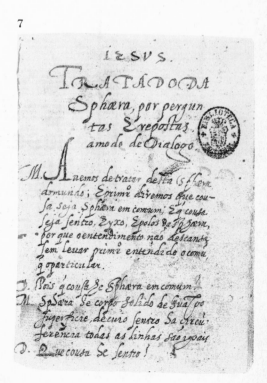

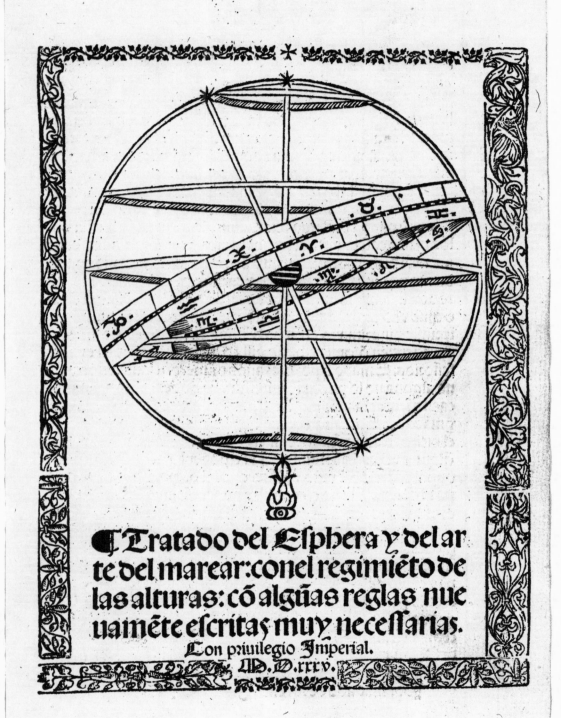

℄Tratado del Esphera y del ar
te del marear: conel regimiéto de
las alturas: có algũas reglas nue
uaméte escritas muy necessarias.
Con priuilegio Imperial.
M.D.xxxv.

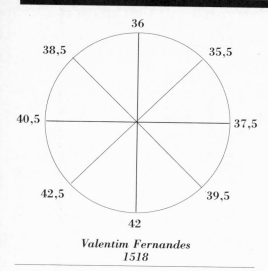

Valentim Fernandes
1518

The directions that are taken into account on this wheel are N and S, NE and SW, E and W, and SE and NW, even though the navigators designated them by other names. When the values assigned to them were correct, the averages of the numbers corresponding to the paired directions would lead to the correct latitude.

The result is that, with any one of the altitudes marked on the figure, the latitude could be found by adding or subtracting a corrective factor provided by the wheel at a glance. These corrections turn out to be +3° or -3° (for directions N and S), +3°30' or -3°30' (NE and SW), +1°30' and -1°30' (E and W), and +30' and -30' (NW and SE). These indications refer to Polaris, but this star's location with respect to the north pole itself was inferred from the simultaneous position of the Guards of the Little Dipper. Once these values were obtained, and admitting that they did not undergo variations from place to place, pilots could use them to determine latitude as they navigated in the Atlantic. For this reason, the numbers were included *in extenso* and constituted the rules for the "North Star Regiment" or

"Polaris Regiment"; or else they were transferred to new wheels in texts and in graphic depictions that were transcribed or traced innumerable times throughout the sixteenth century, without alteration.

Two observations must be made: First, Pedro Nunes called attention in one of his works to the fact that the corrections included in the North Star Regiment depend on one's latitude. The observation was sound, but for the latitudes in which the pilots of that time navigated in the northern hemisphere, and as far south as the limit of visibility of the North Star, such variations were insignificant – in the most unfavourable case they did not amount to two minutes of arc – and doubtless were absorbed by errors of observation, which in general were decidedly greater. Second, navigators paid no attention to the fact that the North Star was moving closer to the north celestial pole and, as the years passed, they would have to revise the corrections in their Regiments. As late as the end of the sixteenth century, this need was not felt. By the end of the following century, however, an anonymous author corrected the numbers written on the wheel of the North Star Regiment in Lazaro Luis's atlas of 1563 (in the Academy of Sciences of Lisbon). He replaced them with others referring to the year 1700, and stressed that they could be used for another half-century, as one reads in this note: "I corrected the old figures that used to be here, erasing them from the parchment and substituting the correct ones for the coming year 1700; and these latter can serve for twenty-five years before and twenty-five after without appreciable error,

8. Tratado del Esphera y del arte del marear.
Treatise on the sphere and the art of sailing.
1535. Francisco Faleiro

Francisco Faleiro, a Portuguese cosmographer, emigrated to Seville with his brother Rui Faleiro to join Fernão de Magalhães (Ferdinand Magellan) on the voyage which became the first circumnavigation of the globe. When Rui's agreement with Magalhães fell through, Francisco remained in Seville, plying his profession as cosmographer. The result was this book. It includes astral and solar rules, nautical solar tables, and instructions for measuring magnetic declination similar to those put forth by Pedro Nunes. The last pages of the work refer to the use of Arabic numerals, suggesting that they were not widely employed in Spain at the time.

The John Carter Brown Library at Brown University, Providence RI
(Facing page)

9. Tratado da sphera com a Theorica do Sol e da Lua.
Treatise on the globe with the Theory of the Sun and the Moon.
1537. Pedro Nunes

Pedro Nunes (1502-1578) is considered the greatest Portuguese mathematician of the 16th century. Appointed chief cosmographer of the kingdom in 1547, his duties included technical preparations for voyages of exploration and the screening of all candidate pilots, cartographers and instrument-makers. Practical sailors criticized him for his theoretical bent, evidenced in this book. But as the quotation on page 24 shows, Nunes could rise eloquently to the defence of those who disparaged him, while stressing that they would have achieved little without the aid of theoreticians.

Biblioteca Nacional, Lisbon
(Page 52)

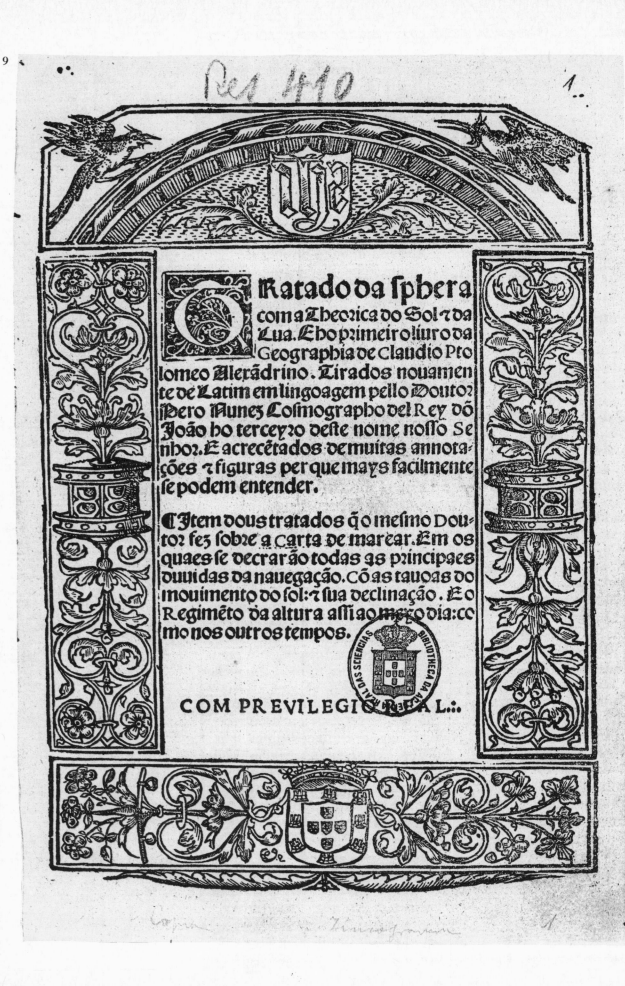

Ratado da sphera
com a Theorica do Sol e da
Lua. E ho primeiro liuro da
Geographia de Claudio Pto
lomeo Alexãdrino. Tirados nouamen
te de Latim em lingoagem pello Doutor
Pero Nunez Cosmographo del Rey dõ
João ho terceyro deste nome nosso Se
nhor. E acrecẽtados de muitas annota
ções e figuras per que mays facilmente
se podem entender.

Item dous tratados q o mesmo Dou
tor fez sobre a carta de marear. Em os
quaes se decrarão todas as principaes
duuidas da nauegação. Cõ as tauoas do
mouimento do sol: e sua declinação. E o
Regimẽto da altura assi ao meyo dia: co
mo nos outros tempos.

COM PREVILEGIO REAL.

or at least without a great one, in the practice of navigation." Various authors of nautical treatises, Portuguese as well as Spanish, also revised the Regiment so as to take this matter into account. Among them we can cite Rodrigo Zamorano (1591), Andres Garcia de Céspedes (1606), Manuel de Figueiredo (1608), and Luis Serrão Pimentel (1681): and no two of them agree with each other. Because of the proximity of the dates of the revisions that they undertook, it would have been natural for at least Figueiredo and Céspedes to have converged or come close; but no such thing.

Fourth Phase: Latitude from Sun's Meridian Altitude and Declination

The North Star Regiment, as we said, represented an important step forward in the development of navigation. Pilots could now measure, at sea, one terrestrial coordinate. In other words, they had leapt from an art to a technique. Nevertheless, sailors of those days knew full well that, to reach a perfect solution to the problem of obtaining a fix at sea, they also had to determine, simultaneously, the value of the other terrestrial coordinate, longitude. They worked out various methods without success, and they accepted various principles without any basis. We shall speak of those unsuccessful attempts and those unrealized dreams a little later. Nonetheless, to know one's latitude day by day was already an excellent development. Eventually, all pilots could make the observations needed to obtain this value, provided, of course, that it were possible. However, as the voyages extended southward, Polaris

approached, and finally sank below, the northern horizon. When that happened, and in spite of written references that would lead one to suspect the contrary, pilots were not accustomed to have recourse to other stars. Pedro Nunes, appointed chief cosmographer of the Portuguese kingdom in 1547, and ever critical of men who went to sea in ships, even wrote that such men were acquainted with very few stars, in spite of the fact that a man like astrologer Mestre João (Master John), who embarked on Pedro Álvares Cabral's fleet, had made note of some of the brightest stars of the southern hemisphere (Item 91). At any rate, it became essential to find an alternate method of determining latitude at sea.

In this sense, no innovations had to be introduced because, in the medieval treatises on the astrolabe – such as Msha'allah's, written in the late eighth or early ninth century and the oldest that is known – a chapter was already included on how to determine latitude from the meridian altitude of the sun and its declination on the same day. Nevertheless, certain hurdles obviously had to be cleared. First, many precepts or Regiments in those books are not applicable on all parts of the globe. This is true of the above-mentioned treatise by Msha'allah, which is useful only for observers located north of the tropic of Cancer, that being the relevant case for the time and place in which the work was drawn up. Consequently, it became necessary to analyze those texts and complete them whenever they were found to be limited to particular situations. Second, the rules that theoretical books proclaimed had to be put

10. Livro de Marinharia.
Book of Seamanship.
16th c. André Pires

Judging from the contents, Pires was a pilot thoroughly acquainted with problems of navigation. The book contains sailing directions, rules, solar tables, guidelines for determining solar declination on the basis of rather complicated instructions that reference the sun's day-to-day position on the elliptic, etc. Most important are the solar tables, lucid instructions on the oriental method of navigating, and the first correct mention of the correspondence between the Arabic "isba" (lit. "finger", cf. Portuguese "polegada", "inch") and the sexagesimal units of arc used in the West.

Bibliothèque Nationale, Paris
(Pages 40-41 and 54)

11. Livro de Marinharia.
Book of Seamanship.
1563. Manuel Álvares

Manuel Álvares was a pilot on the India Route, and commanded the ship Grifo in the fleet of 1538 under the command of viceroy Dom Garcia de Noronha. The signature and date "Thevet 1567" on the title page indicate that this manuscsript copy belonged to André Thevet, a Franciscan monk who spent time in Brazil and wrote two important books on that region, both of which are included in this exhibition and catalogue.

National Maritime Museum, Greenwich England
(Below)

11

Janeiro

dia do mês	grãos	menudos	grã	me nu
1	21	4	21	52
2	21	6	21	44
3	23	7	21	32
4	24	8	21	22
5	25	9	21	10
6	26	10	21	0
7	27	11	20	47
8	2	12	20	35
9	29	13	20	22
10		14	20	10
11	1	15	19	57
12	2	16	19	42
13	3	17	19	28
14	4	18	19	13
15	5	19	19	0
16	6	20	18	45
17	7	21	18	28
18	8	22	18	12
19	9	23	17	57
20	10	24	17	40
21	11	25	17	22
22	12	26	17	5
23	13	27	16	48
24	14	28	16	30
25	15	29	16	13
26	16	30	15	55
27	17	33	15	37
28	18	33	15	19
29	19	34	15	1
30	20	35	14	42
31	21	36	14	21

Fevereiro

dia do mês	grãos	menudos	grã	me nu
1	22	35	14	0
2	23	35	13	40
3	24	36	13	20
4	25	36	13	0
5	26	37	12	39
6	27	37	12	18
7	28	37	11	58
8	29	38	11	37
9		38	11	16
10	1	38	10	54
11	2	39	10	31
12	3	39	10	10
13	4	39	9	47
14	5	39	9	26
15	6	39	9	4
16	7	39	8	41
17	8	39	8	19
18	9	39	7	57
19	10	39	7	34
20	11	39	7	12
21	12	39	6	49
22	13	39	6	26
23	14	39	6	2
24	15	38	5	39
25	16	38	5	15
26	17	38	4	51
27	18	37	4	28
28	19	37	4	44
00	20	0	0	0
00	0	0	0	0
00	0	0	0	0

Março

dia do mês	grãos	menudos	grã	me nu
1	20	37	3	41
2	21	36	3	18
3	22	36	2	54
4	23	36	2	31
5	24	35	2	7
6	25	34	1	44
7	26	44	1	20
8	27	33	0	55
9	28	32	0	32
10	29	31	0	9
11		31	0	15
12	1	30	0	39
13	2	29	1	3
14	3	28	1	27
15	4	27	1	51
16	5	26	2	15
17	6	25	2	38
18	7	24	3	1
19	8	23	3	25
20	9	22	3	47
21	10	21	4	10
22	11	20	4	34
23	12	19	4	56
24	13	18	5	20
25	14	17	5	43
26	15	16	6	5
27	16	15	6	28
28	17	13	6	50
29	18	12	7	12
30	19	10	7	36
31	20	9	7	57

Abrill

dia do mês	grãos	menudos	grã	me nu
1	21	4	8	20
2	22	3	8	41
3	23	1	9	2
4	24	0	9	24
5	25	58	9	47
6	26	57	10	7
7	27	56	10	29
8	28	53	10	51
9	29	51	11	12
10	19	49	11	32
11	1	47	11	52
12	2	45	12	17
13	3	43	12	31
14	4	41	12	49
15	5	39	13	8
16	6	37	13	28
17	7	35	13	47
18	8	33	14	7
19	9	30	14	24
20	10	28	14	43
21	11	26	15	0
22	12	23	15	16
23	13	21	15	43
24	14	19	16	0
25	15	16	16	16
26	16	14	16	31
27	17	12	16	48
28	8	9	17	4
29	19	7	17	20
30	19	5	17	36
00	0	0	0	0

to practical test, in order to evaluate the degree of safety with which they could be used at sea. Finally, as the calculation of solar declination presented difficulties that were generally beyond the reach of pilots, ways had to be found to avoid them. We will discuss these three problems successively, and speak as well of the instrument that was adopted for solar observations, namely, the mariner's astrolabe. To evaluate the range of rules at hand, to extend them when necessary, and to judge their applicability at sea, kings John II (reigned 1481-1495) and Manuel (1495-1521) turned to the knowledge possessed by Jewish astrologers. This probably began at the latest in 1485.

In a note that Christopher Columbus placed in the margin of a book he used, the Genoese navigator declares that "the King of Portugal sent to Guinea in the Year of the Lord 1485 Master Joseph, his physician and astrologer, in order to observe the altitude of the sun throughout Guinea. . .". The allusion to the "altitude of the sun" should be understood as in relation to the determination of latitudes by meridian altitudes of that celestial body. The Master Joseph referred to here was doubtless the Jewish scholar José Vizinho. He was involved in these matters, and later, perhaps at the beginning of the last decade of the century, he translated into Castilian the Latin canons of the *Almanach Perpetuum* of Abraham ben Solomon Zacuto *(Item 3)* a work that certainly played a key role in the activity which Columbus attributes to Master Joseph. This activity was certainly effected on land, but probably at sea as well. In fact, when

Bartolomeu Dias undertook the celebrated voyage during which the link between the Atlantic and Indian Oceans was proven for all practical purposes, his pilots were equipped to determine latitudes. Obviously, this was accomplished on the basis of measurements of the sun's altitude at its meridian transit (the moment when it reaches its highest point in the sky), for it is not known that at that time anyone had taken careful sights of the stars of the southern hemisphere. That they took sights for latitude we know, again, from Columbus, who in another note in one of his books states the following: "Note that in this year '88 Bartolomeu Dias arrived at Lisbon in the month of November. He was the captain of three caravels that had been sent by the Most Serene King of Portugal to Guinea on an exploring expedition; and he reported to the same Most Serene King that he had navigated six hundred leagues farther than anyone else, that is, four hundred and fifty leagues to the south and two hundred and fifty leagues to the north, as far as the promontory called by him 'of Good Hope', which we suppose is located in Agensiba [*Terra Austral*, to use Ptolemy's terminology] and he knew from the astrolabe that this place is distant 45° from the equator. . .". There is an error of more than 10° in this latitude, if it perchance refers to the Cape of Good Hope. Accordingly, the Columbus excerpt gave rise to innumerable commentaries, even live polemics, that have gone so far as to hypothesize that Dias intentionally exaggerated the number in order to deceive Columbus. (In a later remark, Columbus affirms that he was present at the interview

Letter of Alessandro Zorzi.
1517.

In a margin note in this letter, Zorzi, a Venetian, provides the first known depiction of a nautical astrolabe and points out the things that distinguish it from the terrestrial version of the instrument. The major functional change is that the sighting vanes are closer together, facilitating its use for sun-sights aboard ship without the navigator's having to actually look through the sighting holes. Instead, the vanes, when aligned with the sun, create a bright spot in the middle of the shadow cast by the vanes on a small board or card held behind the astrolabe.

Biblioteca Nazionale Centrale, Florence (Pages 56-57)

---

12. Portuguese Astrolabe.
1555.

The nautical astrolabe served to measure the altitude of celestial bodies, mainly the North Star and the sun. After taking a sighting, navigators would apply a correction factor (for the North Star) or consult a table similar to that of Abraham Zacuto's Perpetual Almanac (for a sun-sight), to calculate their latitude. During the Age of Discoveries, the other necessary measurement – longitude – was calculated by dead reckoning.

With the expansion of underwater archaeology in recent years, many astrolabes have been found in wrecks of vessels that sank in the 16th and 17th centuries. There are now over five dozen astrolabes known, about half of which are of Portuguese origin.

Dundee Art Galleries and Museums (Page 42)

---

13. Magnetic Compass.
1711. José da Costa Miranda

Navigational use of compasses may date from as early as the 13th century. In Portugal, these instruments were definitely part of seafarers' gear even before the beginnings of navigation along the west coast of Africa. The first known Portuguese text dealing with the mariner's compass dates from 1514 and is the work of a pilot, João de Lisboa. However, no Portuguese mariner's compass from the 15th-17th centuries has survived; the one exhibited here is a later model built by cartographer and instrument maker José da Costa Miranda.

Whipple Museum of the History of Science, University of Cambridge (Page 43)

et che p[er] fugir lo corretie fu dicto capo
p[re]dicto che alaestate n[ost]ra di la sono gra[n]
fredi et che sono navicati i[n] fin a .46. gr[adi]
et ch[e] trovo[n] l[e] insole asai et ch[e] verso
lo altro polo antartico sono alcune
stelle lucide i[n] figura di croce
navico co[n] squadra[n]te et Astrolabio
ma il s[u]o astrolabio ha il suo medica-
rio che le sue due pinule p[er] forera[n]
sono sopra ladicta linea della fiducia[?]
sono molto apresso alpolicer del astrolabio et ch[e] sono ch[e] i[n]fusino di stato
verso il lombo p[er]il moto dello have[r]
ch[e] stano sul mare andegriate no[n]
lasano posar dicto astrolabio i[n] modo
ch[e] il sol possi penetrar iusto p[er] tal mo[do]
il p[er] ch[e] e piu comodo asonar tal pinul[e]
poco distante p[er] aver hauisto il s[u]o Ast[rolabio]

Marginal note:

※

Astrolabio

babio ilquale nõ ha sopr̃ el limbo
cõ numeri et cosi lglidada Et
nõ havẽ Il zadiaco cõsequẽtẽ
su la sua rota nõ era il ciel
ĩpresso cõ sui azimut et helmicadar
nr scala i dorso cõ quadrãte
et grossissimo di brõgio straforato
come qui povo la figura et cosa
semplice La lorcarta si ha da
lisbona et tirãdo p lo oceano
alle isole del Cao verde et capo
di bona sperãcia ĩ fino al capo
di guardafini al mar Rosa. Et
cõ il Re de suo nõ vol sopr̃ pena
della vita che niũ habino piu inãci
et dico quãdo mãda le barchi ĩ Jndia
et da due carte l al piloto e
laltra al nochier et subito sõ tor-
nati gliela toglie dicõ che il capo di

14. Cross-staff.
1718.

The cross-staff appeared in the first quarter of the 16th century, post-dating the astrolabe; it was an upgrade of the "Jacob staff", a surveying instrument widely used during the Middle Ages.

The cross-staff was chiefly used by navigators to measure the altitudes of stars, including the sun. In this latter case, to prevent injury to the user's eyes, the sun was viewed from the side or with the observer's back turned toward it (using an appropriately positioned mirror) or else was blocked by the sliding crosspiece. Then one-half degree was subtracted from the altitude reading, resulting in a value which was very roughly correct.

The instrument exhibited here dates from the 18th century and was made in England; no Portuguese cross-staffs are known to have survived, although they are mentioned by numerous writers of the Age of Discoveries.

The Peabody Museum of Salem, MA (Below)

14

conceded by King João II to the recently returned Dias, at which the aforementioned latitude was cited.) It has even been supposed – and perhaps this is the most plausible explanation – that 45° would have been the most southerly latitude reached by the tiny fleet under the command of Dias. Perhaps the matter can be definitively resolved through a minute examination of the map made at the time by Henricus Martellus Germanus *(Item 28)*, but for the moment this is beyond our purview. What interests us is to place on the record that, in accordance with Columbus' testimony, in 1487-1488 Portuguese pilots were navigating with the aid of so-called "sun sights".

To which rules did they have recourse, and how did they know the solar declinations to which those rules referred? To be honest, we do not know. Perhaps we would not be wandering very far from the truth if we admit that at that time they were still following the first of the two Regiments published in the so-called *Munich Nautical Guide* of circa 1509. This Regiment doubtless represents an out-of-date form of the text, one that was soon followed by another, perfectly satisfactory, form. We would also be near the truth if we admit that the table of declinations available to the pilots, if it had been worked out, was of the type known as *Tábua Única* or "Single-Year Table", as appears in the text of the *Munich Guide* itself.

There is no doubt that doubts existed about the Regiment and the exact nature of its practical applications. On one of the vessels of Pedro Álvares Cabral's fleet, King Manuel ordered the presence of an astrologer, his "physician and surgeon", the

Castilian Mestre João (Master John), with the intention of revealing the value of the astrolabe, and therefore of the Solar Regiment, as well as of having recourse to the "kamal" or *Tábuas da Índia* (Tables of India) that Vasco da Gama had found in the hands of Asian pilots, and of which he had brought back to Lisbon at least one example. Master John criticized the use of the *kamal*, but he also had reasons to deride the results obtained with the astrolabe. He was wrong. Concerning the *kamal*, his doubts might have been due to an imperfect acquaintance with that rudimentary altitude-measuring device. As for his doubts regarding the astrolabe, they were in part due to the difficulties of operating it aboard a tiny vessel filled with passengers, frequently pitching and rolling heavily, and also on occasion because of his own sickness, of which he complained. They also must have been largely the consequence of his own desire for absolute or almost absolute rigour, something that might preoccupy the astrologer that he was, but that certainly would not worry a practical pilot in the same circumstances.

Tables for Determination of Sun's Declination
Let us speak now of tables of the sun's declination. As has been said, sun tables exist in traditional astronomical texts, e.g., the *Almanaques Astronómicos de Madrid (Item 2)*, in part written in or translated into Portuguese in the first half of the fourteenth century. They exist of course in Zacuto's *Almanach Perpetuum, (Item 3)* prepared possibly in 1472 but published in Leiria only

in 1496, when its author, a Jew who had refused to convert to Catholicism, was being welcomed in Portugal after having been expelled from Spain.

From the first of these writings one could extract the *Lugares do Sol* (Places of the Sun), as they were called in those days. For each day of a cycle of four years, these gave the sun's zodiacal sign and the number of degrees, minutes, and seconds the sun had advanced into it. That was the equivalent of indicating the coordinate that is today called the "celestial longitude" of a body. In the Madrid manuscript, however, an element is missing that would be essential in navigation, namely, a rudimentary table that, given the Place of the Sun, would make it possible to determine its declination. In other words, if the pilot knew a Place of the Sun in degrees, minutes, and seconds, he had to have recourse to the numbers provided by the table of declinations (or "Tabula declinationis planetarum & solis ab equinoctiali", as Zacuto called it) and make an interpolation on the basis of them. This required him to carry out multiplications and divisions that were certainly beyond the reach of the majority of the navigators, because their mathematical preparation was elementary and the means of performing those arithmetic operations were not noted for their simplicity.

The solution was to have recourse to an expert in arithmetic and ask him to work out, on the basis of the Places of the Sun, all the declinations for a year (giving rise to the so-called *Tábua Solar Única* or "Single-Year Sun Table") or for a four-year period. We know that this latter was the path followed to get around the difficulty, because the four-year tables of the *Tractado da Spera do mundo...*, that is, the so-called *Évora Nautical Guide* of circa 1516, are repeated in the 1518 edition of the *Reportório dos Tempos* printed by Valentim Fernandes, and there they carry an indication that they had been calculated by Gaspar Nicolas, "a master well trained in that art". Indeed, Nicolas was the author of the first treatise on arithmetic published in Portugal, in 1519. On the other hand, there are residues of previous four-year tables, for the periods 1493-1496, 1497-1500, and 1501-1504, in the so-called *Livro de Marinharia de André Pires (Item 10)*. We do not know who calculated these; perhaps Zacuto had been the calculator of those first four-year tables, as a passage by the chronicler Gaspar Correia suggests.

It was the four-year form that survived, remaining for years as it appeared in the *Munich Nautical Guide*, even while certain discrepancies cropped up between the Julian calendar, in use in those times, and the apparent movement of the sun. These required corrections to be made at the end of each four-year period, corrections that were in fact foreseen in the Madrid *Astronomical Almanacs* as well as in the *Almanach Perpetuum*. At the end of the sixteenth century, corrections were deemed essential and appropriate ones were undertaken. Earlier, Pedro Nunes had recognized the mistake that was being made. He advised a return to the use of four tables of Places of the Sun, one for each year of a four-year period, and to one table of declinations, as can be seen in one of the works annexed to his

15. Model of a Latin Caravel.
1988. Francisco Ferreira Da Conceicão

It is in ships of this type - the two-masted lateen-rigged caravel - that the Portuguese embarked on systematic exploration of the Atlantic in the 15th century. These were relatively light vessels (about 50 tons burden), easy to manoeuvre, and capable of sailing under adverse conditions. They were also distinguished by their large sails, which enhanced their performance. This won them the reputation among navigators of other nationalities as being the finest ships of their day.

Comissão Nacional para as Comemorações dos Descobrimentos Portugueses, Lisbon (Below)

---

16. Plan of the Works of Cape Saker and St. Vincent in Portugal.
1587. Anonymous drawing on paper

This drawing shows some of the installations on the capes of Sagres and St. Vincent in southern Portugal where, according to tradition, the Infante Dom Henrique ("Henry the Navigator") sponsored many innovations in navigation. We can only speculate about which of the buildings shown here may have been the hypothetical centre of operations of Dom Henrique's maritime activities.

The site was strategic, facing towards Africa and also lying along the shipping lanes between the Mediterranean and the Atlantic.

The British Library, London (Page 61)

15

17

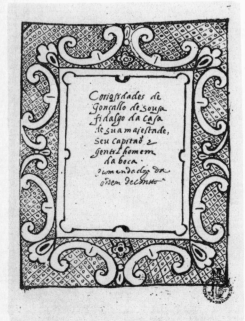

Tratado da Sphera (Treatise on
the Sphere) of 1537 *(Item 9)*, in
which he published a new version
of the five tables, with all the
drawbacks already pointed out.
We do not know of a single
example of the cosmographer's
advice having been taken!

The Problem of Longitude

And what of terrestrial longitude?
We said before that navigators
were concerned about
determining it. Theoretically
correct procedures existed for
finding it, based, for example, on
the moon's movement, even
though this was incompletely
understood at the time. Sailors
were aware of the enormous
errors that such procedures
could generate. Only in
exceptional cases did they turn to
them, and the numbers obtained
did not give them the least
confidence. Dom João de Castro,
an excellent observer, alludes
more than once to his
preparations for observing
eclipses of the moon, to obtain
values for longitudes, but he
never recorded any of the values
he might have obtained.
In the face of such difficulty,
ideas proliferated. The one most
circulated among sailors was
perhaps related to Ptolemy's
having drawn through the
Canary Islands – or through
Atlantic islands that were
identified as such – his prime
meridian for numbering
longitudes, which he counted only
in an easterly direction. When
the phenomenon of magnetic
compass variation was
discovered, and after verification
(or simply the supposition) that it
was zero in that archipelago, the
Ptolemaic reference meridian was
immediately accepted as an
agonic line passing through points
of no variation, and that on
either side of it compass error

was respectively east or west,
and proportional to the longitude
as one sailed in one direction or
the other. Such an idea, in
reality absolutely fantastic, was
expounded for the first time in
João de Lisboa's *Livro de
Marinharia (Item 121)* in the
portion called the *Tratado da
Agulha de Marear* (Treatise on
the Mariner's Compass) of 1514.
Though that same text contains
data that stand in absolute
contradiction to it, the false
notion took hold and was widely
adopted by pilots. This was done
without great risks, let it be
added, for inasmuch as compass
variation did not vary
noticeably, and what was later
called secular change in
variation was then completely
unknown, the value of compass
variation could serve as a
conhecença.
Around 1530, however, strong
doubts began to circulate about
the efficacy of these methods for
determining the second
terrestrial coordinate.
Therefore, Dom João de Castro
was charged with systematically
determining compass variation
through a procedure that he
received from Pedro Nunes, but
to which Francisco Faleiro
before him had referred in 1535
(Item 8). He was also charged
with comparing the "longitudes"
thus obtained with the estimates
he obtained by dead-reckoning.
The task was entrusted to him as
he departed on his first voyage to
India, in 1538 *(Item 7)*, as
commander of the *nau* (a full-
rigged ship) *Grifo*. He sortied
from Belém on the Tagus River
on April 6. Two months later, on
June 10, he felt sure enough of
himself, based on the results of
observations made so far, to
include the following in his
notebook: "From these changes
it is clear that the variation that

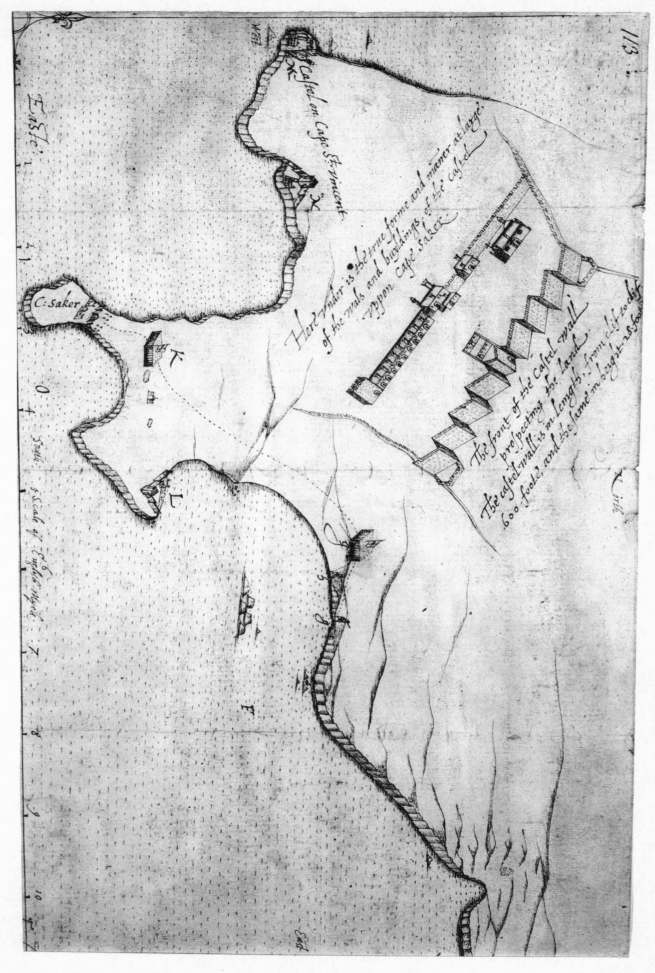

16

113

Easte

The Castel on Cape St Vincent

C. saker

Here vnder is the true forme and manner at large of the wals and buildings of the castel vppon Cape Saker

The front of the castel wall prospecting the land.
The castel wall is in length, from clif to clif 600 footes, and the same in hight 18 foot

North

K

L

Soute Scale of English myles

West

East

18. Livro da Fabrica das Naos.
Book of Shipbuilding.
c. 1580. Fernando Oliveira

Around 1570, Fr. Fernando Oliveira (1507- after 1581) wrote, in Latin, the first European encyclopaedic work on naval subjects, entitled Ars Nautica. *In about 1580 he rewrote the chapter on shipbuilding, in greater detail and in Portuguese. This is the manuscript exhibited here, the* Livro da Fabrica das Naos.

In certain areas, Oliveira was a century ahead of his contemporaries; as late as 1691, Dutch shipbuilding engineer Nicolaes Witsen in his Architectura Navalis *copied the technical drawings directly from the* Ars Nautica.

*Biblioteca Nacional, Lisbon
(Page 48 and below)*

---

19. Livro Náutico ou meio practico da construção dos navios e de galés antigas.
Nautical Book or practical method for the construction of ships and ancient galleys.
Late 16th c. Anonymous

This miscellaneous codex contains a large number of documents related to Spanish and Portuguese naval history. Noteworthy are its figures on the cost of armadas and rules for the construction of naus, *galleons and other types of vessel, as well as one of the most complete descriptions of the "Invincible Armada" with which Philip II of Spain sought in vain to attack England in 1588.*

*Biblioteca Nacional, Lisbon
(Facing page)*

18

compasses undergo is not due to a difference in meridians, for in the city of Lisbon the variation is 7°30'E, and on the meridian where he now is [from the dead-reckoning position that he was estimating] it is 19° or 20° E". If compass variation were proportional to longitude, then his measurements should have been lower as he sailed west, towards the supposed line of zero-variation.

Regardless of this, the practice of guessing longitude by observing compass variation was not abandoned. The value obtained was accepted, as we said, as a *conhecença*. By the beginning of the seventeenth century, no practical and certain means of determining longitude at sea had been found, although tempting pecuniary awards awaited their would-be discoverer. At that point, an Italian Jesuit named Cristoforo Bruno, who resided in Portugal and was a teacher in the *Colégio* of Santo Antão, seized on the idea of having charts drawn with parallels of latitude and with isogonic lines; the latter was in a sense a substitute for meridians. The simultaneous determination of latitude and of compass variation would fix the position of the vessel.

Bruno's fantasy is forgiven, because he was unaware that compass variation changed in a given place with time. Let it be credited to his memory that the determination of longitude would be assured once the problem of the conversion of time was resolved. He even says as much in an *Arte de Navegar* that he wrote. From the first quarter of the sixteenth century on, navigators knew this. An example is Fernão de Magalhães (Ferdinand Magellan), who took a supply of hourglasses on his

journey, in the hope of getting around the difficulty. But only the tenacity of the Englishman John Harrison, inventor of the first true chronometer, would succeed in reaching the definitive solution of a problem that had defied the sagacity of a Galileo or a Huygens.

Variations in Design of Altitude-Measuring Devices

One word more, so that we can speak of the "sea astrolabe" *(Item 12)*. Its precursor, the medieval planispheric astrolabe, disk-shaped and containing various graphics on its two surfaces, served mainly to solve problems of fixed-position astronomy, usually for astrological ends. The alidade or sighting bar was affixed to the centre of the disk and capable of moving in a complete circle. At its extremities were two square or rectangular sighting vanes with holes in their centres, through which aim could be taken at heavenly bodies. Once the instrument was suspended by the ring at its top and the alidade duly aimed, a scale on the outer edge of the disk furnished the value in degrees of the astronomical altitude of the observed body.

From medieval references to the use of the plansipheric astrolabe, these kinds of observations would have been the exception. However, a passage in a treatise by John of Holywood (Sacrobosco) does reveal that in the thirteenth century the instrument was used to observe the North Star. Other bodies eventually would have been observed.

With the advent of nautical astronomy and recourse to measurements of the sun, the astrolabe turned out to be the best instrument for observations, and with good reason: it was not necessary to look directly at the sun, but merely to rotate the alidade until the solar rays passed through the holes of the sighting vanes and produced a small circle of light in the middle of the superimposed shadows created by the vanes. For this, only the alidade and the peripheral scale of the instrument were of any importance, leading to modifications that produced the so-called sea astrolabe. This came to consist merely of an outer ring with four radial supports, the alidade being affixed to the centre, where the supports intersected. The suspension ring was retained, but the sighting vanes of the alidade were moved closer together to facilitate the indirect observation of the sun. The latter peculiarity is discussed explicitly for the first time, as far as we know, in an informational note about the Portuguese made in Venice in 1517 by Alessandro Zorzi. Zorzi declares that Portuguese pilots navigated by quadrant and astrolabe; but, although their astrolabe had the two perforated sighting vanes, these "were not at the ends"; in this way, lining up the sun was facilitated "despite the rocking motion of the vessel". The description is accompanied by a drawing that, in spite of its crudeness, shows very clearly the features that attracted Zorzi's attention *(Pages 56-57)*. All that now needs be said is that one other alteration was introduced on Portuguese astrolabes, and only on them. Pilots, and the astrologers who helped them, must have realized very early that, in the calculations required to utilize the Regiment of the Sun, the astronomical altitude of the body

did not come into play but rather the complement of that angle, called its "zenith distance". To avoid one more useless subtraction, it was realized that the astronomical coordinate of interest could be read directly on the instrument. To do so, it was only necessary to alter the direction of the scale that ran along the perimeter of the device, with the upper quadrants of the instrument graduated from 0° to 90°, the 0° being inscribed next to the ring at the point where the perpendicular of the centre of suspension passed. The astrolabe that Portuguese pilots used in the sixteenth, seventeenth, and eighteenth centuries was constructed in this fashion.

20. Livro de traças de Carpintaria.
Book of Carpentry Drawings.
1616. Manuel Fernandes

This work, though not always technically rigorous, is the largest and most beautifully illustrated Portuguese naval construction document from this period, which saw the appearance of the first formal writings on naval architecture. Shown are the first technical drawings of a caravel and a Portuguese galleon.

*Biblioteca da Ajuda, Lisbon
(Pages 44-45, 46-47)*

19

Section II

Francis M. Rogers
Exploring the Atlantic

Introduction by
Wilcomb E. Washburn

*The reasons why the Lord Infante was moved to search for the
lands of Guinea:*
*First, because he had desire to know the lands that lay beyond
the Canary Islands and Cape Bojador. . . for until that time
not by writing nor by memory did any man ever know for
certain the quality of the land that lay beyond that cape.*
*The second reason was because he considered that, if they
found Christians living in those lands. . . they would be able to
bring much merchandise . . . and the traffic would bring great
profit to its inhabitants.*
*The third reason was . . . to determine the extent and power of
his enemies, the Moors.*
*The fourth reason . . . was that he wanted to know if any
Christian princes were to be found in those parts.*
*The fifth reason was the great desire he had to increase in the
holy faith of Our Lord, and bring to Him every soul that had
wish to be saved.*
*And it appears that the root of all the other reasons is to be
found in the paths of the heavenly orbs . . . by force of such
natural influence, this honorable prince was inclined
to such deeds.*

From Gomes Eanes de Zurara, Crónica do Descobrimento
e conquista da Guiné. *(Item 30)*

*. . . whereas a certain controversy exists between the said
lords, . . . for the sake of peace and concord they agreed that a
boundary or straight line be determined and drawn north and
south, from pole to pole, on the ocean sea, from the Arctic to
the Antarctic pole.*
*This line shall be drawn straight . . . at a distance of three
hundred and seventy leagues west of the Cape Verde
Islands. . . . And all lands . . . on the eastern side of the said
bound . . . shall belong to . . . the said King of Portugal and his
successors. And all other lands . . . shall belong to . . . the said
King and Queen of Castile.*

From the Treaty of Tordesillas, *June 7, 1494. (Item 63)*

Europe's view of the world changed rapidly as a result of the Portuguese explorations. Indeed, the advance of geographical knowledge was explosive, as every ship captain brought back new information from the hitherto unknown borders of the Atlantic. That Western Sea was found to be a broad highway leading to the discovery both of Brazil and of a route to India around the southern tip of Africa. Castile was Portugal's fiercest competitor at that time. To keep their explorers out of each other's way, the two Iberian kingdoms obtained, in 1493, a papal division of the earth from pole to pole in the Atlantic, on either side of which line each agreed to limit its activities. Amended by the two kingdoms in 1494 when the initial line proved unsatisfactory, this agreement kept relative peace between the two powers as they pursued their goals of trade, settlement and conquest, as opportunities allowed, in the newly discovered lands. When Portuguese explorers reached the Asian lands (the true "Indies") which were their original goal, debate arose as to whether the line of demarcation extended around the other side of the world to the Pacific. To satisfy questions about the location of the rich spice islands in that area, Castile commissioned the Portuguese Fernão de Magalhães (Ferdinand Magellan) to seek those islands by sailing west, beyond the New World. Although Magellan himself was killed by Pacific Islanders during the voyage, one of his five ships, aptly named the Victoria, returned triumphantly to Seville on September 6, 1522, thus completing the first circumnavigation of the globe.

W.E.W.

Many Americans are aware that Portuguese is the language of Brazil. Knowing that Spanish serves most of the rest of South America, they wonder about the uniqueness of the largest country of that continent. Columbus returned to Castile in the late winter of 1493 after stopping off in the Azores and Lisbon. The Portuguese had hitherto considered the Atlantic, in part at least, as their own preserve, a path around southern Africa en route eastward to the fabled Indies. They immediately became concerned lest a rival power violate their area of action. Negotiations between Portugal and Castile proceeded apace. They resulted in the Treaty of Tordesillas, of June 7, 1494. It defined a Line of Demarcation or "Mark" 370 leagues west of the

21. Replica of Monument (Padrão) of Cape Cross.
1988 (Orig.: 1485). Acrylic cast.

The padrões ("standards") were stone monuments which Portuguese navigators carried on board for placement in lands they discovered to claim and indicate their dominion. The original of this padrão, which is now in the Museum für Deutsche Geschichte, Berlin, was placed in 1485 by Diogo Cão, at latitude 21° 47' S, a point now known as Cape Cross, in Namibia.

It bears the coat-of-arms of Dom João II and an inscription in Latin and Portuguese which reads: "In the year 6685 of the creation of the earth and 1485 after the birth of Christ the most excellent and serene King Dom João II of Portugal ordered this land to be discovered and this padrão to be placed by Diogo Cão, nobleman of this house".

Comissão Nacional para as Comemorações dos Descobrimentos Portugueses, Lisbon (Below)

21

22. Replica of 1492 Terrestrial Globe of Martin Behaim.
1892. Made by Gigot de Grandpré, under the direction of Henry Vignaud.

This globe is significant because it reflects the reigning world-view prior to the discovery of the New World, in which Asia is separated from Europe by a relatively narrow ocean, with no other continent in between. The original globe of 1492 was made under the direction of Martin Behaim. The 1892 replica was made to commemorate the four-hundredth anniversary of the first Columbus voyage to America, and follows an exact copy produced in 1847 for the Bibliothèque Nationale, Paris.

Behaim was a German who was active in Portuguese maritime affairs. He was knighted by the king, Dom João II, in 1485, and purportedly made an Atlantic voyage as a member of a Portuguese fleet. During a period of residence in his native Nuremberg, the City Council there ordered the globe constructed and covered with identifying legends under his guidance.
Smithsonian Institution, Washington DC
(Below)

22

Cape Verde Islands. To the east was the Portuguese preserve, to the west that of Castile. The north-south line, or meridian, placed Brazil, because of its eastward location in relation to the rest of South America, within the Portuguese zone. Portugal subsequently rendered Brazil a Portuguese colony whose means of communication became the Portuguese language. The Tordesillas Line also placed the eastern portion of Newfoundland, or so it was believed, within the Portuguese zone.

Early Atlantic Maritime Subculture

Portugal has been called Europe's garden planted at the side of the sea. The southwesternmost of European countries, it faces both west and southwest.

Once their land was established as an independent Christian nation born of the Reconquest in 1040, Portuguese fishermen and coastwise merchant sailors ranged out into the Atlantic as far as they dared, as far as the art of navigation available to them permitted. They may have gone so far as to perceive real islands, if not continents, especially in the mists to the west and northwest. They certainly were in contact with Europeans to their north whose ancestors – specifically the Norsemen – had in fact come upon land in the west. Informal contact between Norsemen and Portuguese must have existed as the Middle Ages proceeded. Indeed, an entire Western European maritime subculture – the "private sector", to use a modern phrase – undoubtedly was in place; this voiced rumours of islands out in the Atlantic, islands whose precise location the mariners were unable to ascertain, islands

that they made no attempt to claim for their respective sovereigns. The early seafarers did use specific names for them, like Legname (Italian for wood), Corvi Marini (Italian or Latin for cormorants or marine ravens), and S. Zorzi (northern Italian dialect for St. George). These and other islands and names like St. Brendan's Isle, the Island of Brazil, and that of the Seven Cities turn up on early maps executed by Europeans, and notably Italian and Catalonian including Mallorcan cartographers, even as early as the 1320's *(Item 1)*. A beautiful example is the 1424 map made by the Venetian Zuane Pizzigano *(Item 23)*. Among others, it depicts four spectacular islands: Antilla, Ymana, Satanazes and Saya. Examples of a slightly later generation of Atlantic maps are Grazioso Benincasa's Portolan chart of 1463 *(Item 24)*, which reflects accurate knowledge of the Canary Islands and Selvagens and the recently discovered Madeiras and possibly some Azores, and his chart of 1468 *(Item 25)*, which portrays the very recently discovered Cape Verde Islands. A formal and very real contact between Portugal and the Northern countries involved the Church's great ecumenical councils of the fifteenth century: Pisa (1409), Constance (1414-1418) and Basel (convened in 1431), the latter of which changed its location to become the Council of Ferrara (1436-1438), Florence (1439-1442), Rome (1442-1445).

To these councils, among considerable other news, came echoes of a Christian province as far away as Greenland. Nevertheless, when all is said and done, none of the aforementioned maritime knowledge of Atlantic islands and of lands to west and northwest, and possibly also southwest, entered the main historical record. No legal claims were made. The slate remained clean until Columbus reported the event of October 12, 1492. And he did not report it just privately. A letter of his was printed at once and widely disseminated.

Columbian knowledge became widespread in a different and extraordinary way. In 1513, the Turkish scholar Piri Reis drew a map of the Atlantic. It was based in part on information furnished by a Spanish sailor who had sailed with Columbus.

Infrastructure for Portuguese Atlantic Exploration

The heads of Western European countries, all of them Christian, once had been accustomed to respect the authority of the popes, not only in purely ecclesiastical affairs but also in certain secular matters. The latter category included the right of the pope to award newly-discovered lands – that is, non-Christian territories – to European nations.

Development of a solid infrastructure for future Portuguese maritime activity took place as early as the reign of King Dinis (1279-1325). Pine forests were planted, especially in the Leiria region, in anticipation of later demands by shipwrights. A system of marine insurance was devised to minimize the risks of shipowners. To ensure real expertise for his fleets, Dinis arranged to import Genoese seamen, as is evidenced by the contract with Pessagno (Item 65).

Most significantly, in 1288 Dinis married Isabel, the daughter of King Pedro III of Aragon, the

St. Elizabeth of Portugal of the Catholic Church's calendar. He therefore had a family connection with one of the Christian kingdoms of Iberia, which in the mid-sixteenth century came to form "Spain" as we know it. This connection led him to have close relations with that other Christian kingdom lying between him and Aragon, adjacent Castile. He, or at least his successors, was thus receptive to the contributions of his near-contemporary, King Alfonso X "el Sabio" (ruled Castile 1252-1284).

Alfonso "the Wise" sponsored translations of Arabic scientific treatises that in turn went back to the work of the Ancient Greeks. He was particularly interested in astronomy – the ultimate pinion of high-seas navigation – and his *Alfonsine Tables* were widely regarded and formed a link in a chain of such tables that led directly to later Portuguese capabilities.

Two examples manifest the ultimate impact of Alfonso X's circle on later Portuguese navigational theoreticians. The one concerns the obliquity of the ecliptic, the angle between the plane of the earth's orbit around the sun (the ecliptic), and the plane of the equator. The scientists of the later Middle Ages accepted this quantity as 23° 33', and Zacut employed it in his Almanac of 1496 (Item 3). The later Pedro Nunes adopted 23° 30' for his 1537 treatise (Item 9). The other example concerns the length of the tropical year, 365 d 05 h 49 m 26s – that is, the time it takes for the earth to complete one revolution around the sun. This was the value used by Alfonso X's men and by both Zacut and Nunes and was based on the fact that it takes approximately 23 h 56 m 04 s of

23. Nautical Chart.
1424. Zuane Pizzigano
Manuscript map on parchment

The map of Zuane Pizzigano is a portolan chart with various hypothetical islands drawn in the western Atlantic (e.g., "Antilia" and "Satanazes"). One of the most eminent scholars of this map, Armando Cortesão, maintained that those islands actually correspond to the West Indies and America, presumably reconnoitred by Portuguese navigators seven decades before Columbus. No other historian of cartography has accepted Cortesão's thesis. Most believe the islands to be mythical or imaginary.

The James Ford Bell Library, University of Minnesota
(Page 81)

24-25. Portolan Charts.
1463 and 1468. Grazioso Benincasa
Manuscript maps: ink, hand-coloured, gold leaf on vellum

There exist a number of charts made by the Italian cartographer Grazioso Benincasa; these are either dated or datable between c.1461 and c. 1482. They were drawn according to Mediterranean cartographic techniques. In plotting the west coast of Africa, Benincasa used data from Portuguese voyages and possibly even from Portuguese charts. Besides these direct sources, Benincasa is thought to have referred to Cá da Mosto's account of travels in Africa, as well as to the Chronicle of the Deeds of Guinea by Gomes Eanes de Zurara (Item 30). Benincasa was the first cartographer to show certain key results of Portuguese voyages: the Cape Verde Islands and the entire West African coast south of Cabo Roxo as far as Cabo de Santa Maria.

The British Library, London
(Pages 82, 83)

---

26. Portolan Chart.
15th c. Cristofalo Soligo
Bound manuscript map: hand coloured on vellum

This set of charts in the British Library is ascribed to a presumed Italian cartographer, Cristofalo Soligo. Among them are several which shed light on the Portuguese navigations, particularly those in the Gulf of Guinea in the decade 1470-1480. One of these records places visited as far as Cabo de Santa Catarina, showing three of the four gulf islands, but fails to indicate the fortress of São Jorge da Mina, definite evidence that the chart was drawn on the basis of data pre-dating 1482, when that fortress-trading post was built.

The British Library, London
(Pages 84-85)

27. Map of Africa and the Atlantic.
c.1485. Pedro Reinel
Manuscript map: ink and paint on parchment

Pedro Reinel is one of the earliest Portuguese cartographers of whom we have a signed work – this chart, undated, but which could be dated either c. 1485 (the date preferred here) or c. 1483. Noteworthy is the plotting of part of the African coast on the inland portion of the continent. This suggests that the map had already been nearly completed when new geographic information became available, forcing Reinel to append the extra portion of the coastline in this fashion, to prevent his work from becoming immediately obsolete.

Archives Departementaux de la Gironde, Bordeaux
(Page 86)

---

28. World Map.
In:"Insularium Illustratum"
c.1489. Henricus Martellus
Bound manuscript map: hand-coloured, gold leaf on vellum

Upon completion of Bartolomeu Dias' voyage (December 1488), the news that the Atlantic and Indian Oceans were connected spread throughout Europe. In Italy soon afterward, cartographer Henricus Martellus Germanus produced this planisphere in which the part of Africa covered by Dias' voyage is quite precisely drawn, while beyond that point the old Ptolemaic model prevails.

The British Library, London
(Pages 88-89)

---

29. Map of the Atlantic.
c. 1534. Jorge Reinel
Manuscript map on parchment

Jorge Reinel was the son of Pedro Reinel, and learned the art of map making from his father. After perfecting his craft, he worked in Seville for the kings of Spain, and there his father came seeking him on orders from the king of Portugal, as corroborated by other documents in this exhibition (see No. 73).

All that exists of Jorge Reinel's work today is the so-called "Miller Atlas" made jointly by his father and another cartographer, in the National Library, Paris; a chart of the Indian Ocean, and this Atlantic chart from c. 1534.

The James Ford Bell Library, University of Minnesota
(Page 87)

solar time, the length of the sidereal day, for the stars to appear to make one trip around the earth. In other words, the sun at a given moment is 1' 46" farther east along the ecliptic than four years earlier. Accordingly, at the end of thirty-four four-year cycles, or 136 years, this correction, vital for Zacut's tables, amounted to a whole degree.

In 1291, the expedition of the brothers Vivaldi left the Mediterranean, headed south and passed the Canaries, having obviously sighted, on the island of Tenerife, Teyde, which is that archipelago's and the Atlantic's loftiest peak, 12,198 feet high (3,718 meters).

In 1341, a Genoese expedition first put into Lisbon and received King Alfonso's support. It then headed directly for the Canaries and returned. The account of it, namely, a letter written in Seville and dated "Mcccxlj", is contained in a famous miscellany of jottings, or *Zibaldone*, said to have been assembled by none other than Boccaccio.

Europe thus restored its acquaintance with the *Insulae Fortunatae*, an archipelago already inhabited by an indigenous population known as Guanches and, moreover, known to Antiquity.

Expansion in West Africa

In 1415, King João I, assisted by his three oldest sons, led an expedition that conquered a city and great trading centre in Morocco opposite Gibraltar, the aforementioned Ceuta, the southern Pillar of Hercules. The entire affair was a masterfully planned and carefully executed amphibious operation that should figure high on the list of such operations studied by the U.S. Marine Corps. It placed

Portugal in Africa, overseas. The King of Portugal was now the "King of Portugal and of the Algarves on This Side of and Beyond the Seas in Africa". Portuguese mariners followed up the conquest of Ceuta by exploring southward along Africa's Atlantic coast. Whether at this early stage Portugal was aiming at circumnavigation of the African continent and sailing on to India is a greatly debated subject. In any event, following his return from Ceuta and from a second visit to Morocco in 1418, Henrique (referred to in Portuguese simply as "O Infante," short for "O Infante Dom Henrique" d. 1460) assumed the function of sponsor of Portuguese maritime exploration. He set up a centre on Sagres Point, just east of Cape St. Vincent *(Item 16)*. There, among other preoccupations, he interested himself in research and development, specifically of naval architecture, naval ordnance, nautical science and cartography. He brought in masters of these subjects from abroad. He welcomed the information brought him by his brother Pedro following the latter's travels over the years 1425-1428, including a world map and a manuscript of Marco Polo's travels. He of course absorbed with alacrity any news brought back to his country by the high-level delegations to the Council of Florence, the centre of convergence of real information concerning the "East", including the various Christians of Eastern rites. Pedro's travels greatly excited the popular imagination later in the century. A certain Gomez de Santisteban wrote a little tract in Spanish about the infante's wanderings over the four parts of the world *(Item 31)*. It took him to the shrine of the Apostle Thomas and the court of Prester John, thus outlining Portuguese goals and motivations. It even took him to Norway! Incidentally, in view of Sagres' contributions to terrestrial marine exploration, it is only natural that Portugal has pioneered a movement to link the European Sagres, via today's international sister-cities' programme, with Cape Canaveral, the American centre of twentieth-century space exploration. The phrase "exploration and discovery" is the hallmark of both places.

The Portuguese thrust was to the south, ever farther south along Africa's western coast. The push continued throughout Henrique's life and for several decades after his death. A notable event first took place in 1434, with the rounding of Cape Bojador. In 1441, Nuno Tristão came upon Cap Blanc and three years later the Portuguese sailors reached Cap Vert. Down the coast the Portuguese continued, around the Gulf of Guinea, and still beyond. In 1471, João de Santarém and Pero de Escobar explored the Gold Coast. There, in 1482, the great castle known as São Jorge da Mina was built, in present-day Ghana, where it still stands and is known as Elmina. Another landmark occurred in 1482, when Diogo Cão came upon the mouth of the Congo River. At the time of Henrique's death, the Portuguese had reached what is now Sierra Leone but had not turned the corner into the Gulf of Guinea.
In spite of concentration on South and Southeast, Henrique did not neglect Portuguese interests in other directions. His

fifteenth-century biographer and panegyrist Zurara in the *Chronicle of the Discovery and Conquest of Guinea (Item 30)* even tells of contact with Galway on the west coast of Ireland. By 1482, João II had vigorously assumed the role played by his granduncle Henrique. Whether or not the latter had had a passage to India in his mind, King João certainly did have, as Professor Boxer makes clear in his essay in this volume. Certainly Eastern Christians – St. Thomas Christians in South India and Prester John of the Indies' Christians in Ethiopia, and even the remote Nestorian Christians of Central and Eastern Asia – were well known to the rulers of Portugal because Marco Polo, followed by the Council of Florence, confirmed stories about them. A desire to initiate a quest for those Eastern Christians, combined, of course, with an overwhelming interest in effecting ever greater foreign trade, figured among the motivations at work on Sagres Point. Such at least was Zurara's conclusion.
The chronicler lists six motivations that impelled his hero overseas:
1) to expand knowledge;
2) to trade;
3) to know the extent of the Moorish enemy;
4) to make contact with Eastern Christians;
5) to convert heathens to Christianity, and
6) to follow the decrees of the revolution of the heavenly spheres.

Updating Ptolemy's "Geography"
Advancing ever farther southward along the African coast, the Portuguese naturally determined, as best they could,

30. Portrait of O Infante Dom Henrique (Prince Henry "The Navigator")
in: "Crónica do descobrimento e conquista da Guiné."
Chronicle of the Discovery and Conquest of Guinea.
Dated 1453; partly composed after 1460. Gomes Eanes de Zurara

Prince Henry "The Navigator" (1394 - 1460) made sea exploration an instrument of Portuguese national policy, and encouraged the growth of new methods of navigation.

In Zurara's words: "The noble spirit of this Prince was ever urging him both to begin and to carry out great deeds. . . . He had also a wish to know the land that lay beyond the Isles of Canary and that Cape called Bojador, for that up to his time, neither by writings, nor by the memory of man, was known with any certainty the nature of the land beyond that Cape . . . . It seemed to him that if he or some other lord did not endeavor to gain that knowledge, no mariners or merchants would ever dare to attempt it, for it is clear that none of them ever trouble themselves to sail to a place where there is not a sure and certain hope of profit."

Bibliothèque Nationale, Paris
(Pages 90-91)

---

31. Libro del infante don Pedro de portugal: el qual anduuo las quatro partidas del mundo.
Book of Prince Pedro of Portugal who travelled the four corners of the Earth.
c.1520. Gomez de Santisteban

In the third decade of the 15th century, while his brother Dom Henrique occupied himself as governor of the Algarves and patron of Portuguese navigational enterprises, Dom Pedro – Duke of Coimbra – undertook an extended trip through Europe. His journey was described by Gomez de Santisteban in this book, which was to see numerous editions. Santisteban's narrative blended reality and fantasy, recounting visits Dom Pedro never made, to places like Abyssinia and Norway. In fact, though, Pedro brought back much information which was valuable to his brother, including perhaps a world map, and a manuscript of Marco Polo's travels.

Cleveland Public Library
(Page 72)

32. Obedience Oration.
1485. Vasco Fernandes de Lucena

The oration of obedience delivered at the papal court in 1485 by Vasco Fernandes de Lucena, envoy of Dom João II, includes mention of the Portuguese discovery voyages, which is not unusual in speeches of this kind. In it, Lucena is quite clear: the king is convinced that he could reach the Indian Ocean, and hastened to announce the fact to the Curia. In fact, certainty of being at the "gates of India" was not to materialize until 1488, when Dias returned from his voyage around the Cape of Good Hope. But this speech shows that the Perfect Prince had made a plan and was bent on carrying it to a successful conclusion.

The James Ford Bell Library, University of Minnesota
(Facing page)

---

33. India Recognita.
India Rediscovered.
1492. Poggio Bracciolini

This treatise by the papal secretary Poggio Bracciolini contained information brought back from South Asia by the Venetian, Nicolo de' Conti. It mentions that "the sea [Persian Gulf] rises and falls as does our sea", an observation relevant to the question of whether the Indian Ocean was a closed or open body of water. The possibility of a sea route to India hinged on this fact.

Houghton Library, Harvard University
(Page 74)

31

Libro del infante don Pedro de portugal: el qual anduuo las quatro partidas del mundo.

the position of prominent landmarks, reported them to Sagres, and contributed to ever more accurate mapping of Africa as it was becoming known to Europe. Actually, the Portuguese had to "dis-map". They had to correct, or better, update the vision some writers held of Africa, an apparently erroneous vision inherited from Antiquity. Claudius Ptolemy had written his *Geographia* (also known as the *Cosmography)* in Greek in the middle of the second century A.D. It circulated in Latin translation at the Council of Pisa in manuscript. It was first printed, with its maps, in 1477 *(Item 48)*. In this work the author included a world map and a series of individual maps, one of the latter depicting the Fortunate Islands *(Item 49)*. The world map presented the entire world known to him, that is, the Eurasian land mass from the Atlantic eastward to East Asia. Ptolemy was most uncertain of the southern extension of Africa below the Sahara. Curiously, he carried Southern Africa around to the east and connected it with a projection of Asia beyond the Malay Peninsula. He thus seemed to have made of the Indian Ocean an enclosed lake and suggested that it was impossible to circumnavigate Africa.

The Carmelite John of Hildesheim in 1375 wrote a charming "novel" about the Three Holy Kings. He mentioned the Red Sea and unassumedly pointed out: "And that water is thre cornerde, and it ebbyth and floweth in to the grate sea of Occean". Early on his European tour, the Infante Dom Pedro prayed at the shrine of the *Heilige Drei Koenige* in Cologne. Possessing a trained mind, he would have read Hildesheim in

preparation for his trip and would have passed on this important observation.

At the Council of Florence, Nicolo de'Conti, a Venetian just returned from a long sojourn in South Asia, was interviewed by the humanist and papal secretary Poggio Bracciolini, most active in conciliar circles. In Part IV of his treatise *De Varietate Fortunae*, first printed in 1492 as *India Recognita (Item 33)*, he reported what he had learned there. Commenting on the information from Nicolo de'Conti, he mentions the Persian Gulf, "ubi fluit mare: ac refluit mare oceani nostri" (where the sea rises and falls as does our sea). These texts imply the recognition of tides and an open Indian Ocean rather than an enclosed inland body of water.

Ptolemy in his *Geography* portrayed latitude. He also very cleverly portrayed longitude by running it from zero in the west ever increasingly to the east. His westernmost point, the basis of his prime meridian, as Professor Albuquerque suggests elsewhere in this volume, was interpreted to be the island of Hierro, also known as Ferro, in the Canary Islands. This Ferro meridian remained a prime meridian for many nations and navies down the centuries, even after the Greenwich Meridian was formally adopted at the International Meridian Conference in Washington in 1884.

As the Portuguese progressed in their delineation of Africa, they had to divest themselves of the notion that the continent had no southern tip. The true shape gradually became clear, as is shown by the great Fra Mauro Mappamundi of 1459 *(Pages 36-37)*.

The Portuguese held on to other Ptolemaic notions until much later. They knew that the Greek geographer called the Red Sea the Sinus Arabicus, and designated as the Sinus Barbaricus a great indentation of the coast of what today we know as Kenya and Tanzania, the southern tip of which, in Mozambique, he knew as the Prassum Promontorium. For example, in the oration by which Vasco Fernandes rendered King João II's obedience to the new Pope Innocent VIII on December 11, 1485, and printed at once *(Item 32)*, he referred to Diogo Cão's explorations of 1482-1483, saying quite accurately that this navigator had almost reached the Sinus Barbaricus, meaning he had reached the latitude of that body of water but on the opposite coast of Africa.

Latitude Navigation and Being "Disnorthed"

From 1415 to 1482 the Portuguese explored the West African coast from the Strait of Gibraltar to the mouth of the Congo River. They were poised to finish their task and finally sail around the continent's tip and on to the East. Over that span of sixty-seven years they learned much. Not only had they surveyed a considerable stretch of coastline and become acquainted with new peoples but they also had observed, and the more curiously inclined among them plotted, new skies. Portuguese writers waxed eloquent on this point. In 1485, Vasco Fernandes affirmed that the Portuguese had already provided Europe with "new provinces, new kingdoms, new islands, and as it were, new and unknown worlds". In 1537, the proud Cosmographer Major, Pedro Nunes, could extend the

description: "new islands, new lands, new seas, new peoples, and what is more, a new sky, and new stars". Decades later, the poet Luis de Camões in his epic *Os Lusíadas* of 1572 compressed the description into a single verse: "As nouas Ilhas vendo, e os novos ares" (We saw the new isles and the climates new). Moving south, the Portuguese broke a tradition. Not only did they sail under skies never seen before by Europeans but they also adjusted to new relationships with the noonday sun. In the process they found that, if they became confused, or even lost, they became not "dis-easted" (disoriented, or *desorientados)* but "dis-northed". They added a new word to the Portuguese vocabulary, which today is still very much alive, *desnorteado*. Whereas ancient and medieval sailors were liable to become disoriented within the east-west confines of the Mediterranean Sea, Atlantic sailors became *desnorteados* by sailing so far south as to lose sight of the North Star. For voyagers of the quattrocento, a great thrill was provided by the discovery of an antarctic equivalent of the North Star. This was the Southern Cross, known as *Crux*, with the bright stars Rigil Kent (α Centauri) and Hadar (β Centauri, also called Agena).

Discovery of the Portuguese Atlantic Archipelagoes

The greatest advance in knowledge stemming from the Portuguese north-south movement came from ever increasing acquaintance with the Atlantic's winds and currents, as well as with the flotsam and jetsam, movement of birds and marine life, colour of the water, cloud formations, values of

34. Oration to King Manuel,
August 20, 1501. Pietro Pasqualigo

Pietro Pasqualigo, ambassador from Venice to Portugal, arrived in Lisbon in 1501 and on August 20 of that year delivered an oration in Latin before the king, Dom Manuel, which was printed in Venice on December 22 of that year. In the oration he extols the Portuguese discoveries of regions unknown to Ptolemy and never attained by Alexander, Carthage or Rome. Pasqualigo also makes oblique reference to Brazil, making this little publication the first ever to mention that land. This work exists in only two copies in Portugal, one in the United States, another in London and another in Rio de Janeiro.

The James Ford Bell Library, University of Minnesota
(Page 75)

35. Marco paulo.
Marco Polo.
Lisbon, 1502. Valentim Fernandes

The Portuguese translation of the Book of Marco Polo has been ascribed to a German, Valentim Fernandes, who printed it in his typography shop in Lisbon in 1502. At the time Vasco da Gama had established the sea passage from Europe to India, the celebrated story of the 13th-century Venetian merchant was definitely fascinating reading. To the Marco Polo story, Fernandes appended two up-to-date accounts, making the work a compendium of the best material available on the "Orient" which King Manuel of Portugal claimed as part of his dominion.

Houghton Library, Harvard University
(Page 76)

32

¶Galasci ferdinandi vtriusq; iuris consulti Illustrissimi Regis Portugallie oratoris ad Innocentium octauum pontificem maximū de obedientia oratio.

E si non sum nescius. Pater beatissime Pontifex maxime omniq; christi ihesu pastos beati Petri dignissime successor et dei nostri generalis vicarie.quanta doctrina et quantis laudibus prestare debeat. is qui coram cospectu vestre beatitudinis et prestantissimorum horpatrum verba facturus aut orationem habitur sit.Et si me quoq; non lateat q; grandem prouinciam et q; impar humeris meis muni celebrandū susceperim.qui et dicendi consuetudine eloquētie copia ingenij acumine et omni prorsus doctrina destitutus sum. Cum preterea loci dignissimi ac ornatissimi amplitudinem et maiestatem intueor qui non nisi a peritissimis et grauissimis viris oc cupari solet Cum deniq; tremēdum et gloriosam vestre beatitudinis:et sacri huius senatus conspectum: et rei de qua agendum est magnitudinem et splendorem hinc considero.Inde serenissimi ac illustrissimi principis Johannis secundi. Regis portugallie et algarbiorum citra et vltra mare in affrica et domini guinee:vestre beatitudinis obsequentissimi filij:qui nos ad eandez sanctitatem legatos misit in hanc sanctam et apostolicam sedem deuotiōem fidem et obseruantiam. Josolens profecto et velut amens et temerari9 horreo totus.fra ctus et eneruatus tota mente ac artubus contremi sco totus et vox faucibus heret et dicere cum bye

36. Cosmographia breue introductoria en el libro d(e) Marco paulo. . . .
Brief introduction to cosmography, in the book of Marco Polo. . .
1503. Rodrigo Fernandez de Santaella

The popularity of the Book of Marco Polo was in no way eclipsed by the appearance of more up-to-date accounts of Asia beginning in the early 16th century. This Spanish version of 1503 is modelled after the 1502 Portuguese edition, and includes the Venetian's portrait on the frontispiece, along with a depiction of the Indian port of Calicut.

This version is especially interesting because its compiler added his own "Brief introduction to cosmography", in which he seeks to prove, by referring to old literary sources, that the Indies reached by Columbus and others are not the true Indies: ". . . they be deceived therein, to call it by the name of the Indias *. . . it appeareth that Asia . . . be in the east, and Antilla and Spanyola in the west, in place and condition much different."*

*The British Library, London
(Page 77)*

33

compass variation, and all the other items of which a skilled navigator instinctively takes cognizance including, when possible, the all-important soundings. It was awareness of these oceanic *conhecenças* that enabled Portuguese mariners truly to explore that ocean. Henrique's mariners were of course familiar with the Northeast Trade Winds, blowing south from Eastern Europe and on past the opening to the Mediterranean, and with the south-setting current that moved in the same direction. They could not help but be familiar with the refreshing Prevailing Westerly Winds that struck Iberia's Atlantic coast. What is remarkable in retrospect is how quickly they learned to take advantage of this combination in order to sail down the Moroccan coast and beyond and efficiently return to Cape St. Vincent and the home port of Lagos. An introduction to this lesson was obviously provided by the returned Italian seafarers of the previous century.

The return route explains the new discoveries. The pilots would tack out to sea across the northeast wind and southerly current, then gradually curve around, enter the zone of the westerlies, reach the latitude of their destination, and – to use a hallowed nautical phrase – "run their easting down".

In 1418, or maybe 1425, on an early sweep to seaward from the coast of Africa, a group of Portuguese headed by João Gonçalves Zarco and Tristão Vaz Teixeira discovered the Madeira Archipelago, two large and three small uninhabited islands, unknown to Europeans and Africans, and therefore unlike the Canaries. It is said, and with logic, that they first landed on

Porto Santo, which lies to the northeast of the much larger and higher island known as Madeira. On the first clear day, they would have become familiar with the outline of the latter. Life on the archipelago promptly followed Portuguese economic and social life patterns.

Associated with the Madeiras is the group of deserted islets known as the Selvagens lying between that archipelago and the Canaries. A navigational hazard, they may have become known to Europeans before Porto Santo and Madeira.

In 1431, to take another traditional date consecrated on a modern postage stamp, Portuguese under the leadership of Gonçalo Velho – or possibly as early as 1427 under Diogo de Silves – apparently circled farther out to sea from farther down the African coast and discovered the southeasternmost of the Azores Islands. They labelled it Santa Maria. This uninhabited and unknown archipelago they named after the goshawks that had made their way there earlier than man.

On the first clear day the Portuguese would have discerned São Miguel lying to the north and trending to the west, although the traditional date for landing on it is 1444.

The central Azores lie over the horizon northwest of São Miguel. Courageous navigation revealed Terceira (the Third Island), Graciosa, São Jorge, Pico, and Faial, all mutually visible. Pico is the most visible of all and the third highest island in the Atlantic, with its beautifully symmetrical peak rising to 7,615 feet (2,321 m).

The orientation of the Azores is southeast-northwest. Having reached the western shore of Faial, the Portuguese naturally

PETRI PASCHALICI VENETI ORATORIS AD HEMANVELEM LVSITANIAE REGEM ORATIO.

Etus hospitiũ:mutuiq; amoris studiũ qd' a maioribus acceptũ cũ maiestate tua Veneto nomini itercedit Rex Se, renissime:magnã spem attulit Augu, stino prícipi nõ:& uniuerso Senatui: quũ primũ regni te huius potitũ esse cognouimus:fore ut omni tpe tã amicus Venetæ reipub. & esse:& uideri uelles:tã omni officiox genere cóiũctus: q̃ quiuis alius Regũ:qui hodie sunt in terris:aut unq̃ fu, erunt cóiunctissimus & amicissimus. In quã sententiam nó modo nos cófirmauit:uetus Lusitanox Regum beni uolentia:usq; ad hunc diem mutuo inter nos sanctissime conseruata.sed uirtus tua in primis:iam longe lateq; per orbé terrax cognita ac diuulgata:Quæ etiã in spem ma ximã:præter Venetam ciuitaté:omnes Europæ gentes: populos:regna:nationes cómouet atq; excitauit. Nemo enim fuit:qui ob ea:quæ assidua hominũ p̃dicatione de tuis uirtutibus ferebantur:non persuasum haberet:breui futurum:ut christiana religio plane intelligeret:datũ sibi dei optimi maximi munere:unũ ex omni regũ numero: qui uirtute:cósilio:felicitate:nó solũ ré christianã fessam labantéq; tueretur:sed longe etiã lateq; ppagaret:Quã qdé cómuné omniũ de tua uirtute ac sapientia opinioné Rex illustrissime magis ac magis cófirmauit:& hominũ animis impressit:catholicorum ac inuictissimox castellæ regũ socerũ tuox p̃stantissimox auctoritas atq; iudiciũ: qui certe:nisi tantus esses:quãtũ te omnes prædicant:nó

A

37. Livro das obras de Garcia de Reesende, . . .
Book of the works of Garcia de Reesende, . . .
1554. Garcia de Resende

This book, composed in 1533, contains an account of the discovery of the Congo by the Portuguese and the conversion of the king of that land and the high nobles of his kingdom to the Christian faith. It went through several editions in Portuguese, of which the rare second edition is on display here. It was never published in any foreign language. The portion that refers to the Congo was taken up in the book, also in this exhibition, of Duarte Lopes and Filippo Pigafetta.

Houghton Library, Harvard University (Page 79)

35

wondered what lay beyond the horizon. In 1452, probably by following birds, Diogo de Teive and companions found out: the two islands of Flores, still replete with beautiful flowers, and Corvo, possibly a misapplication of cormorant or raven, possibly a reminiscence of Corvi Marini from early maps.

The Azores did not as promptly become an integrated part of Portugal. Lying much more distant from the mainland, they also lay in the zone of the Prevailing Westerlies. Reaching them made for a more difficult voyage, and the passage from Faial to Flores, especially in mid-winter, can be rough indeed. Accordingly, mainlanders were reluctant to migrate to the Western Islands, as the latter archipelago became known to New England whalemen. The authorities were forced to look elsewhere for "peoplers", especially at the leadership end of the social scale. Henrique's sister Isabel, who had married Philip the Good, Duke of Burgundy, in 1430, reached the islands from Cascais via two ports in Galicia to Plymouth, thence across to Sluys (l'Ecluse). The Infante therefore looked to her for help, and arrangements were made for Flemings to move to the Azores, especially to the central islands of Faial, Pico, and São Jorge. Many went, to the extent that on the Martin Behaim Globe of 1492 (depicted in replica, *Item 22*), Fayal is labelled "neu flandern oder Insula de faial" (New Faial is labelled "neu flandern Slightly Lusitanized, Flemish family names still survive, like da Rosa and da Silveira.

The circular or "arc" sailing practiced by the Portuguese

necessitated new designs of sailing vessels, undoubtedly worked out at Henrique's Sagres centre by mid century. Billowing square sails needed to run before the wind ("rounded sails," as the Portuguese called them, *velas redondas*) of necessity gave way to fore-'n-aft rigged vessels with lateen sails (*velas latinas*). There thus arose two broad classes of vessels: ships (*naus*), full-rigged ships as New Englanders would say, and caravels (*caravelas*), lateen-rigged vessels (*Item 15*). Eventually the naus would be fitted with a lateen sail, aft, to aid in getting under way or coming about, providing the model for New Bedford's whaling barks of the 1800's.
On their sails, especially the spectacular "rounded" sails, the Portuguese affixed the red-bordered cross of the religious Order of Christ, of which Henrique was administrator and whose funds he used to finance his various ventures. The Cross of Christ joined another great Portuguese symbol spread around the globe on rock inscriptions such as those of the Yelala Rocks up the Congo River and on markers (*padrões*) set up in strategic locations (*Item 21*). This other symbol was the coat-of-arms (*escudo* or escutcheon). It consisted of five shields (*quinas*) each with five bazants.

By the middle or late 1450's, native Portuguese, or foreigners sailing under Henrique's auspices or at least with his approval, were poised to make another sweep out to sea. The result was the revelation of a new archipelago, the Cape Verde Islands, which were uninhabited and unknown to Africans and Europeans. The nearest, Boa Vista, is located some 326 nautical miles off Cape Verde,

Cosmographia
breue introdu
ctoria enel libro
ô Marco paulo

Marco   paulo.   Micer   pogio

S.domingo.
êla ysla Jsabela

Calicu

El libro del famoso Marco paulo
veneciano ôlas cosas marauillosas
q̃ vido enlas partes oriétales. côuie
ne saber enlas Jndias. Armenia. A
rabia. Persia ꝗ Tartaria. E ôl pode
rio ôl grã Eã y otros reyes. Eõ otro
tratado de micer Pogio florétino ꝗ
trata delas mesmas tierras ꝗ yslas.

38. Relaçam verdadeira dos trabalhos q̃ ho gouernador dõ fernãdo d(e) souto e certos fidalgos portugueses passarom no d(e) scobrimẽto da prouincia da frolida. Agora nouamẽte feita per hũ fidalgo Deluas.
A truthful report of the work that the Governor Fernando de Souto and certain Portuguese gentlemen performed in the discovery of the province of Florida. Now newly-made by a gentleman of Elvas. *1557*.

The range of Portuguese involvement in New World discoveries is demonstrated here by the fact that the best narrative of Hernando de Soto's expedition through the southeasternmost portion of the United States, 1539-1543, was written by one of the "Portuguese gentlemen" who accompanied de Soto's army. It is impossible to say which of these "gentlemen" is the author of the work, though it has been attributed to Álvaro Fernandes. The account was printed in Évora, Portugal in 1557, fourteen years after the remnants of de Soto's force reached Mexico. An English translation was published in 1603 to serve as a spur to the English settlement of Virginia.

The John Carter Brown Library at Brown University, Providence RI
(Below)

38

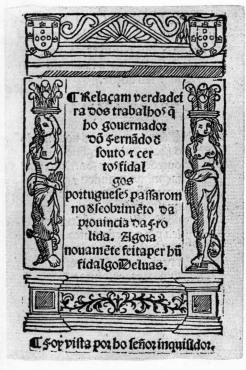

Africa's westernmost promontory, on which modern Dakar is located. The largest of the islands, Santiago, was discovered first. The others rapidly came into view, including lofty Fogo (Fire), with its peak towering to 9,281 feet (2,829 m). Today, the nine islands form the Republic of Cape Verde, independent from Portugal since 1975.

As Professor Albuquerque points out, Diogo Gomes used a quadrant in connection with the discovery of the new archipelago. At just about the same time, specifically the end of 1451, another document seems to hint at celestial navigation by Portuguese, this time in the Mediterranean. However, it probably refers to checks on courses as steered: "*magistris astrologis, iuxta stellas et polum viarum bene doctis*" (professional astrologers who were well-trained in the matter of courses determined from stars and pole).

Bartolomeu Dias and Understanding Atlantic Winds and Currents

Following Henrique's death, a Portuguese ship which was skirting and crossing the Gulf of Guinea came upon four islands. The outer two, Annobon and Fernando Pó, ultimately became Spanish in accordance with the provisions of the Treaty of San Ildefonso of 1777. The inner two, São Tomé and Príncipe, remained Portuguese as a formal colony. They also became independent in 1975.

With the Congo River explored, King João II now affirmed a decisive policy, the *plano da Índia*. This "Perfect Prince", also known as "King of Portugal and of the Algarves on this Side of and Beyond the Seas in Africa, and Lord of Guinea", in 1487 sent forth two expeditions, one by sea, the other mainly by land, both aimed at the "Indies". Bartolomeu Dias sallied forth to complete the sailing along the west coast of Africa, rounded what soon came to be called the Cape of Good Hope and also Cape Agulhas to the east and slightly south of the better known Good Hope, and entered the Indian Ocean. Shortly after this, Dias was forced to turn back.

Simultaneously, Afonso de Paiva and Pero de Covilhã headed east through the Mediterranean and Red Sea. Covilhã reached the "Indies" of Ethiopia and of India proper, in particular the Malabar Coast in the southwestern portion of the subcontinent.

The information brought back by Dias and presumably sent back by the Paiva-Covilhã expedition enabled the theoreticians of John II's high command to piece together a broad picture of the flow of winds and currents not only of both North and South Atlantic but also of the Indian Ocean, including the Arabian Sea.

It was becoming apparent that the Atlantic pattern was a vast figure-8, the top loop (North Atlantic) running clockwise, the bottom loop (South Atlantic) counterclockwise. Eventually, the return home would take advantage of the Gulf Stream (when known and plotted), to the east of which lay the Bermudas, first visited by the Spaniards in 1515 and named for Juan de Bermudez, and first populated by the British in the early seventeenth century.

In parallel fashion, from the equator to the southern tip of Africa one sailed southwest,

LIVRO DAS

obras de Garcia de Reesende, que tracta da vida & grandissi
mas virtudes & bõdades: magnanimo esforço, excelentes
costumes & manhas & muy craros feitos do christiani
ssimo: muito alto & muito poderoso principe el rey
dom Ioam ho segundo deste nome: & dos Reys
de Portugal ho trezeno de gloriosa memoria:
começado de seu nacimẽto & toda sua vida
ate ha ora de sua morte: cõ outras obras
q̃ adiante se seguẽ. Vay mais acrescẽ
tado nouamente a este liuro hũa
Miscellanea ẽ trouas do mes
mo auctor & hũa varieda
de de historias, custu
mes, casos, & cousas
que em seu tẽpo
accõtescerã.

1554

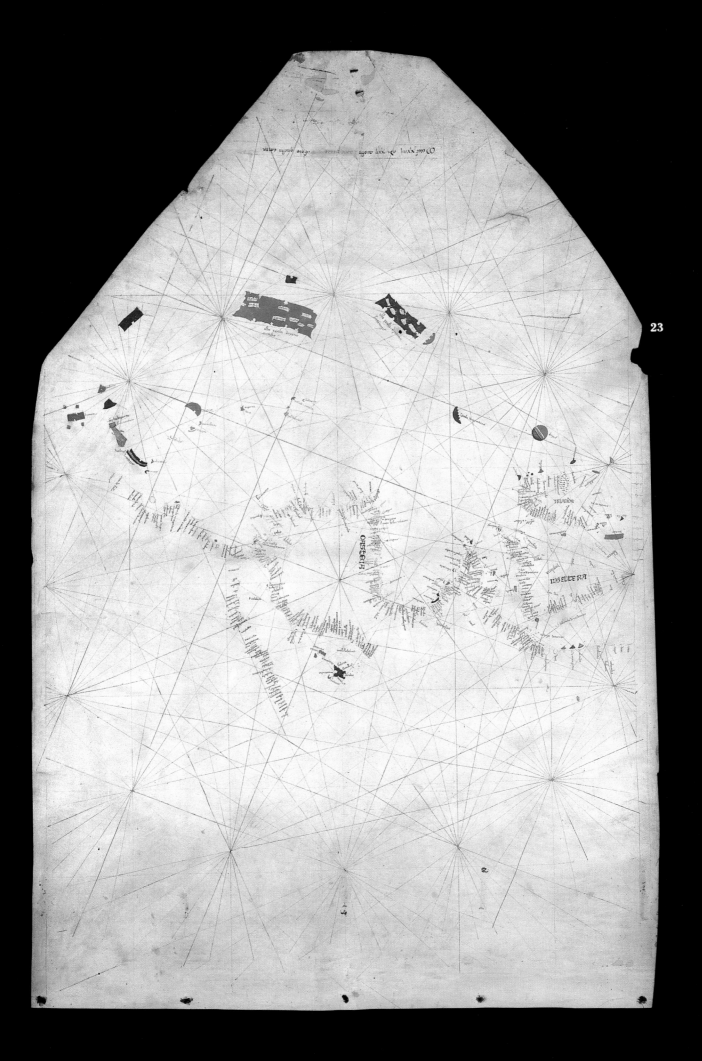

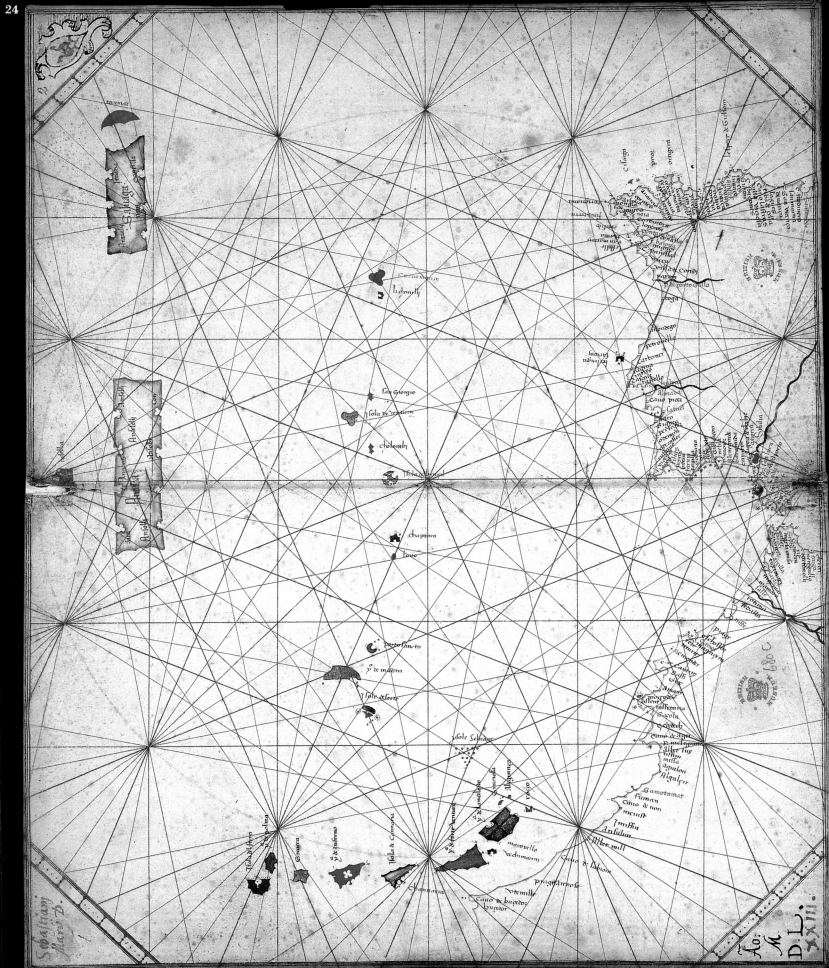

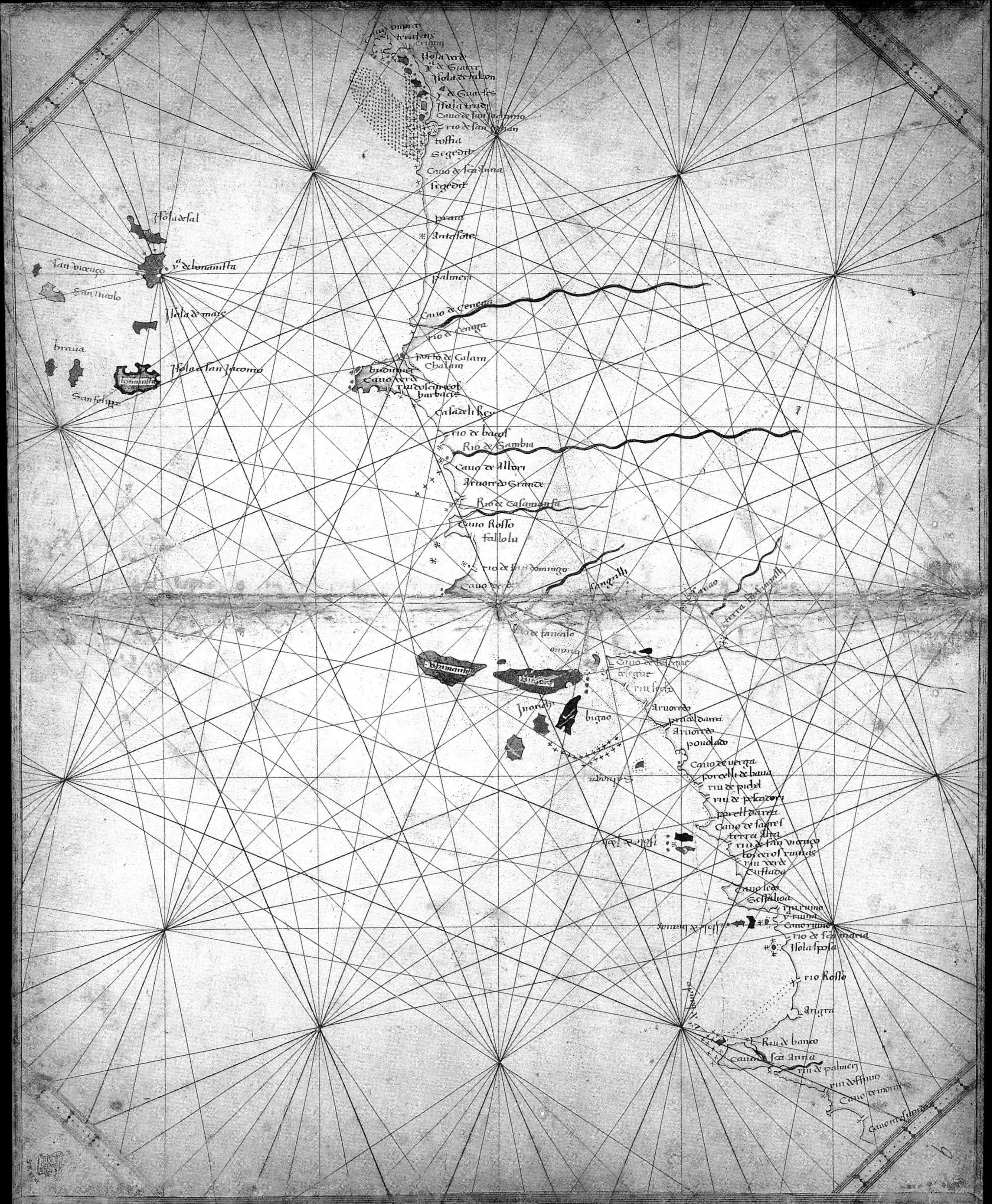

23

Cauo blanco
brasanj
erigini
Hola yrra
y.a de Siatre
Hola de falion
y.a de Guaftes
Hola traci
Cauo de San jutintino
rio de San jutian
toffia
Segedit
Cauo de Sca Anna
Segedit

praui
Antafote

palmen

Hola de sal
Cauo de cenega
rio de cenga
San viacnço
Porto de Calam
San incolo
Chalam
Hola de mais
buomer
Cauo yera
rui oiscanco
braua
harbuge
Hola de San Jacomo
Casa di Rey
branua
rio de bagos
San felipo
Rio de Sambia
Cauo de Allori
Aruores Grande
Rio de casamanfa
Cauo Rosso
fallolu
rio de San Domingo
Cauo rosso
Sangalli
tarao
terra de foundi

rio de taneato
oruna
Criuo de lestegue
lestegue
Hamauki
Aruinan
panacoj
Aruores
Inonoli
prisa danei
bigao
Aruores
poudaco
Cauo de uerga
forcelli de baua
riu de picbal
riu de pescaton
porelli danci
Cauo de fagref
terra alta
riu de San viacnço
tereiros ruinas
riu nera
cuftada
Hola de lofi
Cauo lcdo
Eslaluoa
prurina
ruina
cauo ruino
rio de San maria
Hola sposa
Sanua de Hesi

rio Rosso

Angra

riu de banco
cauo de Sca Anna
riu de palmen
riu doftian
Cauo de moru
Cauo de Silmon

CRISTOFALO·SOLIGO

ihns

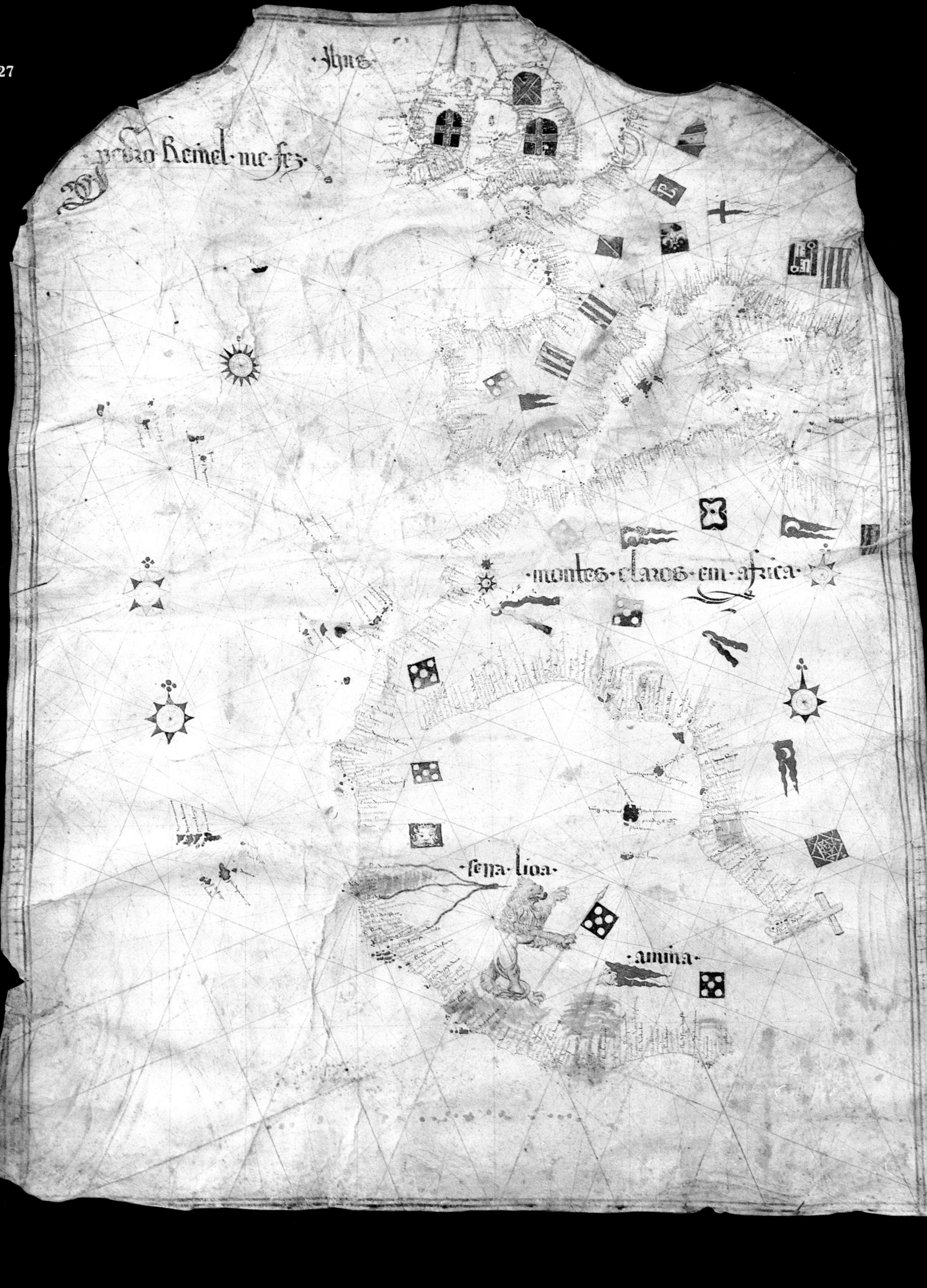

pedro Reinel me fez

montes claros em africa

seta lioa

amina

IHVS

REINEL

EVROPA

TROPIC⁰ CANCRJ

AFRICA

AM...INA

EQNOCTIAL IS

TROPIC⁰ CAPRICORNJ

- *Mare glaciale*
- *OCEANVS*
- *OCCIDETAL*
- *OCEANVS*
- *LIVONIA*
- *mare germanie*
- *Pontus euxinus*
- *hircanum f. caspium*
- *MARE MEDITERRANEVM*
- *MARE*
- *SINVS PERSICVS*
- *mare arabicū*
- *AFFRICA*
- *Insule Portugalesiū*
- *Mare rubrum*
- *MONTES LVNE*

Cartouche texts:

hec est vera forma moderna affrice secundum descriptione Portugalensium inter mare Mediterraneum et oceanum meridionalem

Ad hunc usq̄ montem qui vocatur niger pervenit classis secūdi regis portugalie cui classis pfuit erat duq̄i camū qui in memoriam rei erexit colūpnam marmorea cum cruce in signe et ultra prorexit usq̄ ad terram pardam que dicta ab mōte nigro mille miliaria et hic moritur

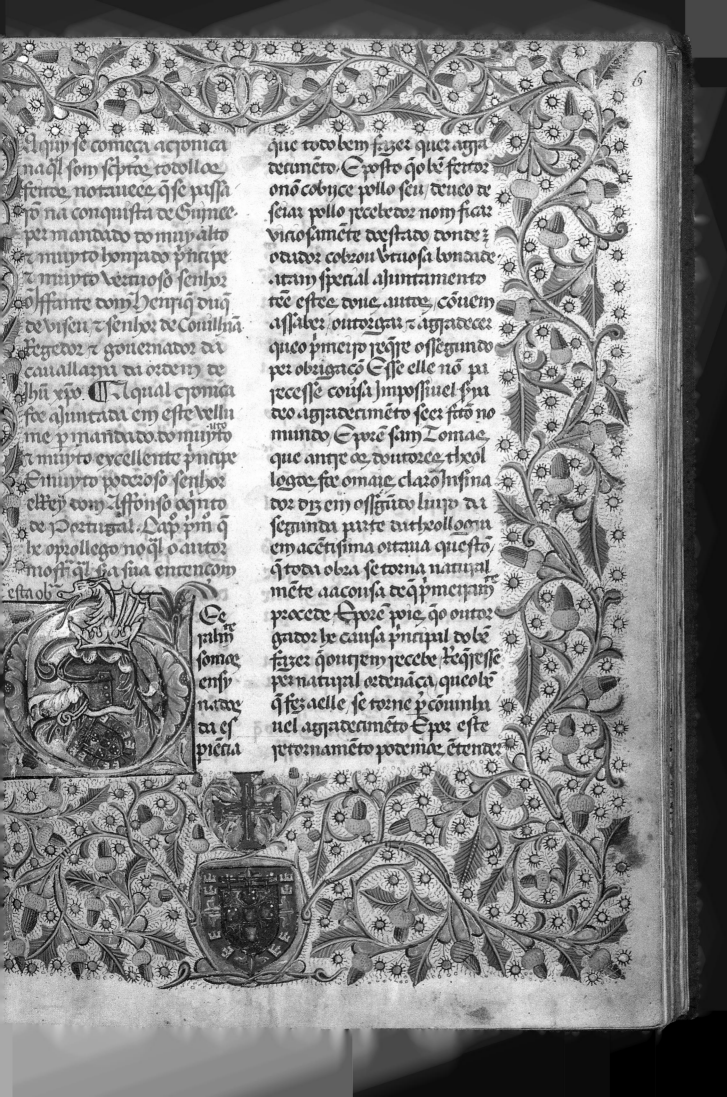

Aquy se começa a coronica na ql̃ som scriptos todollos feitos notaueez q̃ se pssa rõ na conquista de Guynee per mandado do muy alto τ muyto honrrado pr̃ncipe τ muyto vertuoso senhor õsfante dom Henrriq̃ duq̃ de Viseu τ senhor de Couilhãa Regedor τ gouernador da caualaria da ordem de Jhū xp̃o. ¶ Aqual coronica foe ajuntada em este vollu me p̃ mandado do muyto τ muyto excellente pr̃ncipe τ muyto poderoso senhor elRey dom Affonso o q̃nto de Portugal. Cap̃ pr̃m q̃ he o prollego no ql̃ o autor mostra ql̃ he a sua entençom desta obr̃

Se julgam some en sua natureza da es pritual

que todo bem fazer quer agra decimẽto. E posto q̃ he feito ono cobyce pollo seu, τ nõ se seiar pollo recebedor nom fica vir tuosamẽte do estado donde o dador cobrou vertuosa bondade. Ora em especial ajuntamento tẽ estes dous autos, cõuem a saber outorgar τ agradecer que o pr̃meiro rege o segundo per obrigaçõ. E sse elle nõ pa recesse cousa impossiuel fru to agradecimẽto seer feito no mundo. E porẽ sam Tomaz que antre os doutorez theol logoz foe o mais claro Jnsina dor diz em o segundo liuro da segunda parte da theollogia em a cẽtisima oitaua questõ q̃ toda obra se torna natural mẽte a acousa de q̃ pr̃mciam procede. E porẽ pois q̃ o outor gador he causa pr̃ncipal do bem fazer q̃ outrem recebe Requeresse per natural ordenãça que o be q̃ fez a elle se torne p̃ cõuinha uel agradecimẽto E por este retornamẽto podemos ẽtender

DOVASCODAGAMA·
VISOREÉ COMDE·

Partio Vasq̃ da gama pera a Jndia a oyto de Jnego por capitão mõr cõ quatro vellas, 3 pera ҫequir
ho descobrimento da Jndia & hũa carregada de mantimentos pera se cõ elle & cõ a gente della
Reformarẽ, das quaes estes erão os capitães /—

.S. Raphael

℄ Paullo da gama ⅅ

Jrmão de Vasco da gama, á tvenada pera por
baҫa, aos quaes Antre quiloa & mõ
da Mar assise chamaua, & a gente della
se Repartio pellas duas da companhia /—

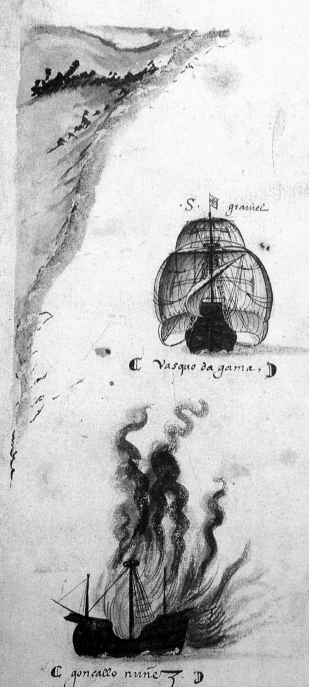

.S. grauiel

℄ Vasquo da gama, ⅅ

berrio

℄ Nicolao coego ⅅ

℄ goncallo nuñ℥ ⅅ

Criado de Vasq̃ da gama, depois de não ter passado
ho cabo de boa esperança & ser pouco avante da agoada
della pellas outras da companhia, & depois de despe
jada lhe poserão fogo /—

47

south, and southeast in a broad sweep to the prevailing winds of the southern hemisphere. The Cape of Good Hope is only at 34° 50' S, whereas those winds are farther south, basically in the 40-degree zone. (Later, Americans knew them as the Roaring Forties.) Therefore, the first courageous mariner to apply this figure-8 theory would have had to sail not only southeast but then east and northeast. He would have taken great care to make his landfall well north of Africa's southern tip, turn to starboard, run down the coast line to the Cape, round the latter, and enter the Indian Ocean.

As will be seen, Vasco da Gama applied the figure-8 theory upon sallying forth from Lisbon on July 8, 1497. Between Dias' return and Gama's departure, however, momentous events of a different nature had taken place, with a resultant pause in Portugal's official quest for the Indies. There may, however, have been informal sailings, for a contemporary Arabic nautical treatise mentions Portuguese activity in East Africa in the mid-1490's.

Delimiting the Zones of Portugal and Castile

It is commonplace to affirm that four major events took place in Spain in 1492:
1) Queen Isabel of Castile and her spouse King Fernando of Aragon reconquered Granada from the Moors;
2) they expelled the Jews, many of whom fled to Portugal;
3) she sponsored Columbus's revelation of America to Europe;
4) Antonio de Nebrija published his grammar.
Fernando and Isabel had been married since 1469, and their union had created a de facto

"Spain". Their Catholic Majesties were fully acquainted with Portuguese doings, including papal documents beginning in 1455 that gave high-level backing to Portugal's aspirations in accordance with established medieval theory. The first example of this was the bull *Romanus Pontifex* issued by Pope Nicholas V in 1455 (*Item 57*). It granted Portugal exclusive rights of conquest and possession in Moslem or pagan lands along the African coast "from the capes of Bojador and of Nam as far as through all Guinea, and beyond toward that southern shore".

Romanus Pontifex was confirmed in 1456 by Pope Calixtus III's bull *Inter Caetera*, which specified "from capes Bojador and Nam as far as through all Guinea, and past that southern shore all the way to the Indians." This latter phrase – "usque ad Indos" – could well have referred to all Christians beyond encircling Islam, the exotic Christians of the "Indies".

Their majesties were only too well aware of the Treaty of Alcáçovas (in south-central Portugal near Évora) of September 4, 1479 (*Item 60*), for they had jointly negotiated it with King Alfonso V of Portugal (reigned 1438-1481). It terminated a war over the Castilian succession. Of immediate relevance is the stipulation attributing to the King of Portugal the lordship of Guinea, Madeiras, Azores, and Cape de Verdes and the conquest of the kingdom of Fez (in Morocco), and to Spain the lordship of the Canaries. This treaty clearly incorporated, at an early date, the notion of demarcation between Portugal's and Spain's possessions.

39. Tratado dos Descobrimentos.
Treatise on the Discoveries.
1563. Antonio Galvão

The Treatise, which records events up to 1550, was published by the author's friend and executor, Francisco de Sousa Tavares. In it Galvão compiled information on discoveries made by the Portuguese, the Spanish, and even those of the Frenchman Jacques Cartier and the Englishman Richard Chancellor. He showed particular interest in the voyages of Gaspar and Miguel Corte Real to North America, and in the ventures of the Portuguese in the Orient.

António Galvão was the son of Duarte Galvão, secretary to kings Dom Alfonso V and Dom João II, and chief chronicler to Dom Manuel I. He began his military career in 1522. Having demonstrated his valour and sound judgement in Africa and the Orient, he was appointed captain of the Moluccas. On returning to Portugal, he failed to receive the rewards he deserved, and died in poverty.

The John Carter Brown Library at Brown University, Providence RI
(Below)

39

TRATADO.
Que compôs o nobre & notauel capitão Antonio Galuão, dos diuersos & desuayrados caminhos, por onde nos tempos passados a pimenta & especearia veyo da India ás nossas partes, & assi de todosos descobrimentos antigos & modernos, que são feitos ate a era de mil & quinhentos & cincoenta. Com os nomes particulares das pessoas que os fizeram : & em que tempos & as suas alturas, obra certo muy notauel & copiosa.

Foy vista & examinada pela santa Inquisição.

Impressa em casa de Ioam da Barreira impressor del rey nosso senhor, na Rua de sá Mamede

40. Itinerario.
Itinerary.
1596. Jan Huygen van Linschoten

Jan Huygen van Linschoten, a Dutch geographer, wrote this work in Flemish in 1596, at the end of the period of Portuguese ascendancy in discovery. The author spent seven years in the Portuguese outpost of Goa, and thus speaks from first-hand experience, though he may have borrowed some material from Portuguese cartographers.

Shown is an engraving of Angra do Heroismo on the island of Terceira in the Azores, one of the earliest Atlantic archipelagoes to be discovered and populated by the Portuguese. Angra became an important port of call for ships returning from India, Africa and Brazil, and Linschoten himself lived there for a time.

The New York Public Library
(Below)

41. Discourse of Voyages.
1598. Jan Huygen van Linschoten

English translation of the Itinerario *of Jan Huygen van Linschoten (Item 40). This work was extremely well received in its time, as evidenced by its subsequent French and Latin versions, as well as this English-language printing. Shown is one of its magnificent fold-out engravings; this one depicting the South Atlantic island of St. Helena, "of sweet and pleasaunt ayre", a much-appreciated stopping-point for ships on the return trip from the Indies.*

The New York Public Library
(Pages 100-101)

40

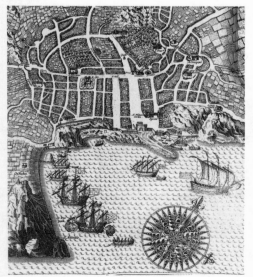

Immediately upon Columbus' return, Fernando and Isabel persuaded Pope Alexander VI to issue a bull establishing a formal line of demarcation between respective spheres of influence. Known also as *Inter Caetera* (from, as in all bulls, the first words of its Latin text), it was dated May 4, 1493 *(Item 59)*, and affirmed: ". . . the said line to be distant one hundred leagues towards the west and south from any of the islands commonly known as the Azores and Cape Verde. . .". This text, drawn up in accordance with the earlier medieval theory of great papal power and prestige in international affairs, actually suggests two lines of demarcation, from Azores and Cape de Verdes respectively, toward the west and the south (*not* the west and the north).

Whatever the length of the league and mariners' ability to determine longitude at sea, this line obviously gave the Spaniards too much and the Portuguese too little; nobody was surprised, for the Pope was an Aragonese, Alexander Borgia (that is, Borja), father of Caesar and Lucretia. In spite of papal authority, the nationalistic João II challenged the location of the line. Negotiations between nations now took place independent of the papacy. The resultant Treaty of Tordesillas, a forerunner of modern international relations, was signed by royal representatives in Tordesillas in north-central Spain near Valladolid on June 7, 1494. The Spanish ratification is dated July 2, 1494 *(Item 63)*. This text mandates categorically that the line of demarcation be a single meridian 370 leagues west (*not* west and south) of the Cape

Verde Islands. It makes no mention of the Azores, which lie to the west of the more southerly archipelago, nor does specify a point of origin in the Cape Verde area, which extend over some 2° 23' of latitude and 2° 42' of longitude .

Determining the meridian of the line on the face of the globe proved virtually impossible at the end of the fifteenth century. We can go along with the widely accepted 17 1/2 leagues per degree of the meridian (60 n. mi.), that is, 3.43 n. mi. per league. The famous 370 leagues work out to 1,269.1 nautical miles. From the westernmost point of the Cape Verde Islands (Ponta Oeste Light, Santo Antão, at 17° 04' N, 25° 22' W of Greenwich), such a distance *at that latitude* results in a line of demarcation at 47° 27' W.

It is possible that after Tordesillas, Portuguese seafaring and practicing navigators would have remembered the 1493 bull with its reference to the Azores as well as the Cape Verde Islands. Bartolomé de Las Casas did just that when, writing his *Historia de las Indias*, he attributed to Columbus the statement that "it was decided that the king of Portugal should have 370 leagues from the Azores and C. Verde Islands on the West to the North, from pole to pole". The Portuguese would have concluded that the new and definitive line of demarcation was at two longitudes and not a single meridian in spite of Tordesillas' stipulation that it be so.

This conclusion would have been most acceptable to Azorean seafarers, many of whom were from Terceira and seekers of codfish (*bacalhau*, the Italian *baccalà*). They would have been encouraged to continue, in their unofficial way, in their thrust to the northwest, thus prolonging what had been a long tradition.

Exploration of the northwestern Atlantic by Azoreans has been much discussed by historians and others, and the details are not at all clear. What seems certain is that Azoreans had come upon Newfoundland ("Terra Nova" in Portuguese) and Labrador ("Lavrador," meaning literally "farmer"), or at least their offshore fishing grounds, years before 1493 or 1494. Indeed, Labrador, today a part of Newfoundland and not a separate province, is named for a Terceiran, João Fernandes "o Lavrador" – João Fernandes "the Farmer" *(Pages 150-151)*. Another favourite bone of contention among historians attempts to determine the reason why, immediately after *Inter Caetera*, the Portuguese crown pushed for a movement of the line of demarcation 270 leagues farther west. Had Portuguese mariners secretly explored areas beyond the 1493 line and come upon Brazil without such events having become part of the official record? Had there been an official "Policy of Secrecy", what in Portuguese is known as a *Política de Sigilo?*
A more logical explanation of King João's desire for more Portuguese *Lebensraum* would relate to the reports on winds and currents received from Bartolomeu Dias and the realization that the next royal expedition aimed at the Indies would have to make a wide sweep to the west in the South Atlantic, a sweep that might take it well west of the *Inter Caetera* line, into Spanish territory.

Vasco da Gama and the Monsoons of the Indian Ocean

King João died in 1495. His son and heir Prince João had died in a riding accident four years before, so the late king was succeeded by his cousin and brother-in-law Manuel, who ruled until 1521. And "Fortunate" he certainly was, for he inherited the maritime lore accumulated by his predecessors. This heritage included the art of navigation. Meanwhile, the royal families of Portugal and Castile had become enmeshed in a series of dynastic marriages, such that relations between the two nations were friendly and did not reflect whatever hostility or rivalry had lain behind the drawing up of a line of demarcation. In early 1497, Portugal, in obedience to family prompting from across the border, expelled those Jews not converted to Christianity.
As already noted, at the beginning of the summer of 1497 Vasco da Gama *(Item 43)* and his fleet departed, bound for India's Malabar Coast. The day was July 8 according to the Julian calendar day at that time running from noon to noon. It if had occurred in the morning, the Julian July 8 would be our Gregorian July 17. We know this fact about departure time from the basic document of the voyage, the journal kept by Álvaro Velho.
Gama's pilots were providentially equipped with the equivalent of a full-scale nautical almanac, Zacut's *Almanach perpetuum (Item 3)*. Gama must have had one exemplar with him, although it is likely that, well before sailing, the professional pilots in the fleet had used Zacut to precompute the declination (d) of the sun at high noon for every day of the projected voyage and

42. Panoramic View of the Monastery and Plaza of Belém.
1657 or 1658. Felipe Lobo
Oil on canvas

King Dom Manuel had this edifice built in thanksgiving for the discovery of the sea-route to India. Since the nineteenth century, Vasco da Gama has been buried there, as is Luís de Camoes, author of Portugal's great epic poem, The Lusiads, which is based largely on Gama's accomplishment.

Museu Nacional de Arte Antiga, Lisbon
(Page 92-93)

43. Portrait of Vasco da Gama.
In: "O Successo dos Visoreis"
Mid 16th c. Lizuarte de Abreu
Coloured ink drawing

This portrait of Vasco da Gama, captain-major of the first fleet to reach India by sea, is contained in a so-called Book of Armadas attributed to Lizuarte de Abreu. It contains various types of documents: copies of written texts, portraits of governors and viceroys up through Dom Constantino de Bragança and depictions of the fleets of the India route as of 1563, with illustrations of accidents suffered by some of their ships.

The Pierpont Morgan Library, New York.
M. 525, vol.II, fol.7
(Page 94)

44. The Fleet of Vasco da Gama.
In: "Memoria das Armadas que de Portugal Pasaram ha India e Esta Primeira e ha com que Vasco da Gama Partio . . . e no do (Ano) de Nacimento de xp̄o de 1497."
Memoire of the Armadas that Journeyed from Portugal to India, and This First one is the one in which Vasco da Gama Departed . . . and in the (year) of the Birth of Christ of 1497.
16th c. Anonymous

The armada of Vasco da Gama departed from Lisbon with four vessels on July 8, 1497, and the first vessel to return, that of Nicolau Coelho, arrived in Lisbon on July 10, 1499 with the news that a direct route around Africa to India had been found.

This manuscript portrays all the armadas which set sail from Portugal for India from 1497 until 1556. Each page identifies the captain-major of the armada and the number of ships; in addition, each individual vessel has a legend indicating her captain and, in many cases, her fate.

Academia de Ciências, Lisbon
(Page 95)

Quem capiant cœlum lymphęque salubria tellus,
Queque novo semper gramine parturiat,
Que facilé admittat gremio et producat alendo,
Quod peregre intulerit providâ cura solo:
Fanum Helenę capiat teneatą nisi arctius ingens,
Orbe procul nostro clauderet occanus

41

ANNO DNI. 1598

elenæ sacra cœli clementia et æquabilitate
te aquarum salubritate nulli secunda sed
a hic receptus nauium ex Or.India rede=
n altitudine 16 graduum ad austrum li=
nex æquinoctialis.
of St. Helena full of Sweet and pleasaunt ayre
ound and fresh water, but not inhabited: a god re=
those ÿ come ovt of east India it lyeth vnder 16.
the south syde of the equinoctiall lyne

Illustribus ac Generosis Dominis DD. Phillippo
Eduardo et Octauiano secundi Fuggeris.
Dnis in Kirchberg et Weissenhoren.
Nobilibus itidem præclaris ac prudentibus
Dnis. Marco Matthæo Welsero ac sociis Dnis
suis clementiss. ac honorandis. honoris et ob=
sequii ergo D.D Ioännes Hugonis a Linschoten.

St. Helena

The Gallion of Mallacca

The Conception of over Lady

The St Christopher Admirale

The holy Crosse

The St Anthonye

Imprinted at London by John Wolfe.
Grauen by Raygnald Elstrake

45. Two Drafts of the Letter of Dom Manuel to the Kings of Castile and Aragon giving notice of the Discovery of India.
1499.

Two days after the return of the ship Berrio under the command of Nicolau Coelho, Dom Manuel hastened to communicate to the Catholic kings that the discoverers whom he had sent to sea two years earlier, under the command of Vasco da Gama, had returned, having found and surveyed "India and other kingdoms neighbouring upon her and they entered and navigated her sea, where they found great cities and great edifices, rich and of great population, wherein is fully practiced the commerce of spices and gems"; they had also discovered "land possessed of mines of gold". The news was sent post-haste, because of Dom Manuel's certainty that the Castilian monarchs would be "happy and well pleased to receive it".

Arquivo Nacional da Torre do Tombo, Lisbon
(Facing page)

---

46. Copia de una littera del Re de Portogallo madata al Re de Castella del viaggio & successo de India.
Copy of a Letter from the King of Portugal to the King of Castilia about the Voyage to India.
1505.

When Vasco da Gama's fleet, reduced to two ships, straggled into Lisbon after reaching India, Dom Manuel I used all means at his disposal to spread the news to all Christian countries. Drafts of two letters on the subject are preserved in the National Archives in Lisbon. This one addressed to the Catholic Kings of Spain, whose original is also on exhibition, was reprinted as a pamphlet in 1505, in an Italian translation.

The James Ford Bell Library, University of Minnesota
(Page 104)

---

had jotted down the results on slips of paper. Combining this "d" with "z" in accordance with the well-known formula still very much in use, the navigator would take his sight and determine his "L" (latitude) as of high noon. The fleet of four vessels *(Item 44)* sailed before the Northeast Trades, passing between the African coast and Madeira, then among the Canaries.

It proceeded to Praia, the capital of today's independent Cape Verdean republic, on the island of Santiago. It remained there a week.

On August 3 (Julian calendar), the vessels continued before the wind and with most favourable current to approximately the southwestern corner of the West African bulge. At that point on August 14, one vessel, commanded by Bartolomeu Dias, was detached and proceeded to the Gulf of Guinea. The remaining vessels made a hard turn to starboard and initiated their broad sweep to the west around the lower half of the figure-8. They made their landfall on the coast of what is now South Africa well north of the southern tip. On November 8, they settled in at St. Helena Bay (32° 40' S, 18° 10' E), where pilots went ashore with a large surveyor's astrolabe and determined their latitude. Gama knew the latitude of the Cape, possibly inaccurately, from Dias. He therefore had made certain that, coming in from the west, he had aimed well off to the left, to port. If he had aimed for the Cape and sailed too far to the right, to starboard, he would have unwittingly entered the Indian Ocean, run out of supplies, and been lost forever. This principle of "aim-off" may have been adopted by Juan Sebastian de Elcano as he

brought Magellan's vessel *Victoria* westward across the Indian Ocean from the Spice Islands to the southern tip of Africa. It is definitely known that Drake used it in 1580 as he sailed from Tjilatjap on the south coast of Java to a point well to the right or north of the African tip and then coasted south to it. The technique would even turn up again with Portuguese air navigators of the 1920's.

Gama's passage from the turn off Sierra Leone to the landfall in South Africa is possibly the most dramatic and the most courageous in maritime history, since it followed what was in reality an unconfirmed theory about navigation in the South Atlantic. Just how far west Gama went, how near the hitherto unknown coast of Brazil, we do not know.

Gama proceeded from St. Helena Bay south, rounded the Cape, and sailed up the East African coast. He then crossed to Calicut on India's Malabar Coast, aided in this undertaking by an Arab pilot. After rounding Africa on his return, he followed the figure-8 pattern, sailing northwest off Africa, on across the equator, out to sea on a sweep to the west, north to the latitude of the Azores, and east to Lisbon. Along the way, Vasco da Gama arrived at the island Terceira in the Azores, in a caravel he had chartered in Santiago (Cape Verde Archipelago) while trying to reach Lisbon in time to save his seriously ill brother, Paulo da Gama.

The city of Angra do Heroismo, on Terceira, later became an important port of call for vessels returning from the Indies, from Brazil as well as Asia.

The importance of Angra was

45

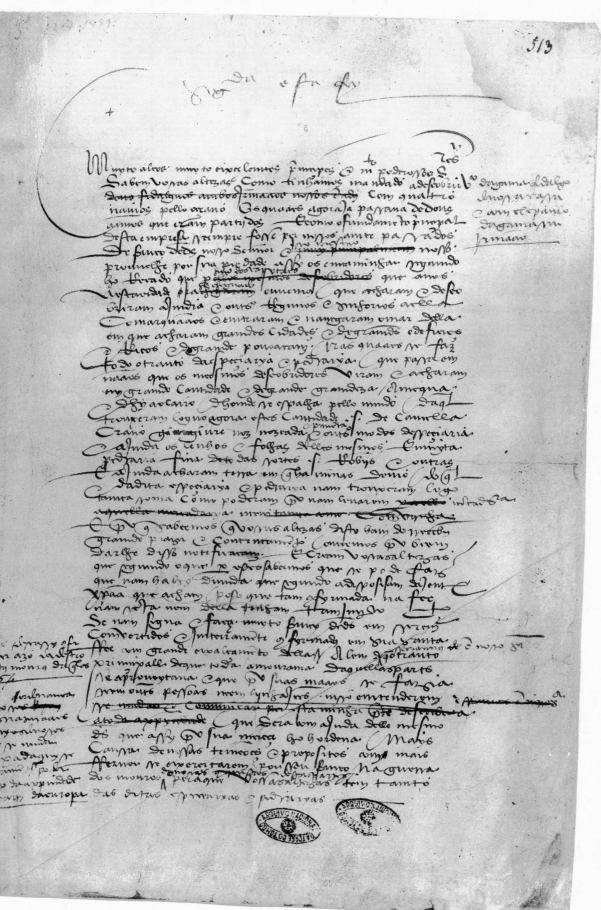

Muyto altos muyto excelentes prinçepes e poderossos
Sabem vosas altezas como tinhamos mandado a descobriir
dous fidalgos ambos estimados nosos criados com quatro
navios pello oçeano Esguardes agora ja pasada de dous
annos que eram partidos Como o fundamento primçipal
desta empresa sempre fose per nos ante pasados
de sempre deos nosso Senhor por nos
premitisse por sua piedade elhos emcaminhar segundo
lho teuera por bem que per meeos de soldados que amos
justamdade e [...] convinha que achasem descobriram
a india e outros thermos e emformos aelles
comarquados centraram e navegaram o mar dela
em que acharam grandes çidades de grandes edefiçios
e titos de grande povoaram vras esguardes per ser
todo oriamte das peçiarya e pedarya que parte em
naaos que os mesmos descobridores viram carregaram
em grande cantidade de grande grandeza Almegna
de fir acario e home de espaça pello mundo dagl
trouueram segundo agora estes cantidade s de canela
crauo [...] nuz nozada segundo modos despeçiarya
e ainda os tenhos e folhas delles mesmos Emmyta
pedraria fina deto das pertes s Robys e outras
e ainda acharam terra em que as minas domo bel
A dita espeçiarya e pedraria nam trouueram con
tanta soma como poderiam de nam leuarem [...]
aquella [...] moritama [...]
E de que sabemos vosas altezas Asto ham de preceber
grande prazer e contentamento Conuemos de bem
darlhe diso notificaram E eram vosas altezas
que segundo o que [...] vos sabemos que se pode fazer
que nam hara duuida em segundo ad posam seem
Xpaa que acharam pois que tam esmerada na fe
eram pera nom della perligam e tam syndo
se nam segura e farz muyto seuro deos em preto
Convertidos Anteriamente o formad em hua santa
fee em grande enxalçamento delas A lem negoçiando
prinçipall dignos da amouoma daquellas partes
Na apromytana e que de suas maaos se fazia
per outras pessoas mem lynguas nos entendiam
[...] Comuniçar per esta mingoa que descobriira
dito a aprendido que sera bem ainda delle mesmo
de que [...] de sua meçe lho hordena Mais
Cansas de nosas teneçoes e propositos vms mais
Afeenos se exerçitarem per seu [...] naquerra
de mouros peraqui [...] e a [...] fez tanto
das ditas espeçiarias e pedrarias

47. Armillary Sphere
Armillary Sphere
1543. Caspar Vopell Medebach

Armillary spheres were instruments designed to solve astrological problems. The term "armillary", from the Latin word for "bracelet", refers to the rings surrounding the world globe, representing meridians, polar circles, the equator and the ecliptic, among other things. Portugal's King Dom Emmanuel (Manuel) adopted the instrument as his symbol, signifying the importance of astronomical knowledge to the Portuguese explorations.

National Museum, Copenhagen
(Page 96)

---

48. Geographia.
Geography.
1477. Claudius Ptolemy
The Geography of Claudius Ptolemy, a Greek scholar of the 2nd-century, was not widely known in Western Europe until the first decade of the 15th century, when it was translated into Latin from the original Greek. The work was highly successful, reproduced in innumerable manuscript copies, and later printed after Gutenberg's invention of the printing press.

This 1477 Bologna edition is the first printed edition to include maps. The map on display depicts the entire world as it was known to Ptolemy, and as it was assumed to be until the voyages of discovery proved it wrong.

The New York Public Library
(Pages 114-115)

46

saliented late in the sixteenth century by the Dutch traveller to Portuguese Asia, Jan Huygen van Linschoten. He left Cochin in a Portuguese fleet on January 20, 1589, rounded the Cape of Good Hope on April 23, spent nine days on St. Helena, passed Ascension, and arrived at Terceira on July 24. He left the fleet and stayed in Angra for two and a half years, arriving home in September, 1592. The Dutch and English editions of his *Itinerario* included a superb plan of the city *(Item 40)*.

Vasco da Gama brought back to Portugal an Arab altitude measuring instrument known today as the *kamal* and of course had much to report. He certainly provided details of his wide sweep to the west in the South Atlantic for the use of commanders of subsequent fleets bound for India. He also furnished information on another meteorological phenomenon of great interest to those commanders, the periodicity of the monsoons in the Indian Ocean. This subject was most relevant in determining the month of departure from Portugal in order best to reach India.

The moisture-laden southwest monsoon blows from the southern reaches of Africa northeast to the west coast of India from roughly April to September. The dry northeast monsoon blows in the reverse direction from approximately October to March. The inexperienced European navigator would be tempted to arrive in Southeast Africa during the southwest monsoon and ride it comfortably across to Malabar. Unfortunately, however, Malabar and the west coast of India in general have few usable ports. The ports with which the

Portuguese were to become familiar – e.g., Cannanore, Calicut, Cochin, Quiloa – were, in their day, mere open anchorages. They were unusable when the rains and winds of the southwest monsoon beat in upon them.

The trick that Gama quickly learned and passed on to his successors was this: arrive in Southeast Africa toward the end of the southwest monsoon – late August or early September – and ride on its tail to India at a time when the anchorages become functional again; departure from Lisbon in March is advised.

Pedro Álvares Cabral and the Discovery of Brazil
The second fleet to sail from Lisbon to Malabar was commanded by Pedro Álvares Cabral *(Item 89)*. Reflecting the rapidity with which the Portuguese absorbed strategically important information, Cabral departed on March 9, 1500. He made his sweep to the west and made it very wide, so wide that on April 22 he literally bumped into Brazil, at Porto Seguro (16°26' S, 39° 04' W), south of the present-day city of Salvador da Bahia, or, more accurately as today seems proven, at Baia Cabrália (16° 16.0' S, 39° 01.5' W). Portuguese voyagers, including sweltering marines sporting heavy helmets and breastplates, went ashore and initiated the encounter between two worlds. Cabral's mission, however, was to reach India. One of his staff, Pero Vaz de Caminha, sent back home to King Manuel a letter about the great revelation, dated Porto Seguro of Vera Cruz, May 1, 1500 *(Item 90)*.

Cabral's very large fleet lost little time in continuing on its way.

But it encountered a terrific storm off the Cape of Good Hope. Several vessels were lost, including one with none other than Bartolomeu Dias aboard.

Updating Ptolemy's "Almagest"

On May 1, 1500, another letter was sent to King Manuel from the Land of the True Cross. It constituted an early and major element of yet another great Portuguese contribution to mankind's knowledge. Written by a Castilian scientist in the royal service known as Master John, it recounts details of the observations he and the pilots made ashore on Monday, April 27, 1500, by means of the astrolabe.

Result: observed altitude ("h") 56°, "z" 34° S, "d" (from Zacut) 16° 51' N, "L" 17° S.

On its second page the letter includes a drawing of the Southern Cross and associated stars (Item 91). Its author likens the ensemble of Crux, α and β Centauri, and Triangulum Australe to the Little Dipper, and refers to Crux itself as the Guards.

The Portuguese recognized that Crux was a separate constellation and led other Europeans to that realization. Here again, intrepid Portuguese on the high seas were updating Ptolemy — this time the astronomical notions contained in his *Almagest*. The first important star catalogue, first printed in abbreviated form in 1496 (Item 54), was a companion to the *Geographia* and grouped the stars into forty-eight constellations including Centaurus. It was not possible to distinguish the outline of Crux within Centaurus' hind feet. The Christian name that it later received contrasted markedly with the reference to the fabled

half-man and half-horse.

A Florentine agent with the Portuguese in India, Andrea Corsali, sent two significant letters in Italian back to Italy, both printed immediately. The first, dated Cochin, January 6, 1515 (i.e., 1516), was addressed to Duke Giuliano de' Medici. It contains a drawing of stars near the South Pole, with the five stars of Crux clearly and centrally indicated. These latter, incidentally, are not to be confused with Dante's *quattro stella* (four stars) in *Purgatory*, I, 23, probably a symbol of the cardinal virtues.

Corsali waxes eloquent concerning the new constellation, as is evident from the English translation contained in Richard Eden's *The Decades of the Newe World or West India* published in London in 1555 (Item 55). Following mention of the Magellanic Clouds in the drawing, the Florentine writes: "Aboue these appeareth a marueylous crosse in the middest of fyue notable starres which compasse it abowt (as doth charles wayne the northe pole) with other starres whiche moue with them abowt xxx. degrees distant from the pole, and make their course in .xxiiii. houres. This crosse is so fayre and bewtiful, that none other heuenly signe may be compared to it as may appeare by this fygure."

Corsali, and vicariously the Portuguese because of him, turn up in later astronomical literature. An outstanding example is Johann Bayer's *Uranometria* of 1603, an atlas of fifty-one copper-engraved sky maps (Item 56). The first forty-eight are of Ptolemy's constellations. Map 41 shows Centaurus; and ε, ζ, γ and ξ Centauri represent the Southern

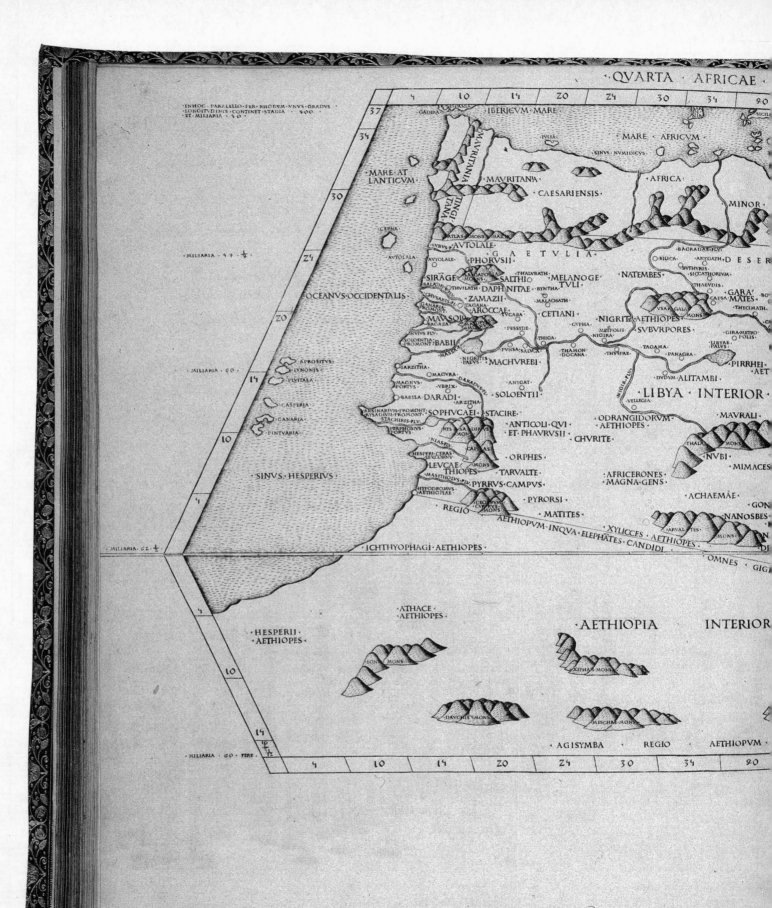

INHOC · PARALELLO · PER · RHODVM · VNVS · GRADVS
LONGITVDINIS · CONTINET · STADIA · 400
ET · MILIARIA · 50

4   10   14   20   24   30   34   90

37

34

30

24

20

14

10

4

IBERICVM · MARE

GADIRA HISPANIA

MAVRITANIA

MARE · AT·
LANTICVM

MAVRITANA

CAESARIENSIS

IVLIA

MARE · AFRICVM

SINVS · NVMIDICVS

AFRICA

MINOR

· MILIARIA · 49 · 1/2 ·

OCEANVS · OCCIDENTALIS

CERNA

AVTOLALA

ATLAS · MONS MAIOR

SVBVS · AVTOLALE

AVTOLALE

PHORVSII

SIRAGE

SALTHIO

MELANOGE·
TVLI

DAPH NITAE

THALVBATH

ZAGATON
MONS

SALATHI

THVILATH

GAETVLIA

SYNTHA

MALACHATH

NATEMBES

BAGRADAS · FLV

SILCA ANYGATH DESER

BVTHVRIS
SICCATHORIVM

THABVDIS

CAPSA GARA·
MATES

THYCIMATH

VSAR GALA MONS

BO

ZAMAZII

· MILIARIA · 60 ·

APROSITVS

IVNONIS

PLVITALA

CASPERIA

CANARIA

PINTVARIA

SINVS · HESPERIVS

CHRYSARIS · FL

GANARIA
PROMONT

MAVSOLI

AROCCAE

BAGAZA

INVIVS · FLV

SOLOENTIA
PROMONT BABII

MASSA

MAGVRA

MAGNVS·
PORTVS

VBRIX

BABILA DARADI

ARSINARIVM · PROMONT
RYSADIVM · PROMONT
STACHIRIS · FLV

SOPHVCAEI

PERPHOSIVS
PORTVS

NIAS · FLV

CHESPERI · CERAS
SEVZORVM

LEVCAE·
THIOPES

MASITHOLVS · FLV

HYPODROMVS
AETHIOPIAE

REGIO

VCARA

PESSYDE

THIGA

NIGRITIS
PALVS

DARADVS · FL

ARZITHA

KYS SA
MON

CETIANI

CVFHA

THAMON
DOCANA

MACHVREBI

ANYGAT

SOLOENTII

STACIRE

SADIRVS
MON

CAIRLAS

ORPHES

TARVALTE

PYRRVS · CAMPVS

DEORVM
CVRRVS
MONS

PYRORSI

MATITES

NIGIRA

PVNSA · SADGA

ANTICOLI · QVI
ET · PHAVRVSII

AETHIOPVM · INQVA · ELEPHATES · CANDIDI

METTOLIS

NIGIRA · FLV

NIGRIT AETHIOPES

SVBVRPORES

TAGAMA

THVSPAE

LIBYAE
PALVS

PANAGRA

VELLEGIA

DVDVM · ALITAMBI

ODRANGIDORVM
AETHIOPES

CHVRITE

AFRICERONES
MAGNA · GENS

XYLICCES · AETHIOPES

ARVAL TES

GIRAMETRO
POLIS

PIRRHEI
AET

LIBYA · INTERIOR

MAVRALI

THALA MONS

NVBI

MIMACES

ACHAEMAE

GON

NANOSBES

N

DE

MONS

OMNES GIG

· MILIARIA · 62 · 1/2 ·

ICHTHYOPHAGI · AETHIOPES

ATHACE·
AETHIOPES

HESPERII·
AETHIOPES

10

ION · MONS

AETHIOPIA

XIPHAN · MONS

INTERIOR

14

1/2
1/4

DAVCHIS · MONS

MESCHAE · MONS

· MILIARIA · 60 · FERE ·

AGISYMBA

REGIO

AETHIOPVM

4   10   14   20   24   30   34   90

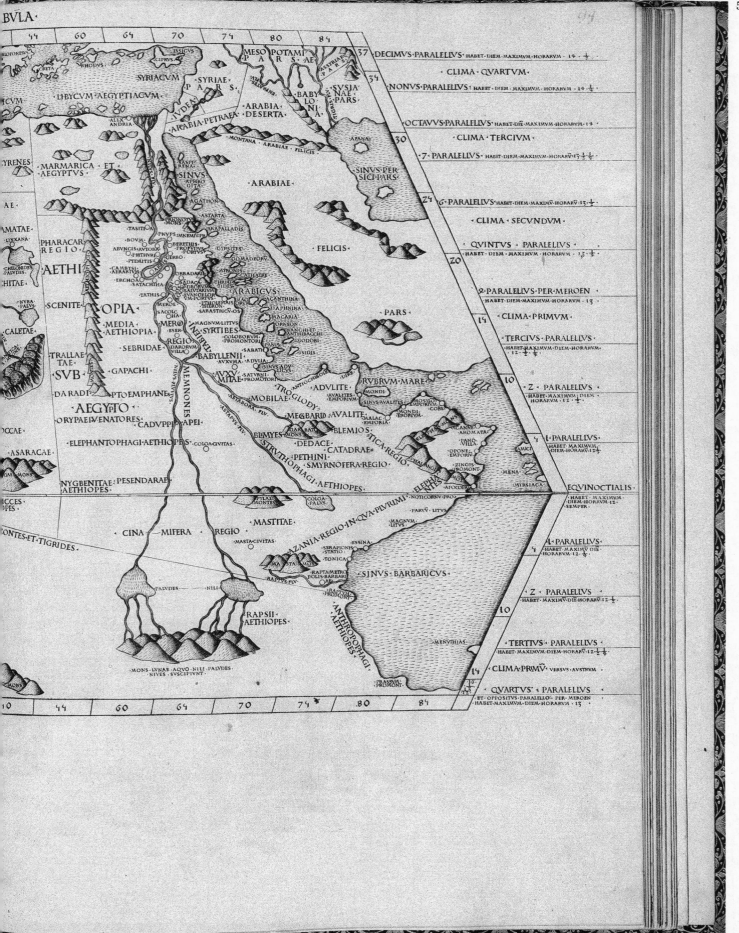

DECIMVS PARALELIVS · HABET · DIEM · MAXIMVM · HORARVM · 14 · ½

CLIMA · QVARTVM

NONVS PARALELIVS · HABET · DIEM · MAXIMVM · HORARVM · 14 · ¼

OCTAVVS · PARALELIVS · HABET· DIE · MAXIMVM · HORARVM · 14

CLIMA TERCIVM

7 · PARALELIVS · HABET·DIEM·MAXIMVM·HORARV·13·½·¼

6 · PARALELIVS HABET·DIEM·MAXIMV·HORARV·13·½

CLIMA · SECVNDVM

QVINTVS · PARALELIVS
HABET·DIEM·MAXIMVM·HORARV·13·½

2 · PARALELIVS·PER·MEROEN
HABET·DIEM·MAXIMVM·HORARV·13

CLIMA · PRIMVM

TERCIVS · PARALELIVS
HABET·MAXIMVM·DIEM·HORARVM·12·½·¼

Z · PARALELIVS
HABET·MAXIMVM·DIEM·HORARVM·12·⅓

1 · PARALELIVS
HABET·MAXIMVM·DIEM·HORARVM·12·¼

EQVINOCTIALIS
HABET · MAXIMVM·DIEM·HORARVM·12·SEMPER

1 · PARALELIVS
HABET·MAXIMV·DIE·HORARVM·12·¼

Z · PARALELIVS
HABET·MAXIMV·DIE·HORARV·12·⅓

TERTIVS · PARALELIVS
HABET·MAXIMVM·DIEM·HORARV·12·½·¼

CLIMA·PRIMV · VERSVS·AVSTRVM

QVARTVS · PARALELIVS
ET·OPPOSITVS·PARALELLO·PER·MEROEN
HABET·MAXIMVM·DIEM·HORARVM·13

52. De Nauigatione Libri Tres . . .
Three Books on Navigation.
1549. Diogo de Sá

This book is a veritable denunciation of cosmographer Pedro Nunes, in the form of a dialogue between "Philosophia" and "Mathematica". The latter sets forth Nunes' ideas, based on a Latin translation of the Treatise on the Sphere which he published in Lisbon in 1537. Sá's criticism is for the most part unfounded; in fact, he lacked the preparation needed to read, much less criticize, the two little treatises authored by Nunes.

The New York Public Library
(Below)

53. Theatrum Orbis Terrarum.
A View of the Lands of the Globe.
1570. Abraham Ortelius

Using knowledge of hand-drawn maps that portrayed new lands with considerable accuracy, or turning for aid to foreign cartographers (principally the Portuguese Luís Teixeira), Dutch map makers issued the first modern, printed atlases. Abraham Ortel (Latinized as Ortelius), author of this Theatrum Orbis Terrarum, is undoubtedly the most representative of these innovative map makers. In addition to noting the parts of Northeastern Canada and South America claimed by Portugal, this map establishes a prime meridian for measuring longitude at a line that runs through the Cape Verde Islands, reminiscent of the line established to separate Portuguese and Castilian spheres of activity in the Atlantic.

The New York Public Library
(Page 118-119)

52

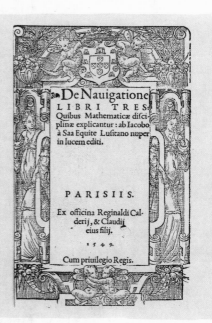

Cross. Of them Bayer writes in the accompanying text in his very clear Latin: "Modernis Crux, Ptolemaeo pedes Centauri" (For us moderns they are Crux, for Ptolemy the feet of Centaurus).

Map 49 is of twelve newly identified constellations around the south pole. Off to the upper right and next to Triangulum Australe is a bright star labelled "Pes laevus Centauri" (Left foot of Centaurus), that is, α Centauri. Bayer's text states that these twelve constellations had been observed by Amerigo Vespucci, Andrea Corsali, and Pedro de Medina, and more recently plotted by "Petrus Theodori nauclerus peritissimus". This latter is a reference to the "most expert" Dutch navigator Pieter Dirkszoon Keyser who in 1595-1597 with Frederich de Houtman charted the stars around the south pole. As for Pedro de Medina, he was the Spanish author of an important *Arte de navegar* published in 1545 *(Item 51).*

The Corte-Real Family and Newfoundland

As the information brought back by Columbus from his first voyage (August 3, 1492 - June 11, 1493) and his second (September 25, 1493 - June 11, 1496) was absorbed by the Portuguese high command, they began to suspect an alternate way of reaching those Indies. Recalled were the Azorean voyages northwest to or toward the lands known as Terra Nova and Lavrador, as well as the location of the Tordesillas Line in terms of the latter. Perhaps one could skirt northward of whatever Columbus had come upon and find a short cut to East Asia, a Northwest Passage to the

lands described by Marco Polo the Venetian.

Like João II in 1487, King Manuel in 1500 sent out two expeditions: Cabral's via the South Atlantic and Indian Ocean to the Indies, and another headed by Gaspar Corte-Real, from an old Terceiran family, across the North Atlantic to the northwest. King Manuel's royal charter, dated Sintra, May 12, 1500, grants to Gaspar any isle or isles or lands that he may reach or discover. It naturally makes no mention of John Cabot's round-trip voyage of 1497 from Bristol, England, to what turned out to be Newfoundland. Historians disagree as to Corte-Real's ultimate objective. Was it the Indies via a Northwest Passage? The best answer is probably the late Admiral Teixeira da Mota's: "Gaspar Corte Real was not . . . in search of Asia. Like other Portuguese before him, he was looking for new lands in the North Atlantic which might be within the Portuguese hemisphere. He found the only land to be sought".

On his voyage, Gaspar Corte-Real came upon Newfoundland and placed it on the European historical record, even though it had been informally known to or its existence suspected by earlier Europeans. Gaspar returned to Lisbon that same year, and then the following year he crossed the North Atlantic once again. This time he failed to return, but two of his vessels did come back, arriving early in October. Their men provided much information soon to be widely disseminated. By royal charter dated Lisbon, January 15, 1502, *(Item 69)* King Manuel sent Gaspar's older brother Miguel on a third expedition to the northwest, hopefully to find the lost Gaspar.

54. "Epytoma in Almagestum Ptolemaei".
An Epitome in the Almagest of Ptolemy.
1496. Regiomontanus (Johann Müller)

Johann Müller was a 15th-century German astronomer. This Epytoma, an updating of the astronomical work of Ptolemy, is the first important star catalogue to appear in the Age of Discoveries, and demonstrates the accumulated results of celestial observations made by navigators during the period.
The illustration shows Regiomontanus (Müller) on the right and Ptolemy on the left, under the armillary sphere which became one of the symbols of the Age of Discoveries and figured prominently in Portuguese royal iconography.

The New York Public Library
(Page 109)

---

55. The Decades of the Newe World or West India.
1555. Richard Eden

This work reflected growing English interest in the deeds of Spain and Portugal overseas. Among other things, the author included a reprinting of a letter by the Italian voyager Andrea Corsali, who had been with the Portuguese in India. This letter mentions the southern hemisphere's most notable constellation, the Southern Cross, as the English text clearly states: "And above these appeareth a marvellous crosse . . .".

The New York Public Library
(Below and facing page)

55

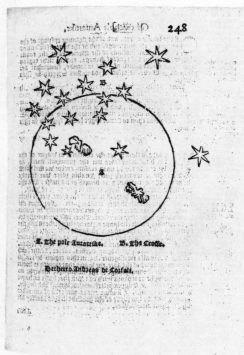

Miguel was never heard of again. In the town of Berkeley, Massachusetts, up the Taunton River just north of Fall River, is America's most famous writing stone, Dighton Rock. Since 1975 it has been protected by the Commonwealth of Massachusetts in a beautifully designed little museum within the Dighton Rock State Park. The rock was known to English colonists and descendants in the seventeenth century, and an illustration of inscriptions on its written side was published in Boston in 1690, in Cotton Mather's *The Wonderful Works of God Commemorated (Item 70)*.

A distinguished psychologist on the faculty of Brown University in Providence, Edmund Burke Delabarre, in late 1913 began to unfold the Portuguese theory. He gave the results of his researches in full in a lengthy and well-illustrated book published in 1923, *Dighton Rock: A Study of the Written Rocks of New England*. He believed he had found evidence on the rock itself that Miguel Corte-Real had been there in 1511, indeed, had been a leader of the Indians. He read : "V. DEI hIC DVX IND.", evidently: "Voluntate Dei hic Dux Indorum", "By the will of God here the leader of the Indians". A fact that makes an objective scholar skeptical of the theory involves the letters OR of MIGV. . CORTER. . . They had earlier been used in the Norse theory to support the reading ThORfinn Karlsefni!

Foreign Agents in Lisbon
Rival powers in Europe were naturally watching with the greatest of interest Atlantic discoveries effected by the Portuguese. This was especially true of Italian city states, notably Venice. Hitherto, this Adriatic power had held the monopoly on the import trade from South and East Asia. It saw itself suddenly threatened, for sea transport was faster and less costly than the overland method. The Italian leaders therefore placed agents – ambassadors or spies – in Lisbon to report on great events as they unfolded. One such agent was the Venetian Pietro Pasqualigo. He arrived in Lisbon in mid 1501 and on August 20 delivered a flowery oration in Latin addressed to King Manuel. Printed in Venice toward the end of the same year *(Item 34)*, it seems to have summarized Portuguese exploration in southern Africa and on to the east but makes no mention either of Brazil or of Newfoundland. To the extent that it does in fact allude to the Gama and Cabral voyages, it may be said to have been the first printed account of the Portuguese discovery of the ocean route to India.

Pasqualigo also sent two letters, dated respectively October 18 and October 19, 1501, from Lisbon to Venice. They quite fully reported on the information garnered from those who returned from the northwest a few days earlier. They were not printed at once, however.

Another such agent was Alberto Cantino, who sent an important letter dated Lisbon, October 17, 1501, to his master, Ercole I d'Este, Duke of Ferrara. Likewise not printed at the time, it did report the return of the two vessels from Gaspar Corte-Real's second expedition and provided news of Newfoundland. Cantino did more. For his master in Italy he had a map made *(Pages 147-149)* which shows the line labelled "Este he o marco dantre castella & portugall," the much-disputed

Of the pole Antartike.

As touchyng the starres and reasons of Cosmographie, I
haue gathered thus much owt of the vyage of Americus
Uesputius. And haue thought good to ioyne hereunto
that whiche Andreas de Corsali wryteth in his vyage to East
India as concernynge the same matter.

After that we departed frome Lisbona, wee sayled euer
with prosperous wynde, not passynge owt of the Southeast
and Southwest. And passyng beyonde the Equinoctial line,
we were in the heyght of. 37 degrees of the other halfe circle of the earth. And trauerlynge the cape of Bona Speran-
za a coulde and wyndy tíme bycause at that tyme the soonne
was in the north signes, wee founde the nyght of. xiiii. houres. Here we sawe a marueplous order of starres, so that in
the parte of heauen contrary to owre northe pole, to knowe
in what place and degree the south pole was, we tooke the
day with the soonne, and obserued the nyght with the Astro-
labie, and sawe manifestly twoo clowdes of reasonable byg-
nesse mouynge abowt the place of the pole continually nowe
rysynge and nowe faulynge, so keepynge theyr continuall
course in circular mouynge, with a starre euer in the myddest
which is turned abowt with them abowte. xi. degrees frome
the pole. Aboue these appeareth a marueplous crosse in the
myddest of fyue notable starres which compasse it abowt
(as doth charles wayne the northe pole) with other
starres whiche moue with them abowt. xxx. degrees distant from the pole, and make their
course in. xxiiii. houres. This crosse
is so fayre and bewtiful, that
none other heuenly signe
may be compared to it
as may appeare by
this fygure.

A. The

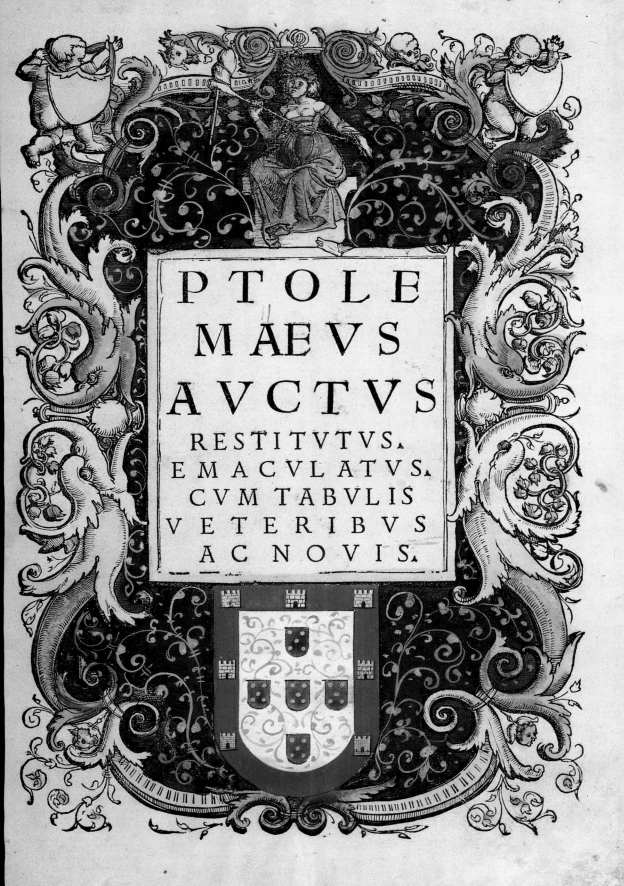

PTOLE MÃEVS AVCTVS

RESTITVTVS,
EMACVLATVS,
CVM TABVLIS
VETERIBVS
AC NOVIS.

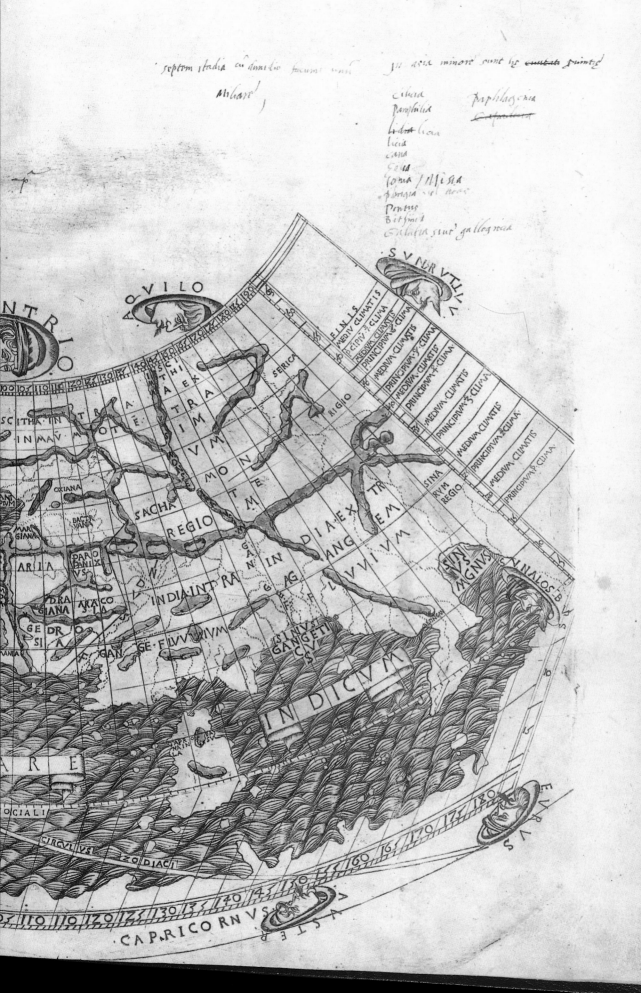

septem stadia cū dimidio faciunt unū   in asia minore sunt hȝ ciuitates prouincie

          milliare

                                        Cilicia   Paphlagonia

                                        Pamphilia

                                        Pisidia licia

                                        Licia

                                        Caria

                                        Ionia / Mysia

                                        phrigia vel ...

                                        Pontus

                                        Bithinia

                                        Galatia siue gallograeca

LIBRO·IIII·DE LA AL
TVRA DEL SOL, Y
COMO SE HA DE RE
GIR POR ELLA LA
NAVEGACION·

Capitulo prime=
ro, en que se declaran diez y siete
principios fundamentales que en
el altura del sol se deuen saber.

De las co
sas mas sub
tiles, y de
mayor en=
tendimien=
to q̃ enel ar
te del naue
gar ay, es
el altura dl
sol, porq̃ esta enseña verdaderamẽ
te el camino q̃ el que nauega haze
o a de hazer. En tal manera, que si
yerro alguno en su viaje a hecho,
por esta altura lo conoce. Y assi por
ser cosa tan excelente y tan subtil,
los antiguos tuuierõ en mucho la
practica della: mayormente aquel
gran Ptholomeo, y otros singula
res auctores. Para la qual, diuer
sos instrumentos vsarõ, assi como
el Astrolabio, y el Triu regularũ,
y otros. Esta altura, es tanta par=
te para la buena nauegacion, q̃ los
que nauegan a partes remotas y
muy distãtes no podriã hazer sus
nauegaciones ciertas si esta faltas
se: porque, puesto q̃ por las reglas
y auisos que yo tengo declarados
eneste arte, y declararc, assi en la al
tura del Norte como en otras que
siruẽ en la nauegaciõ. Esta altura
del sol tiene excelẽcia entre todas,
porq̃ es, como prueua de arismeti
ca, q̃ enseña el yerro q̃ enlos nume
ros ay. Biẽ assi, cõ el altura del sol

toma da precisamente puede el pi=
loto conoscer la falta que en su na
uegacion huuiere. Y porque esta
altura del sol es materia delicada
y subtil (como dicho tengo) Eneste
libro quarto tratare della lo mas
claramente q̃ possible me fuere, se
ñalando las reglas por testo, y dã
doles su declaracion y verdadero
entendimiento, que deuen tener.
Y assimesmo, dãdo a cada vna exẽ
plo y demostraciõ para q̃ mejor se
entienda. Pues para esto se nota=
ran diez y siete principios fũdamẽ
tales, q̃ son los siguientes.
¶ Altura.
¶ Grado.
¶ Orizonte.
¶ Zodiaco.
¶ Linea equinocial.
¶ Declinacion.
¶ Circulos.
¶ Tropicos.
¶ Parte del Norte.
¶ Parte del Sur.
¶ Longitud.
¶ Latitud.
¶ Paralelo.
¶ Meridiano.
¶ Hemispherio.
¶ Cenith
¶ Centro.
¶ Altura, es los grados q̃ el sol o
el polo se leuãtã sobre el Orizonte.
Tãbiẽ altura se ẽtiẽde por los gra
dos q̃ algũa ciudad puerto ysla ꝛc.
esta apartado dla linea eq̃nocial.
¶ Grado, es vna parte de. ccclx. en
q̃ el mũdo es diuidido, tiene. xvij.
leguas y media d camino, por la lõ
gura o anchura dl agua y tierra.

ANIAN.

Ulterius Septentrionem versus hę regiones incognitę adhuc sunt.

SEPT

Tuchana
QVIVIRA
Sierra neuada
Quiuira

TOLM.

Cicuic
Axa
Chucho
Tiguas rio.

TOTO   TEAC.
Tiguex   Totonteac
Ceuola   MARATA
Suala mons

Yn del ripa
Cazones inf.
La Sardinas
Costa blanca
Baia de los fuegos
C. de cruz
Abacus nunc Granata
P. de clara
Camonada
Maruta
Cosina
ASTATLAN
Guaiaual rio
TERLICHICH

R. Palmar
Ometlan
Perlatan
HISPANIA NOVA

Las dos hermanos
Malabrigo
Los bolcanes
La farfana

Inf. Cebri
Los diamantes
C. del
C. California
Baia de la trinidad.
insf. Nalisco
Culuae KALISCO Chicil
Chamet
Ystapa
TOPIRA
MECHVACAN

ARCHIPELAGO DI
SAN LAZARO.

Restinga de ladrones
Zamal
Inf. de los corales.

Rocha parcida
S. Thomas.
La Anabi ada

OCCIDENS.

Los iardines
Inf. de los reÿs

Circulus Aequinoctialis

martyres
y de crespos
Da primo mala gente
V. dos hombres blancos
La barbada
La Caimana
Los bolcanes

Ysola de los tiburones

NOVA GVINEA, Andre:
as Corsalus Florent: videtur eā
sub nomine Terrę Picciuacoli
designare.

Hę duę insulę, infortunatę sunt dictę
à Magellano, quod nec homines nec
victui apta haberent.

S. Petri

MER

AMERICAE SIVE
NOVI ORBIS, NO;
VA DESCRIPTIO.

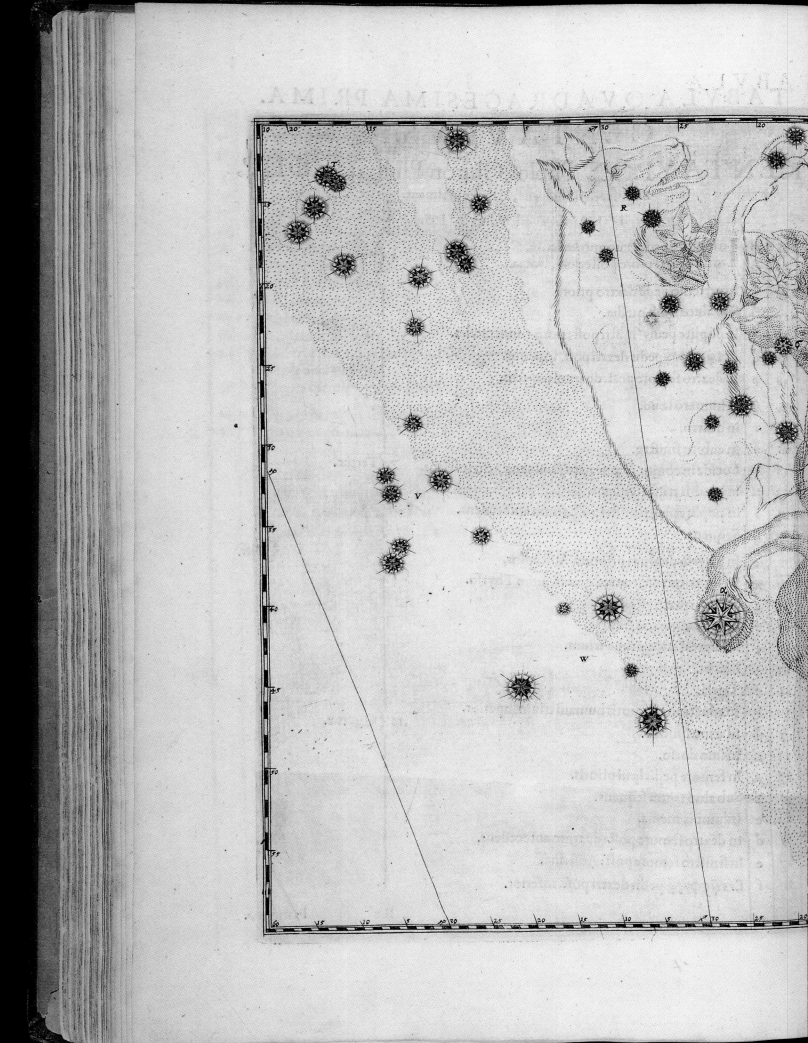

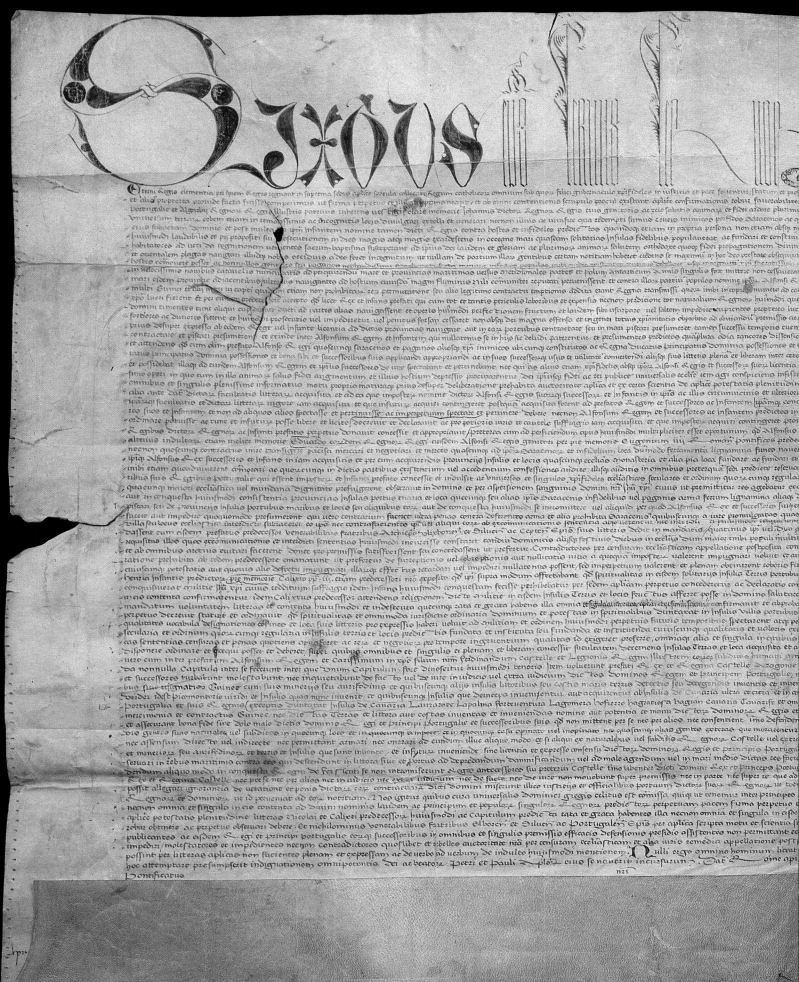

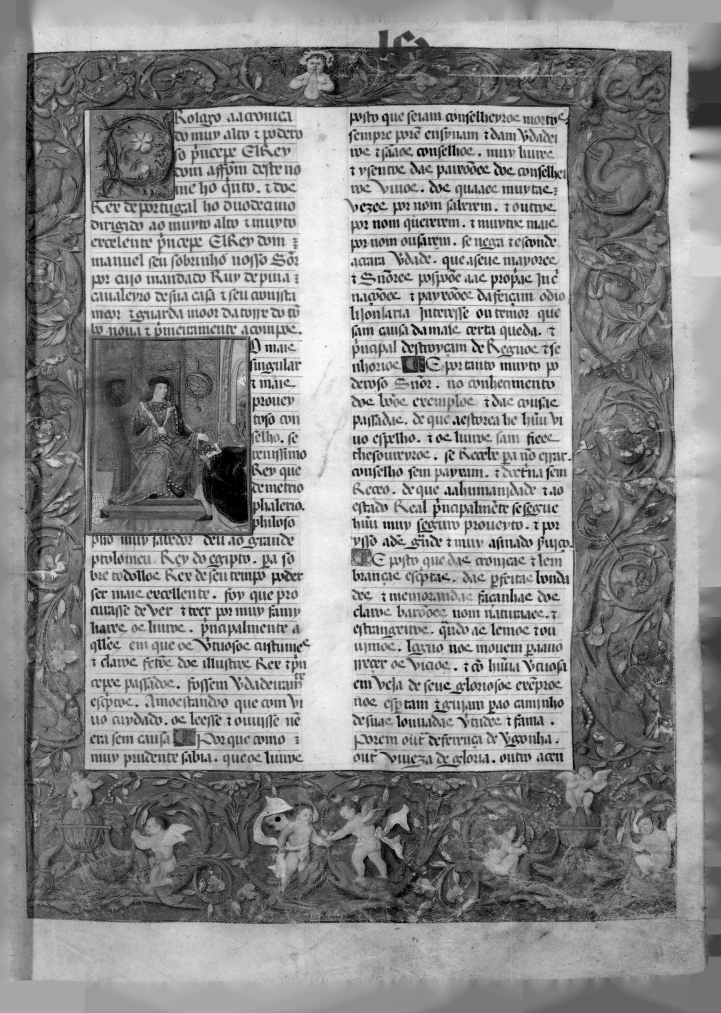

Prologo da cronica
do muy alto e poderoso principe ElRey
dom affom deste no
me ho quinto. e de
Rey de portugal ho duodecimo
dirigido ao muyto alto e muyto
excellente principe ElRey dom
manuel seu sobrinho nosso Sõr
por cuio mandado Ruy de pina
caualeyro de sua casa e seu coronista
mor e guarda moor da torre do to
bo noua e primeiramente acompõe.

O mais
singular
e mais
prouey
toso con
selho. se
rẽ̃issimo
Rey que
demetrio
phalerio
philoso
pho muy sabedor deu ao grande
ptolomeu Rey do egipto. pa so
bre todollos Rey de seu tempo poder
ser mais excellente. foy que pro
curasse de ver e teer por muy familiares os liuros. principalmente a
quelles em que os vertuosos custumes
e clauos feitos de illustres Rey e principes passados. fossem vdadeiram
escriptos. Amoestando que com vi
uo cuydado. os leesse e ouuisse nẽ
era sem causa Porque como e
muy prudente sabia. que os liuros

posto que seiam conselheyros mortos
sempre porẽ ensynam e dam vdadei
ras e saaos conselhos. muy liures
e ysentas das paixões dos conselhei
ros viuos. dos quaaes muytas
vezes por nom saberem. e outros
por nom quererem. e muytos mais
por nom ousarem. se nega e esconde
a certa vdade. que a seus mayores
e Snõres pospõe aas proprias inc
nações. e paixões da feiçam odio
lisonlaria intereysse ou temor que
sam causa da mais certa queda. e
principal destroyçam de Regnos e se
nhores E por tanto muyto po
deroso Snõr. no conhecimento
dos boos exemplos e das cousas
passadas. de que a estorea he huu vi
uo espelho. e os liuros sam seus
thesoureyros. se recolhe pa no espar
conselho sem paixam. e doctrina sem
Recco. de que a a humanidade e ao
estado Real principalmente se segue
huu muy seguro prouveyto. e por
ysso a de e grande e muy asinado fruyto.
E posto que das coronicas e lem
branças escriptas. das perfeitas lounda
des e memorandas façanhas dos
clauos barões non naturaes. e
estrangeiros. quando as lemos ou
uymos. logo nos mouem pratio
prazer de viados. e com huua vertuosa
em veia de seus gloriosos exemplos.
esptam e guiam pao caminho
de suas lounadas virtudes e fama.
porem outros deseruiça de vergonha
outros vmeza de gloria. outros acen

QE OS OI NO SETA SEDREI ME LOUVADO

In principia se ho prollego. A denotar quem os seguintes volumes, ma[n]dou fazer e sob que fundamento. E ielam os ouuintes, e pello uijndoijro tempo. Os possuidores farom como este Senhor fez, e como theudos som. Porque como quer, que todollos, fiees xpaos, tanto obrigados, e theudos somos. Aa santa madre igreja. Porem principalmente os Reys, e Duques. A que a deffensam della he encomendada, lhe stam obrigados. Quanto mais, e mayor graao. Se della temporalmente percebem, e a ssegujo ou administracom della tee nos, seu Rejno e Senhorjos. E porem diz minha Isiuel. Afide pena. Delictens dos auctores, e dignes dos graaos, e incentiuos pa semelhante assoelhar. Portijamte com a beuenca que ao da Altgeza e Real estaado, principalmente, com fiel amor e preuinal temor, sujo, e obedencia, deuemos. Assij aa graao e nobreza, dos grandes Senhores, e deferenca das pessoas, e Comunalmente, Aa todo numero uirtuoso que o presente uerm a Leer ouuyrem, por qualquer modo, e manijra que aa sua noticia ra empanada vier. Que ho muy alto, e muy excellente, e muyto poderoso e espra zemdo Sñor. Dom Johan, por gra de Ds Rey de portugal e dos Algaruees daquem

Don fernando e donna ysabel

por la graçia de dios Rey e reyna de castilla de leon de aragon de seçilia de granada de toledo de Valençia de galizia de mallorcas de Seuilla de çerdeña de cordoua de corçega de murçia de Jaen del algarbe de algezira de gibraltar delas yslas de canaria condes de barçelona e Señores de vizcaya e de molina duques de atenas e de neopatria condes de rrosellon e de çerdania marqueses e condes de oristan e de goçiano ...

...

En el nombre de dios

...

MVNDVS NOWS:

TIERA DEL LABRADOR

TIERA NVEVA DELOS BACA LlAOS:

TIERA DE ESTEVAM COMEZ:

TIERA DEL LICENCIADO AILLON:

TIERA DE GARAY:

ISLAS DELOS ACORES:

TIERA DE PANFILO DE NARBAEZ:

GOLFO DE LA NVEVA ESPAÑA:

ISLAS DELOS LVCAYOS:

ISLAS DELAS CANAREAS

OCCEANVS OCCIDENTALIS:

NVEVA ESPAÑA:

ISLAS DE CABO VERDE:

ISLAS DE CARIBES:

CASTILIA DEL ORO:

MAR DEL SVR:

PERV PROVINCIA:

RIO DE MARAÑON:

ELBRASIL:

MVNDVS NOWS:

ELGRAM RIO DE PARANA

TIERA DE PATAGONES:

Eu nome de Deus amen. Sabham quantos esta carta virem Como eu Don Denis pela graça de Deus Rey de Portugal e do algarve em senhor [...]

ego manuel pezagro

Tordesillas line of demarcation, as a continuous meridian putting a major portion of Brazil and half of Newfoundland on the Portuguese side of the "mark". Newfoundland is labelled "Terra del Rey de portuguall". Another legend states that this "Terra" was discovered by Gaspar Corte-Real. A letter from Cantino to his duke dated Rome, November 19, 1502 suggests that the agent purchased the map in Lisbon for twelve gold ducats. This so-called Cantino Map exemplifies an art form cultivated by Portuguese cartographers both before and after 1502. This is still very much appreciated in Portugal today – the beautifully designed and coloured compass rose (in Portuguese *rosa dos ventos or rosa náutica*).

Another source of evidence – admittedly oblique – about the location of the line of demarcation is provided by a later map. The depiction of America, "Americae sive Novi Orbis, Nova Descriptio" in the 1570 atlas by Abraham Ortelius entitled *Theatrum Orbis Terrarum (Item 53)* runs longitude 360 degrees eastward, in the Ptolemaic manner, from a prime meridian through the eastern Cape Verde Islands at about 23 degrees W of Greenwich. Its 330 degree meridian cuts through the mouth of the Amazon and the western side of Newfoundland. The Cantino map at the beginning of the Portuguese dominion over Newfoundland and the Ortelius map at roughly its end seem in agreement.

Their lesson appears confirmed, *grosso modo*, by the location of Cape Mark, situated above Miquelon off southern Newfoundland; and the Mark Islands near Battle Harbor, Labrador – "Battle" being a

deformation of the Portuguese *batel* (boat). Both are at approximately the same longitude, and support the guess that the mark as shown on the Cantino map stood at 53° 43' west of Greenwich.

Printing and the Dissemination of the New Knowledge

Several criteria may be used for drawing a line of demarcation between the Middle Ages and the Renaissance. For the present exhibition certainly a most important one involves the widespread use of printing by movable type. A specific year for this mark might be 1476, when *Die Legend der heyligen drey Koenig* first appeared, or perhaps better the following year, when Marco Polo's description of the world was first printed, as was the edition of Ptolemy's *Geography* with maps. Lucena's obedience oration enjoyed the new-style dissemination in the mid 1480's. In 1492 appeared the small and extremely rare volume entitled *India Recognita*. In 1493 came Columbus' letter and three years later Zacut's perpetual almanac. Next, in 1501, the new medium disseminated Pasqualigo's Latin oration.

Early in 1502, in Lisbon, a spectacular volume was published in the Portuguese language, the first Portuguese book to allude to the new tidings *(Item 35)*. It was put together and printed by Valentim Fernandes, a German resident in Lisbon. The compiler realized that King Manuel was most excited about Portuguese deeds in the "Indies" of Africa and Asia and that he had gone to the extreme of adding to his already extended title concerning the Algarves and Guinea the words "Lord of the Conquest,

56. Uranometria.
1603. Johannes Bayer

This atlas of 51 copper engraved star maps records the ever expanding knowledge of new skies uncovered by the explorers, particularly by the Portuguese in the southern hemisphere. Shown is Map 41, containing Centaurus; in the legendary beast's hind legs are the stars later called the Southern Cross; Bayer's text even states that whereas to the ancients it was known as Centaurus, the moderns call it "Crux" ("The Cross").

The New York Public Library
(Pages 120-121)

---

57. Papal Bull, "Romanus Pontifex".
January 8, 1455. Nicholas V

This document represents an early recognition by the papacy of the growing politico-geographic dimensions of the Portuguese discoveries. After a lengthy recital of the sacrifices invested by Dom Afonso V in the conquests of Africa and in the discoveries and colonization undertaken by Dom Henrique, the Pontiff grants to the king of Portugal and his successors, and to the infante, all lands conquered from Capes Bojador and Não to Guinea, and all the southern coast of Africa to its tip. They also receive the right of occupation of all lands, harbours, islands and seas which they might conquer, and authority to promulgate laws, impose taxes and build churches and monasteries.

Arquivo Nacional da Torre do Tombo, Lisbon
(Pages 130-131)

---

58. Papal Bull, "Aeterni Regis Clementia".
June 21, 1481. Pope Sixtus IV

This pontifical document confirms previous papal bulls recognizing the rights of dominion assumed by the Portuguese crown over lands it discovered. It also confirms portions of the treaty of Alcáçovas, whereby the king of Portugal and his successors are granted all right to trade and navigation on the coast of Guinea and islands discovered and to be discovered, except for the Canaries, which are recognized as the possession of the kings of Castile.

Arquivo Nacional da Torre do Tombo, Lisbon
(Page 122-123)

NICOLAVS ... ...

Romanus Pontifex Regni celestis clauigeri successor et Vicarius Ihu xpi cuncta mundi climata omniumque nationum in illis degentium qualitates et iura que oues sibi diuinitus creditas ad vnicum ouile dominicum reducat et acquirat eis felicitatis eterne premium, ac veniam impetret animabus que ... et intrepidos pugiles nomine do Saracenorum ceterosque infidelium xpiani nominis inimicos feritatem reprimere sed etiam ipos eorumque Regna ac loca expensis sat tremenda cognoscimus de Regum et Principum xpi sublatis quibusuis dispendiis ad tam saluberrimum tamque laudabile prosequendum opus ...

Carissimus in xpo filius nr Alfonsus Portugalie et Algarby Regnorum Rex Illustris Patruus inherens ur tiuus dare memorie Johannis die ac fortissimis expensis et insuper ... eisdem erationes gloriose efferentur iuxta ... diuersis terris oceani etiam ... remotissimis et in angulis ...
reducta ab eius incunte etate totis asperantis viribus pos t Ceptam Ciuitatem in Affrica consistentem per die tam Johannem Regem eius salute expensis ac rerum et personarum periculum et iac tuta plurimorum qz naturalium suorum vita bella certorumque tanquam laboribus periculis et damnis non fra ...
ac fundari et construi inibi fecit ecclias et alia loca pia in quibus diuina celebrantur officia et die ti quicumque Infantis laudabili opera et industria quamplur ...
ratione animarum salutem orthodoxe quoque fidei propagationem et diuini cultus augmentum Preterea cum olim ad ipius Infantis peruenisset notitiam ...
incertum erat vt nullam de partibus illarum gentibus certam notitiam haberemus credens se maximum in hoc deo prestaturum obsequium si eius opera et indu ...
hostes comouere posset ac nonnullos Gentiles seu Paganos nefandissimi Machometi sec ta minime infectos populos inibi mediociter tentes contrario ...
Regnorum gentibus maximis cum laboribus periculis et expensis in velocissimis nauibus Caruelis nuncupatis ad perquirendum mare et Prouincias marit ...
trassent et occupassent ad Guineam prouinciam tandem peruenire occupassetque nonnullis Insulas portibus ac mari eidem Prouincie adiacentibus ulterius ...
Annos quatuor habita extitit et in illa quamplures inibi mense Insule debellate ac pacifice possesse fuerunt prout adhuc cum adiacenti mari possidentur, exinde ...
in copioso numero ad catholicam fidem conuersi extiterunt speraturque diuina fauente clementia qz si huiusmodi cum eis continuetur progressus uel populi ip ...
sis necno perditione tot naturalium Regnorum quod inibi quamplures peribant ipsos naturalium duntaxat fren auxilii, Prouincias illas perlus ...
huiusmodi perfectionem fru tum et laudem sibi usurpare uel saltem impedire cupientes propriorio seu lucri commodo aut malitia ferrum arma lignamina aliasque ...
uel impediretur uel forsan penitus cessaret non absque dei magna offensa et ingenti totius xpianitatis obprobrio ad euitandum remissa se prouis uris et ...
... super extructa iis eidem Regi uel Infanti licenciam ad illas huiusmodi Prouincias nauigare aut in earum portubus contra tare seu in illis exercitari presum ...
ablutione huiusmodi ad dictas Prouincias accedere et in sic acquisitis Prouincias portibus Insulis ac mari nauigare contra tare ac piscari presumerent uel ...
in maximam dei offensam et animarum periculum verisimiliter subsequi possent et subsequuntur, Nos premissa omnia et singula debita meditatione penso ...
Dominia possessiones et mobilia ac immobilia bona quecumque per eos detenta ac possessa, inuadendi conquirendi expugnandi debellandi et subiugandi, illo ...
ac in suos successores qz suos usus et utilitatem conuertendi, aliis nris litteris plenarie et libere inter cetera concesserimus facultatem, die te fraternitatis obtent ...
Alfonsum Regem et ipius successores de iure spe tant et pertinent nec quisuis alius etiam residuus absit ipoz Alfonsi Regis et successoz suoz ...
et eum eius memoratam dignissimo opere in quo etiam ip illo animarum salus fidei incrementum et illius hos huiusmodi depressio procurentur dei ipiusque fidei ac rei publ ...
conspexerint de premissis omnibus et singulis plenissime et informati motu proprio non ad ipoz Alfonsi Regis et Infantis uel alterius pro eis nobis super ho ...
tenentes de verbo ad verbum presentibus haberi volumus pro insertis cum omnibus et singulis in eis contentis clausulis ad Ceptam a pedis ta quecumque alia etiam inante ...
remotioribus partibus de Insularum seu Paganorum manibus acquiri poterunt Prouincias Insulas portus et maria quecumque extendat et illa sub eisdem fac ...
sores suos ac si Infantem ipsum conquesta tam quam a Capitibus de Boiador et de Naam usque per totam Guineam et ultra versus illam meridionalem p ...
pertinere de iure, necno Alfonsum Regem et successores suos ac Infantem predic tos in illis et circa ea quecumque prohibitiones statuta et mandata etiam ...
presenti decernimus et declaramus, ac pro potiori uiris et cautele suffragio iam acquisita et que imposterum acquiri contigerint Prouincias Insulas port ...
die tos Regnorum ac Infanti prefa tis perpetuo donamus concedimus et appropriamus per presentes, Preterea quia ad perficiendum opus huiusmodi ...
Regum per felicis recordationem Martinum V et alterius indultos etiam inclite memorie Eduardo earumde Regnorum Regi eiusdem Alfonsi R ...
rebus et bonis ac uir tualibus emptiones et uenditiones et quoue contingerit facere negotiis quibusuis contra tus iure transigere prout mercatoriae negotiari et mercer ...
nendere omnia quoque alia et singula in premissis et circa ea opportuna uel necessaria facere exercere ad ipos Alfonsum Regem successores et Infans in iam acquisit ...
icas seculares quoque ius etiam mendicantium eciam regulares de superius tamen licentia ad illa transmittere ipoque persone inibi etiam quoadquiuerint con ...
impendere ac penitentiam salutarem iniungere, necno eccliam ad sacramenta minis trare ualeant libere ac licite decernimus ipsque Alfonso et successoribus suis ...
regulares ubiliter per orbem constitute cuiusuis status gradus ordinis conditionis uel preeminentie fuerant etiam si Archiepali Epali Imperiali Regal ...
mittimus res agitur exhortamur eisque in remissionem suoz peccaminum iniungimus, necno hoc perpetuo prohibitionis edic to districte tus inhibemus, ne de ac ...
Paganos arma ferrum lignamina aliaque a iure Sarracenis deferri prohibita quoquomodo uel etiam absque speciali ipius Alfonsi Regis et successoz suoz et ...
et locis seu aliquibus eorum aut de Conquesta huiusmodi se intromittere uel aliquid per quod Alfonsus Rex et successores sui et Infans predic ti quominus ...
quoquomodo presumant, qui uero contrarium fecerit ultra penas contra deferentes arma et alia prohibita Sarracenis quibusuis a iure promulgatas quas il ...
Ciuitas Cas trum Villa seu locus interdic to subiaceat eo ipo nec contrafacientes ipi uel aliqui eoz ab excommunicationis sententia absoluantur nec ...
aut super amicabiliter concordauerint cum eisdem Mandantes per aplica scripta Venerabilibus fratribus nris Archiepo Vlixbonen et Siluen ac C ...
requisitus uel aliquis pro eis fuerit requisitus illos quos excommunicationis et interdic ti sententias huiusmodi incurrisse constiterit tamdiu Dominicis aliisque fest ...
denuntient necno ab aliis nuntiari et ab omnibus arctius euitari faciant donec pro premissis satisfecerint seu concordauerint ut prefertur Contradic tores ...
littere que a nobis de nra certa scientia et matura desuper deliberatione prehabita emanarunt ut prefertur de surreptionis uel obreptionis aut nullitatis uitio a quo ...
obreptionis uel nullitatis etiam ex ordinarie uel alterius cuiuscunque potestatis aut quouis alio defec tu impugnari illaz ef esse tui iritandam uel infirm ...
contigerit attemptari Et insuper quia difficile foret presentes nras litteras ad quecumque loca deferre uolumus ut ta aut uoritate hoz serie decernimus qu ...
uel ex tense et excommunicationis aliaque sententie in illis contente infra Duos Menses computandos a die qua ipe presentes littere seu carte uel membrane ex ...
intimate ac presentate fuissent Nulli ergo omnino hominum liceat hanc paginam nre declarationis constitutionis donationis concessionis appropriatie ...
creationem omnipotentis dei et beatorum Petri et Pauli Aplorum eius se nouerit incursurum, Dat Rome apud Sanc t ...

59. Papal Bull, "Inter Caetera".
May 4, 1493. Alexander VI

In this pontifical document, Alexander VI, "of his own accord and with full apostolic power", grants to the Catholic sovereigns Ferdinand and Isabella of Castile, Aragon, Sicily and Granada, all islands and mainland, discovered or to be discovered, west of an imaginary line from pole to pole, 100 leagues from the Azores and Cape Verde Islands. The Pontiff's sole exclusion from this edict were lands already possessed by any Christian king or prince. This edict was soon superseded by the Treaty of Tordesillas.

Archivo General de Indias, Seville
(Below)

60. Treaty of Alcáçovas.
March 6, 1479.

This treaty's basic purpose was to settle the Castilian War of Succession, but in one of its clauses Ferdinand and Isabella of Spain pledge not to interfere with the Portuguese trade in Guinea; they also recognize Portugal's possession of the Atlantic archipelagoes of the Azores, Madeira and Cape Verde, thus helping to cement Portuguese sovereignty in much of the Atlantic, and implicitly as far as the Indies. To enforce the treaty, King Afonso V of Portugal immediately ordered his captains to capture all foreign ships in Portuguese controlled waters, and to cast their crews into the sea.

Arquivo Nacional da Torre do Tombo, Lisbon
(Facing page)

59

Navigation, and Commerce of Ethiopia, Arabia, Persia and India." He therefore wished to provide maximum information about those parts for his Monarch's pleasure. He decided to do so by making available in Manuel's native language three narratives from the past that seemed accurate and extensive: Marco Polo's, Nicolo de'Conti's as reported by Poggio, and a letter from Genoese merchant Girolamo da Santo Stephano dated Tripoli (Lebanon), September 1, 1499.

The 1502 *Marco Paulo*, as the book is prominently entitled, had an immediate repercussion in neighboring Seville, where a 1503 Spanish *Cosmographia breue introductoria en el libro d(e) Marco paulo. . .* was published *(Item 36)*. Its compiler, Rodrigo Fernandez de Santaella, modelled his volume after its predecessor but included only the Polo and Poggio narratives. He introduced this material with his own *Cosmographia breue introductoria* in which he discussed what he thought Columbus had really come upon. The Admiral of the Ocean Sea had already been on his third voyage (May 30, 1498 - October 1500), was at the time of publication away on his fourth (May 9, 1502 - November 7, 1504), and was to die in 1506 still adhering to the belief that he had reached East Asia.

In the *Cosmographia* between descriptions of Arabia and India, Santaella presents the following, given here in John Frampton's Elizabethan translation of the Spanish published in London in 1579:

"And wheras the vulgar people, and men for the most part, do thinke that Antilla, or those Ilandes lately found out by commaundemente of the Catholike King Don Fernando, and Lady Isabell Queene, be in the Indias, they be deceyued therein, to call it by the name of the *Indias . . .*". The author was correctly denying what Columbus so dearly believed: the new lands discovered to the west were not the easternmost portion of Asia.

In spite of the precedent set by Valentim Fernandes, Portuguese books, or even pamphlets, concerning the great deeds proved virtually nonexistent until mid century. Almost inexplicably, some of the most basic texts discussed in this introduction saw the light of day in print only in the first half of the nineteenth century, during the Romantic period. In countries of Northern Europe like France and Germany, the literary movement known as Romanticism involved abandonment of Classicism – the cult of writers and other artists of Antiquity – and a sudden burst of interest in the culture of the Middle Ages. But in Portugal, a major facet of Romanticism represented enthusiasm, not for the Middle Ages as such, but for the era of transition between the Middle Ages and the Renaissance, namely, the Age of Maritime Exploration. The first literary work traditionally assigned to the movement is Almeida Garrett's epic poem *Camões* of 1825. Thus is explained the very late publication of the Zurara manuscript with Dom Henrique's portrait in 1842. Álvaro Velho's narrative of Gama's first voyage had appeared in print in 1838 and Caminha's letter revealing Brazil to Europe still earlier, in 1817. Mestre João's letter was published in 1843. These texts,

Don ferrando e dona ysabel por la graçia de dios Rey
e reyna de castilla e de leon de aragon de seçilia de toledo de
valençia de galli. de de mallorcas de sevilla de çerdeña de
cordova de corcega de murçia de Jahen de los algarbes de
algezira e de gibraltar condes e condesa de barçelona señores
de Vizcaya e de molina duques de atenas e de neopatria
Condes de Ruysellon e de çerdaña marqueses de or
istan e de goçiano. fazemos saber a quantos la prese
te carta vieren que por el dicho Rodrigo maldonado oy
dor de la nuestra audiençia e del nuestro consejo como nuestro procu
rador e enbaxador fueron por nos mandado tratadas e asentadas
e concordadas çiertas pazes perpetuas entre nos e nuestros reynos e
partes de una e el muy ylustre Rey de portogal e de los
algarbes de aquen e allen mar en africa por primo
e entre los dichos sus reynos e señorios la qual
e el ylustre prinçipe don juan su fijo de los dichos
les dias partes fueron primera mente tratadas por don Juan da Silveyra baron da lui
e del conejo del dicho Rey e su es e estillano de la poridat e de çerdo de la fa
enda e del conejo e chançeller mayor del prinçipe de portogal e por pero botello e Rodrigo
alfonso alla e e e e dichos Rey de portogal. despues fueron asentadas e
firmadas e juradas por el dicho Rey e don como procurador bastante e sufiçiente
de los dichos Rey e prinçipe de portogal como su procurador e enbaxador Segun
que mas complidamente es contenido en la estçitura de capitulaçio e asiento de los dichos
pazes que sobrello fue fecha. en la qual entre otras cosas se contiene que cada e
quando fuesemos requeridos por parte del dicho muy ylustre Rey de portogal e del
ylustre prinçipe su fijo otorgariamos consentiriamos e juraríamos las dichas
pazes por nuestras personas e porque por ferrando de silva del conejo de los dichos
Rey e prinçipe de portogal e su enbaxador e procurador fuesemos requerido e que
otorgasemos consentiesemos e firmasemos las dichas pazes segunt que por el dicho
otor nuestro procurador e enbaxador fueron otorgadas firmadas e juradas. nos
mandamos venir para ante nos la dicha escritura de la dicha capitulaçio e asie
to de las dichas pazes para las ver e examinar el tenor de la qual de verbo ad
verbum es este que se sigue

nel nombre de dios todo poderoso padre e fijo el spiritu santo tres personas
real mente distintas e apartadas e una sola esençia divina Ma
nifiesto e notorio sea a quantos este publico ynstrumento de capitu
laçion e asiento e reformaçion e retefiçaçion de pazes perpetuas viere
que en el año del nasçimiento de nuestro señor ihesu xpo de mill e quatroçientos e seten
ta e nueve años a quatro dias del mes de setiembre. en la villa de los alcaçovas
en las casas donde posava la muy ylustre señora ynfante dona beatriz en presen
çia de mi el notario publico e general abaxo nonbrados e de los testigos aqui escri
tos estando y el honrrado e discreto don Rodrigo maldonado oydor de la audiençia
e del conejo de los muy altos e muy poderosos señores don ferrando e dona ysabel
Rey e Reyna de castilla de leon de aragon de seçilia de toledo de Valençia de

61. Chronicle of King Afonso V.
15th C. Rui de Pina

This chronicle recounts the life of the Portuguese monarch who signed the Treaty of Alcáçovas, an early attempt to untangle conflicting claims by Portugal and Castile arising from the voyages of discovery. The illumination shows Afonso's nephew, Dom Manuel I, receiving the manuscript of the chronicle.

Rui de Pina succeeded Gomes Eanes de Zurara as chief chronicler of Portugal. Judged by some to be second-rate, he even failed to mention the voyage of Bartolomeu Dias in his Chronicle of Dom João II.

Arquivo Nacional da Torre do Tombo, Lisbon
(Page 124)

62. Portrait of Dom João II.
In: "Livro dos Copos da Ordem de Santiago".
Book of Sword Hilts of the Order of Santiago.
1484. Alvaro Dias de Frielas

Dom João II was chiefly responsible for Portugal's expansionist policy; it was he who set up the technical and political conditions that led to the most important of the 15th-century voyages – the one that culminated in the discovery of the sea route to India. His shrewdness and political acumen won him the name, "Perfect Prince". This book, containing copies of documents relating to the Order of Santiago, was commissioned by Dom João in 1484; its name derives from the hilt of the royal sword visible in this illustration.

Arquivo Nacional da Torre do Tombo, Lisbon
(Page 125)

63. Treaty of Tordesillas.
Ratified July 2, 1494..

Signed on June 7, 1494 by representatives of Dom João II of Portugal and the Catholic Monarchs (Ferdinand and Isabella) of Spain, this was the first attempt to define spheres of influence on a world level. Dom João secured control of the Atlantic (essential for the route to India), and, in demanding that the line of demarcation be drawn along a meridian 370 leagues west of the Cape Verde Islands, he assured possession of Brazil, which was not officially discovered until six years later.
By negotiating directly with Ferdinand and Isabella, the Portuguese king also succeeded in bypassing the Pope who, until then, had been the final arbiter in European international relations.

Arquivo Nacional da Torre do Tombo, Lisbon
(Page 126)

inspired by Romanticism, in effect initiated the era of modern scholarship concerning the Portuguese *descobrimentos*, an era that is still unfolding.

Completion of Knowledge of the Atlantic

Portuguese discoveries in the South Atlantic continued, following Cabral's voyage and even as Valentim Fernandes' book was being printed. Six islands or island groups remain to be accounted for: Ascension, St. Helena, and Tristan da Cunha, all British, while St. Peter and St. Paul Rocks, Fernando de Noronha, and the pair Martin Vaz and Trindade, all are in the Brazilian orbit. St. Helena and Ascension are located on the British Admiral Somerville's inbound or northbound track from southern Africa to Europe. Ascension was most likely discovered on Ascension Day 1501, that is, May 20 of that year. (The day occurs on the Thursday following the fifth Sunday after Easter, May 24 in 1990.) The discovery was made by one or more vessels of Cabral's fleet on its return from India and was duly recorded on the Cantino Map of the following year.
St. Helena is said to have been found by João da Nova on May 21, 1502. According to the calendar of the Eastern Church, it was also the feast day of Constantine's mother (August 18 in the Roman calendar). His fleet departed from Lisbon for India in March 1501, so he would have come upon the island on his return voyage. Linschoten included in the English translation of his *Itinerario* an invaluable depiction of St. Helena and of the Portuguese fleet in which he travelled *(Item 41)*.

Tristan da Cunha was discovered by Tristão da Cunha on his outbound voyage in 1506. Admiral Somerville would take a southbound sailing ship from Europe past the Cape de Verdes and successively by St. Peter and St. Paul Rocks, Fernando de Noronha, and Martin Vaz/Trindade. Fernando de Noronha is said to have been discovered on June 24, 1503, by the mariner of the same name, a reasonable date. As for the Rocks, known affectionately in Portuguese as the Penedos, they were discovered by the Portuguese ship *São Pedro* in 1511.
As for the pair of islands well out to sea off the Brazilian coast at the latitude of Vitoria, capital of the Brazilian state of Espírito Santo, their discovery is credited to João da Nova on his outbound voyage in 1501. The Falkland Islands do not enter into our discussion, for they were not discovered until 1592.
In the years immediately following Cabral's revelation of Brazil to Europe, the Portuguese king and court fixed their attention on India, which they perceived as the focal point of the true objects of their quest: pepper, cinnamon, cloves, nutmeg and Eastern Christians. Only gradually did Brazil's potential become apparent, as the new colony's coastal areas were explored and administratively organized. Significantly, the first book about Brazil published in Portuguese did not appear until 1576, which was Pedro de Magalhães de Gândavo's *Historia da prouincia sãcta Cruz a que vulgarmente chamamos Brasil (Item 124)*. Cold and barren Newfoundland was, not surprisingly, officially neglected.
Non-Iberian observers aboard Portuguese vessels contributed

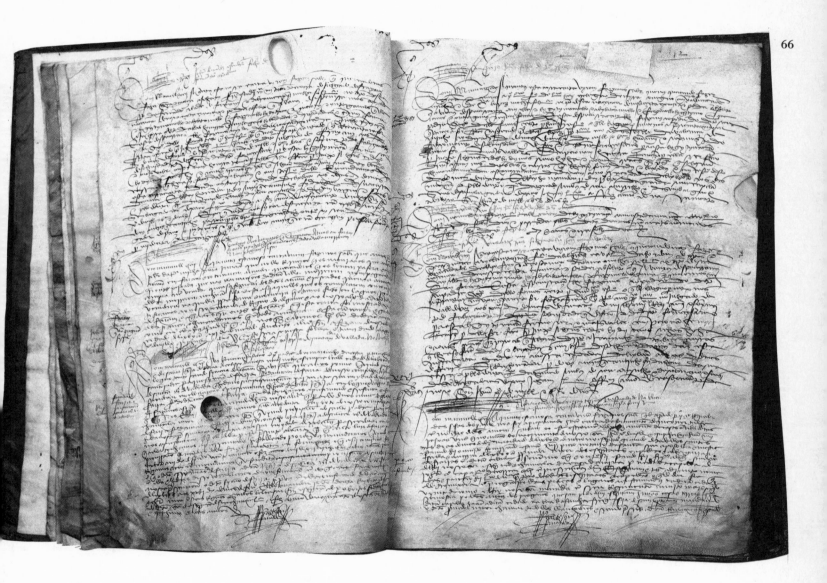

64. Map of America.
c. 1532. Attributed to Diogo Ribeiro
Manuscript map on parchment

This map displays the line established by the Treaty of Tordesillas, separating Portuguese and Spanish spheres of activity in the Atlantic and the New World. In what is now northeastern Canada, the cartographer has indicated the tiera nueva delos bacallaos *and* tiera del labrador *("new-found-land of codfish" and "land of Labrador"). The former refers to the cod exploited by Portuguese fishermen in the waters nearby, and the latter is a reference to João Fernandes "o Lavrador", ("the Farmer"), who was the land's Portuguese discoverer. In South America, the continent's eastward bulge is called "el brasil". The map's presumed maker, Diogo Ribeiro, was a Portuguese cartographer who worked exclusively in Seville.*

Herzog August Bibliothek, Wolfenbüttel
(Page 127)

65. Letter and Contract of Donation between King Dom Dinis and Micer Manuel Pezagno.
Feb. 1, 1317

To reinforce his war armada, Dom Dinis of Portugal sent for a Genovese, Pessagno, accompanied by "twenty men who knew the sea", and signed this contract with him on February 1, 1317. The contract entitles Pessagno (or Pessanha in Portuguese) to certain benefits, in particular the title of admiral, which was passed on through his male descendants. Pessanha was to have galleys at his disposal to guard the coast, but the contract did not exclude privateering, which was considered a legitimate enterprise at the time. Pessanha further committed himself to maintain, on his own initiative, the aforementioned group of twenty Genovese "who knew the sea".

Arquivo Nacional da Torre do Tombo, Lisbon
Page 128)

to the dissemination of information about Brazil. Foremost among them was the Florentine Amerigo Vespucci who became a controversial figure. His tract entitled *Mundus Novus*, although it circulated in many editions beginning in 1504, is used by serious scholars with great caution *(Page 238)*. This, together with other tracts are more properly assigned to Parts III and IV of this exhibition.

It need only be added that the last, or southwest, corner of the South Atlantic was explored in 1519 by a Portuguese, Fernão de Magalhães, whom we know as Ferdinand Magellan. But he was sailing in the service of Spain. Moreover, the Strait that bears his name (Atlantic end at 52° 20' S, well south of the Cape of Good Hope) lies to the west of the line of demarcation, as do Argentina and Uruguay, albeit more to the north.

Magellan died before completing the historic voyage that we associate with his name. The circumnavigation of the globe completed in 1522 by Elcano revealed the need for a second line of demarcation on the other side of the world. The respective Portuguese and Spanish zones were worked out in 1529 by the Treaty of Saragossa. To clarify the matter at the time, the Portuguese cartographer Diogo Ribeiro, in the service of Spain and known as Diego Ribero, drew up a comprehensive map *(Page 156-158)*. It clearly shows the Tordesillas meridian, with the Castilian flag to the west and the Portuguese flag to the east. This mark puts most of the "Tiera Nova de Cortereal" and all of the "Tiera del Labrador" in the Portuguese zone.

By this time, however, the Protestant Reformation was in full force. Papal authority and universal respect for Catholic monarchs were on the wane. At the end of the century Portugal's thalassocracy would be severely challenged by Dutch and English maritime forces.

Such challenge, and the resulting change in the fortunes of Portugal, however, in no way limited the cultural heritage of the Portuguese discoveries. An Atlantic community of independent nations whose international language is Portuguese now flourishes. Portugal (including its two Autonomous Regions of the Azores and of Madeira) and Brazil, of course, constitute its principal axis. The other members are Cabo Verde, Guinea Bissau, São Tomé and Príncipe and Angola, to which must be added, in conformity with the 1485 reasoning of Vasco Fernandes de Lucena, the eastern African nation of Mozambique.

The nation within this community with the greatest number of speakers of the Portuguese language is Brazil, thanks to the Tordesillas modification of *Inter Caetera*. When the Lusophones of the other six members are added, the language of Camões turns out to be one of the world's most important tongues. It follows Arabic, Chinese, English, Hindi, Russian and Spanish in terms of number of native speakers. It is the second most widely-spoken of the Romance or "Neo-Latin" languages, behind Spanish but ahead of Catalan, French, Italian and Romanian.

LE GRAND ROY ⸻ MONO-MOTAPA ⸺

Fort Puissant, et oy Riche en Or ⸻ q. d'aucuns l'apelle l'Empereur de
l'Or, Il à plus.rs Roys ces tributaires, cōpris Sous l'Ethiopie Inferieure, desquels les
Enfans Sont Elevez dans Son palais, po. Con⸻ tenir les Peres dans Son Obbeissance Son
Son royaume est de tres grande Estendüe ⸻ ojant de Circuit pres de 800 lieues, il Soutien.
de fortes Guerres contre le Prête Jan, Empereur des Abbisins, Il fut à Sa Cour à Zimbaoe ou il
Entretien po.r Sa Garde Ord.re des femmes, et 200 Chiens, Grands, et furieux, La Relation de l'anse
1631, nous apprend q. ce Roy Mono-motapa Ces⸻ toit fait baptiser, avec toutte Sa Cour, par les RR.
Peres Jesuistes, ce Monarque n'est Servi qu'à Genoux, il y à en ce Royaume des femmes, quy ⸻
Vont à la Guerre, et rendent aussy bons Service q. les hommes, dans ces Armées, il y à grand nombre
d'Elephans, force Abbondancci de Sucre, plusieurs Mines d'Or. Ces peuples Sont Noirs, Vaillens, et sy disp.s
quils Surpassent à la Coursse, les plus Viste Chevaux; les Idolastres, Sorciers, Adulteres, et larrons, y Sont
tres Rigoureüsement Punis;

à Paris chez P. Bertrand Rüe St. Jacques à la Pomme d'Or, proche St. Severin . Avec Privil. du Roy.

66. Registration of the letter of quit-claim from King Manuel I in favour of the wife and heirs of Bartolomeu Dias.
July 8, 1501.

Historians often wonder why Dom João II did not generously reward Bartolomeu Dias after his history-making voyage around the southern tip of Africa. They attribute this to royal precaution: the Perfect Prince had heaped rewards upon an earlier explorer, Diogo Cão, and that navigator erred in announcing to the king that he had found the route that would lead to the Indian Ocean.

If the Perfect Prince was unfair to Dias, Dom Manuel I belatedly made up for it: Dias died at sea in 1500, when a storm sank his caravel in the South Atlantic; the next year the king established a pension for the navigator's widow and descendants, attested by this document.

Arquivo Nacional da Torre do Tombo, Lisbon
(Page 135)

---

67. Portrait of Dom Manuel I.
1521. Anonymous

Dom Manuel I, king of Portugal between 1495 and 1521, was aptly known as "the Fortunate", and with good reason. Preparations for the voyage in which Vasco da Gama was to discover the sea route to India were nearly complete at the time of his accession; soon afterwards, Brazil was discovered. During Manuel's reign, Portugal laid the foundation for its Eastern possessions, secured domination of the Atlantic, initiated exploration of Brazil, and enjoyed enviable economic success.

This illuminated manuscript also contains the Portuguese coat of arms flanked by two armillary spheres, symbols of the astronomical knowledge essential to the voyages of discovery.

Arquivo Nacional da Torre do Tombo, Lisbon
(Page 145)

68. "Foral" (Statutes) of the Village of Vidigueira.
June 1, 1512.

A foral was a statute that specified the mutual obligations and rights among the residents of a village or region, their lord, and the Crown. As far back as the time of the Crusades, Portuguese kings had granted forals to noblemen who had distinguished themselves against the Moors, granting them lordship over tracts of the Portuguese countryside. In the Age of Discoveries, such grants were made to outstanding explorers. Sometime earlier, the village of Vidigueira, to which this one refers, had been granted by Dom Manuel to Vasco da Gama for discovering the sea route to India. The first page bears the arms of Portugal flanked by two armillary spheres symbolic of Portuguese ascendancy in astronomy and navigation. It also states Dom Manuel's various titles, including "Lord of Guinea and of the conquest, navigation and commerce of Ethiopia, Arabia, Persia and India".

Anonymous Lender
(Page 146)

69. Letter from Dom Manuel I granting to Miguel Corte-Real all the lands or islands that Gaspar Corte-Real his brother may have discovered or reached.
1502.

Under the Treaty of Tordesillas, Portugal had the right to explore portions of North America; this was carried out principally by the brothers Gaspar and Miguel Corte-Real. This letter was written as the younger brother, Miguel, was preparing to depart in search of Gaspar, who had disappeared. The letter grants to Miguel Corte-Real all lands which his brother may have discovered, and reconfers the same grant given earlier to Gaspar, who by then was presumed lost. Miguel Corte-Real, in turn, never returned from this voyage. The Portuguese exploration of the northeastern part of America is little remembered today, though the Portuguese name "Labrador" is one prominent reminder.

Arquivo Nacional da Torre do Tombo, Lisbon
(Opposite)

70

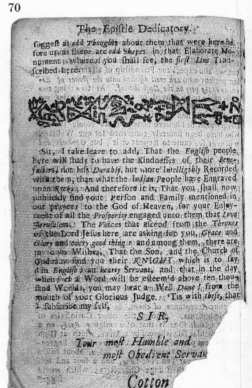

69

70. The Wonderful Works of God Commemorated.
1690. Cotton Mather

One of many works from the prolific pen of the Puritan divine who sought to explain God's Providence through the history of New England. It mentions and illustrates the mysterious Dighton Rock inscription in southern Massachusetts, still the subject of debate by some who think it is evidence that sixteenth-century Portuguese explorers had been there – perhaps Miguel Corte-Real in search of his lost brother. Other experts have decided it was made by local Indians.

The New York Public Library
(Facing page)

71. Transcription of contract and agreements between Fernão de Magalhães (Ferdinand Magellan) and King Carlos of Castile.
May 14, 1518.

Magalhães offered his services to Carlos after the king of Portugal failed to afford him the recognition he felt rightfully due to him. The eastward route to the Indies was already established, and the king saw no need for another route to the land of spices. But for Carlos of Spain, who was prevented by treaty from dispatching ships along the same route used by the Portuguese, a westward route seemed a good alternative. He made this contract with Magalhães to pursue that route, which culminated in the first voyage around the world.

Arquivo Nacional da Torre do Tombo, Lisbon
(Below)

71

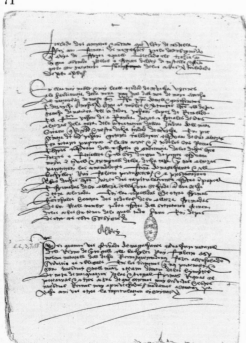

72. Royal Cédula of Carlos V to the Sailors of the Armada of Fernão de Magalhães, that they should follow the indicated route.
1519.

As preparations were being made in Seville for Magalhães' voyage, Portugal pressured the king of Spain to suspend it, on the grounds that it was an invasion of waters reserved for Portugal under the Treaty of Tordesillas. That claim must have prompted this memorandum of Carlos V; in recommending to Magalhães' crew that they should not deviate from the indicated route, the king satisfied the Portuguese without jeopardizing his plan to reach East Asia through seas to which he held right under the 1494 treaty.

Archivo General de Indias, Seville
(Below)

72

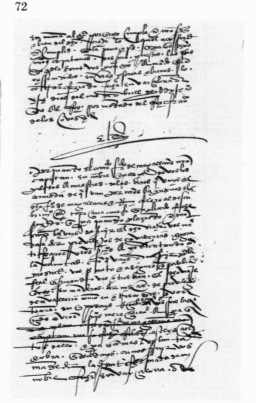

73. Royal Cédula from Carlos V of Spain to Jorge Reinel.
May 27, 1524

Pedro Reinel and his son Jorge are among the first cartographers known by name to practice their art in Portugal. Jorge Reinel fled to Seville because of an incident in Lisbon, and the Portuguese king directed his father to go there to persuade him to return to Portugal. He eventually did return, but in the interim the two worked in Seville, as this note dated May 27, 1524 shows; he is invited to exercise his art for a fee of 35,000 maravedis. On a subsequent page of this codex, the father is also invited to practice his craft for 30,000 maravedis.

Archivo General de Indias, Seville
(Below)

73

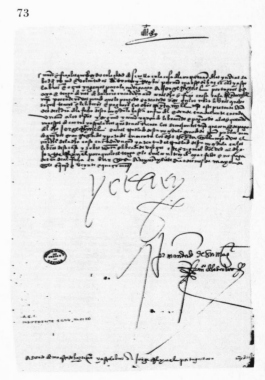

74. Atlas de las costas y de los puertos de las posessiones portuguesas en America y Africa.
Atlas of the Coasts and Ports of the Portuguese Posessions in America and Africa.
c. 1636. Anonymous.
Hand-drawn watercolour maps.

We know neither the author nor the date of this atlas, with its hand-drawn coloured charts, plotted on paper. The eminent historian of cartography, Teixeira da Mota, has remarked that its style "is poor and the plots are often incorrect", and the African parts suggest the author was more "a simple seaman than a professional cartographer". Nonetheless, it evidences the strong Portuguese presence on both sides of the Atlantic.

Biblioteca Nacional, Madrid
(Pages 152-153)

75. Letter of Obedience of the Lord of the Congo to Pope Julius II.
1512.

This letter of obedience to the Pope, in the manner of European monarchs, is signed by the Christianized king of the Congo, who had taken the name Dom Afonso. Political relations between Portugal and the Congo began at the time of the voyages of Diogo Cão, and progressed rapidly thereafter. High ranking Congolese visited Lisbon and other Portuguese towns and learned European ways, while Dom João II and Dom Manuel I zealously sought to export Christian culture to the African kingdoms.
Despite some initial difficulties, the king and his family were converted and baptized, and Christianity became firmly implanted in Congo.

Arquivo National da Torre do Tombo, Lisbon
(Below)

75

76. Liuro da nobreza e perfeiçam das Armas dos Reis christãos e nobres linhages dos reinos e Senhorios de Portugal.
Book of the nobility and perfection of the coats-of-arms of the Christian Kings and lineages of the kingdoms and Lordships of Portugal.
c.1528-1541. Antonio Godinho

This manuscript depicting the coats of arms of the kings of Christendom was ordered by Dom Manuel prior to March 1517, and was completed sometime between 1528 and 1541. In the lower right quadrant of folio 7, alongside those of Scotland, Poland and Bohemia, there appear the arms which Dom Manuel of Portugal bestowed upon Dom Afonso, the King of the Congo, after the latter's conversion to Christianity. This provides an interesting testimony to the fact that Portuguese-African relations were not limited to trade and commerce, but were also characterized by a cultural interchange that affected both societies in deeper ways over the long term.

Arquivo Nacional da Torre do Tombo, Lisbon
(Pages 154-155)

77. Portrait of King Mono-motapa.
c.1631. Published in Paris by P. Bertrand

The engraving is a pseudoportrait that probably portrays the emperor Mavura, baptized in 1630. It is typical of Europeanized conceptions of the rulers of Africa. In their earliest contacts with the coast of Mozambique, the Portuguese learned that gold was extracted in the kingdom of Monomotapa and in nearby dependencies. António Fernandes, a Portuguese convict who was banished to East Africa, undertook two trips to this gold country in the second decade of the 16th century.
The inscription reveals the attributes of the great king: "Most powerful and so rich in gold that many call him the Emperor of Gold.. . . . He wages great wars against Prester John, Emperor of the Abyssinians. He holds his court at Zimboae where he maintains as his Ordinary Guard women and 200 large and fiercesome dogs. . . . this monarch is served only from a kneeling position. . . ."

Bibliothèque Nationale, Paris
(Page 137)

78. Relatione del Reame di Congo.
A report on the Kingdom of the Congo.
1591. Filippo Pigafetta/Duarte Lopes

Duarte Lopes, son of a "new Christian" – a Jew more or less forcibly converted – who had a confectionery business in Lisbon, embarked for the Congo in April 1578. He travelled about the Congo for approximately six years, visiting places and observing people no European had ever seen. Later, as an ambassador of the King of the Congo, he described these curiosities to the Italian Pigafetta, including the boundaries of the Congo and its political and administrative organization, its history, and the customs of the African peoples before and after the onset of Christian influence.

This work was widely distributed and translated in the 16th century, evidence of strong European interest in this part of the world.

The New York Public Library
(Below)

78

79. Istorica Descrizione de' tre Regni Congo, Matamba et Angola sitvati nell' Etiopia Inferiore Occidentale e delle Missioni Apostoliche Esercitateui de Religiosi Capuccini.
Historical Description of the three Kingdoms: Congo, Matamba and Angola situated in Southwestern Ethiopia, and of the Apostolic Mission of the Capuchin Order.
1687. Giovanni Antonio Cavazzi da Montecuccolo

A group of Capuchin friars is shown in their first audience with the king of the Congo; the text describes the king's court, "bizarrely adorned, and all decorated according to the style of the Country".

Cavazzi's work, published in Italian in 1687, is a primary source document on the Congolese (Bakongos), Ambundos (Angola) and Jagas. Cavazzi lived in these regions twice, for a total of about seventeen years. Besides his personal observations, he had available to him missionary letters and reports, and printed books on the Congo, one of which was that of the earlier Portuguese, Duarte Lopes.

Houghton Library, Harvard University
(Below)

80. Ethiopic Manuscript with notes in Portuguese.
15th c.

This bound manuscript from a private collection is assumed to have been brought from Ethiopia by Fr. Francisco Álvares, who was part of the Portuguese diplomatic mission headed by Dom Rodrigo de Lima (1520-1526).

The page highlighted here is a unique personal document of cultural encounter. Found loose inside the front cover of the bound volume, it contains writing exercises by someone who was learning Portuguese. That person may have been Abba Embagon, an abbot and leading functionary of the Eastern Orthodox Church, who became a close ally of Francisco Álvares while both were living in Ethiopia.

Contents of folio:
Portuguese linguistic exercises: the alphabet, followed by consonant and vowel combinations that are similar to the sounds of the Ethiopic syllabary; then, personal names and names of months; at bottom, Arabic numerals and the opening words of the Ave Maria in Latin. At the foot of the page, Portuguese names for the numbers one to nineteen are transliterated into Ethiopic.

Anoymous lender
(Below)

81.Verdadera informaçam das terras do Preste Joam.
Truthful Information of the Lands of Prester John.
1540. Francisco Álvares

This book is a repository of invaluable information on Ethiopian customs and mores, laws, religion, justice and the country's court. Moreover, it is a faithful portrait of the tolerance, moderation and conviviality of its author, a cleric who accompanied the first Portuguese diplomatic mission to Ethiopia. His open-minded approach to the legendary country was unmatched by any other Portuguese of his century.

The James Ford Bell Library, University of Minnesota
(Below)

79

80

81

82. Letter from Galadewos, Emperor of Ethiopia, to Dom Joao III.
16th c.

This letter from the Emperor of Ethiopia is addressed to Dom João III, urging the Portuguese king to wage a crusade against the Moslems surrounding his empire. He

82

በክመ፡እግዚእብሔር፡ኣሉ
ክ፡ዘኢየቅፈ፡ለጥ፤ዘይሬኢ፡
እንተ፡ኣፍኣ፡ወይፈተን፡እንተ፡ወሥ
ጛዛየደ፤ክም፡ለጸኑዕ፡ወያጸንን፡ለ
ቅጥቀጥፉተፈነወት፡ዘቲ፡መጽሐፈ፡
መልእክት፡እምኃበ፡ንጉሥ፡ገለውዩ
ዎክ፡ወልደ፡ወናግ፡ስግድ፡ንጉሠቀወ
ደ፡ናእደ፡ንጉሠቀወልደ፡እስክንድር፡ን
ጉሠቀወልደ፡በእደ፡ማርያም፡ንጉሠቀ
ወልደ፡ዘርእ፡ያዕቆብ፡ንጉሠቀወልደ፡
ዳዊት፡ንጉሠቀወልደ፡ስሎምን፡ንጉሠ
ነገሥተ፡እስራኤል፡ሳዕሌሆሙ፡ሰም
ትብጻሕ፡ናበ፡ዮሐንክ፡ንጉሠ፡ብርት
ጋል፡መፈቀሬ፡እግዚእብሔር፡ወመፈ
ቀሬ፡ሃይማኖት፡ወልደ፡ንጉሠ፡ዘእማኑ
ኤል፡ርቱዐ፡ሃይማኖትቀስማዕ፡በእንተ፡
ሚካኤል፡ገብርኣ፡ዘመጽኣ፡ናቤን፡ዘ፤
ነዖ፡ገብርኣ፡ዳር፡ምስለ፡ደክርስቶቡ፡ደ
ጋማ፡ያደዊ፤፡እዝማዌ፡ክወ፡ይርድ፡ኡ
ጊዜ፡ዐብ፡እቀወዝንተስ፡ሚካኤል፡ተግህ
ጥቀ፡ለኢትዮጵያ፡ወተታተስ፡ምስለ፡ን
ክሳም፡በእንተ፡ክርስቶስ፡እንዘ፡ይዌ
ሙ፡ንፉሱ፡እስክ፡ተስብረ፡ዐጋማደ፡እደ
በንፍጛወበፈቃደ፡እግዚአብሔር፡እ
መደሳረ፡ሐይወ፡እምዴዊሁ፡ናሁ፡ፈኛና
ሁ፡ናቤ ከቀወእንተ፤፡ግበር፡ሎቱ፡ወና
ያት፡ተዘኪረክ፡ፈቅረ፡ክርስቶስ፡ወፉቀ
ረ፡ዚኢንነሃቀወእቱስ፡ፈጸም፡መልእክተ
ክ፡ክመ፡ጴጥሮስ፡ሊቀሐዋርያት፡ወደ
ውሎክ፡ልስን፡ዕፍረትቀወበእንተዝ፡ት
ግሀቱ፡ለሚ፡ኤል፡ክከተኛዝ፡ዘፈኛሁ
ወዳሌክ፡ክመ፡ይትሬናእ፡ወጎዝቲ፡በክ
መ፡እዘዝኩ፡ወኢያብጠሰ፡መልእክተ
ክፈወእንተ፤፡ተዘኪረክ፡ግበር፡ሎቱ፡
ዘሐስየ፡ልቡ፡ዘኢጸሐፍኛ፡ወከት፡ዘ
ንቱ፡መጽሐፈ፡መልእክትቀወንሕንኊ
እበ፡ንእምዕ፡ዜና፡ዘንቱ፡መልእ ክት፤
ትሬሣሕ፡በክ፡ወይክውን፡ፉጹመ፡ፉ
ቅርን፡በዝንቱ፡ግብርꝗ
7

83. Salver with African motifs.
Early 16th c. Anonymous
Wrought silver, gold-plated.

This is a Portuguese work displaying African influence, in the style of the first half of the 16th century. The Portuguese coat-of-arms with open crown is in the centre. It is divided into eight sectors with palm trees, elephants, hunting motifs and figures of native Africans. The circular base has identical motifs.

*Palacio Nacional da Ajuda, Lisbon
(Pages 159-160)*

mentions Dom Cristóvão da Gama, whose brother Dom Estevão da Gama, the governor, had left four hundred Portuguese in Ethiopia to quash an Arab-Turkish invasion that had devastated the country.

*Arquivo Nacional da Torre do Tombo, Lisbon
(Opposite)*

84. Sceptre of a Christian Chieftain of Africa.
16th c.

This sceptre was collected sometime in the 1930's in the Congolese area of Angola; there is no confirmed information as to the ethnic group to which it pertained. Incorporation of the cross motif is unusual, and suggests that this may have been the sceptre of a chieftain strongly influenced by the Catholic centre of São Salvador do Congo.

*Museu Nacional de Etnologia, Lisbon
(Below)*

84

85. African Crucifix.
Guinea, 17th c.
Wood and brass

In Guinea, as in other regions touched by Portuguese commercial and missionary activity, artists incorporated Catholic iconography into their work. Eventually, these images found their way into local tradition and even partially replaced certain older icons, but became endowed with meanings that were not necessarily directly linked with Christianity as Europeans conceived it.

Superior Geral da Sociedade Missionária de Cucujães, Portugal
(Below)

86. African Crucifix.
Angola, 17th c.
Wood and brass

The Portuguese commercial initiative in the Congo was accompanied, as elsewhere, by missionary activity. Over time, the regions's artists adapted Christian iconography – including Christ crucified, the Blessed Virgin Mary and St. Anthony – to local magico-religious tradition. The oldest crucifixes, made of iron or brass, were produced in two-piece molds or by the lost wax method. The one shown was recovered in present-day Angola, which was formerly part of the kingdom of the Congo.

Superior Geral da Sociedade Missionária de Cucujães, Portugal
(Below)

87. African Crucifix.
16th c.
Stone

The preferred medium for sculpture south of the Sahara is wood, which is linked with religious symbolism, the tree being central to African cosmogonies. In Central Africa, however, especially in Angolan territories formerly part of the kingdom of the Congo, there is a type of sculpture done in steatite. The Portuguese exerted enormous influence there. This stone figure of Christ was probably intended for use in a Bakongo funerary rite, reflecting the syncretic intermixture of African and European culture in that region.

Sociedade de Geografia, Lisbon
(Below)

86

85

87

67. Portrait of Dom Manuel I.
1521. Anonymous
Arquivo Nacional da Torre do Tombo,
Lisbon
(Page 145)

68. "Foral" (Statutes) of the Village of
Vidigueira.
June 1, 1512.
Anonymous lender
(Page 146)

Planisphere.
1502. Anonymous. Commissioned by
Alberto Cantino
Manuscript map.

Cantino was an agent of the Duke of
Ferrara working in Lisbon, where he
commissioned a cartographer to produce
this map showing the line established by
the Treaty of Tordesillas, identifying it
with the legend, "This is the mark between
Castile and Portugal". The other legends
specify which parts of the newly-discovered
Americas were claimed by the two Iberian
powers. The island called "Terra del rey
de portuguall" is Newfoundland or
Labrador; while on the eastern side of the
Line, in the Southern Hemisphere, some of
the earliest landmarks of Brazil are noted,
along with three parrots, which continue to
be an unofficial symbol of the country.
Nearby but on the other side of the line, the
legend reads, "All this land is discovered
by order of the King of Castile". While
revealing the latest information based on
voyages of discovery, the map also retains
archaic conventions. For example, the Red
Sea is coloured red, and Jerusalem is given
prominence because of its religious
significance.
Biblioteca Estense, Modena
(Pages 147-149)

Map of Labrador.
c. 1576. Fernão Vaz Dourado
Manuscript atlas on vellum

This map, part of a series of twenty, is
anonymous but clearly the work of Fernão
Vaz Dourado, one of Portugal's many
distinguished cartographers. It reflects the
results of Portuguese voyages to the
northeastern coast of North America. Two
farmers ploughing the soil appropriately
illustrate the "Tera do Lavrador," that is,
the land discovered by João Fernandes, a
lavrador (farmer or small landed
proprietor) from Terceira in the Azores.
The coat-of-arms of Portugal hangs from a
nearby tree. Another legend states that
this is the land discovered by the Corte-
Real brothers, who disappeared while
exploring this portion of the New World.
Biblioteca Nacional, Lisbon
(Pages 150-151)

74. Atlas de las costas y de los puertos de
las posessiones portuguesas en America
y Africa.
Atlas of the Coasts and Ports of the
Portuguese Possessions in America and
Africa.
17th c. Anonymous
hand-drawn watercolour maps.
Biblioteca Nacional, Madrid
(Pages 152-153)

76. Liuro da nobreza e perfeiçam das
Armas dos Reis christãos e nobres
linhages dos reinos e Senhorios de
Portugal.
Book of the nobility and perfection of the
coats-of-arms of the Christian Kings and
lineages of the kingdoms and Lordships of
Portugal.
c.1528-1541. Antonio de Godinho
Arquivo Nacional da Torre do Tombo,
Lisbon
(Pages 154-155)

Planisphere.
1529. Diogo Ribeiro

Ribeiro, a Portuguese cartographer who
worked in Seville, produced this world
map for the King of Spain. The spheres of
influence of the two Iberian powers are
indicated at the bottom, where the arms of
Spain and Portugal are respectively on the
left and rights sides of the line established
by the Treaty of Tordesillas. The legend
along the map's bottom edge explains that
this division was made "by the Catholic
Kings of Spain and by Don Juan of
Portugal at Tordesillas in 1494". The one
along the top identifies the map as a
"universal chart containing all that has
been discovered of the world up to the
present time; made by me, Diego Ribero
[the Spanish form of his name],
cosmographer to His Majesty, in the year
1529 in Seville". A portion of northeastern
Canada is referred to as the "new-found
land of Corte-Real", after the Portuguese
brothers who first claimed it for Portugal.
In insets dispersed over the map, Ribeiro
incorporated navigation rules, an
astrolabe and a quadrant, though some of
the instruments are shown with accessory
scales that are useless for navigation.
Biblioteca Apostolica Vaticana
(Pages 156-158)

83. Salver with African motifs.
Early 16th c. Anonymous
Wrought silver, gold-plated.
Palacio Nacional da Ajuda, Lisbon
(Pages 159-160)

DOM MANVEL

Per graça de dõs, Rey de purtugal e dos
alguarues, da quẽ e dalem mar em africa
Señor deguynee E daconquista nauegaçã e
comercio de ethiopia. ARabia persia e da
Juidia A quantos esta nossa carta deforal
virẽ dado avilla dauidiguerra fazemos saber
que per lê das diligencias Jsames e enquy
ricõẽs que em nossas Regnos e Senhorios
mãdamos Jeralmente fazer pera Justificação
e declaraçam dos foraães delles E per
algũas sentenças e detrimjnaçõẽs que cõ

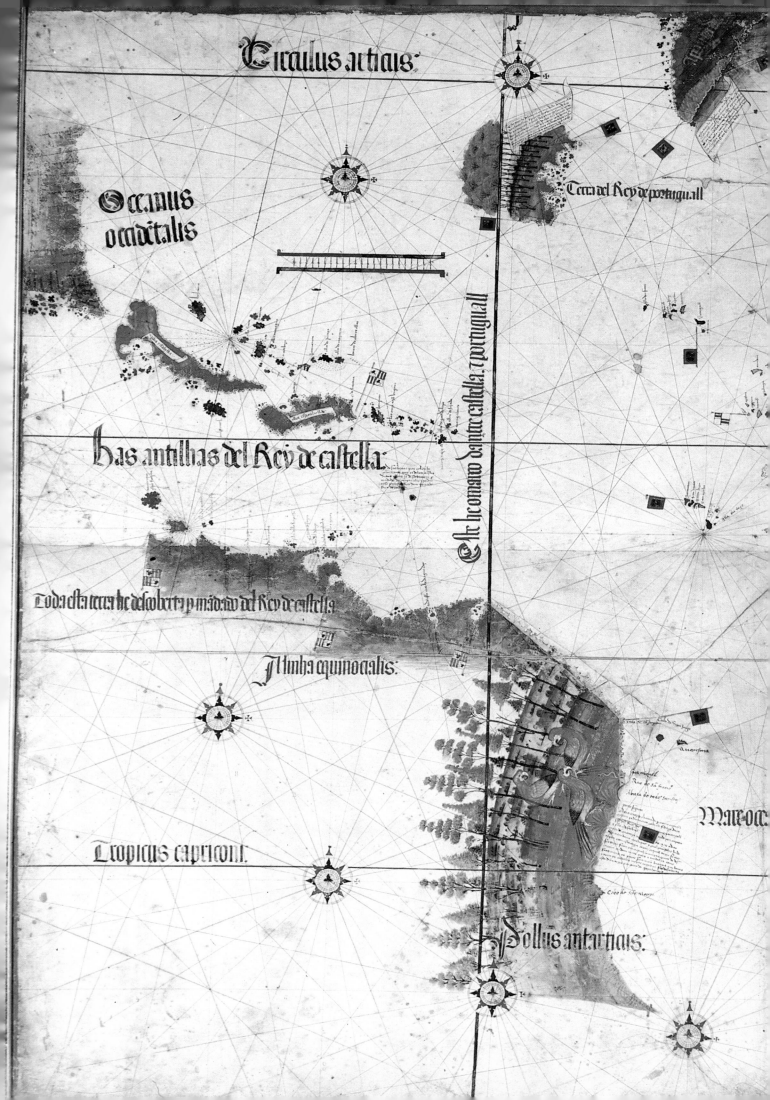

Circulus articus.

Occeanus occidentalis

Terra del Rey de portuguall

has antilhas del Rey de castella.

Esta he o marco da entre castella, e portuguall

Toda esta terra he descoberta y mādado del Rey de castella.

A linha equinoçialis:

Tropicus capricorni.

Mare occ

Pollus antarticus.

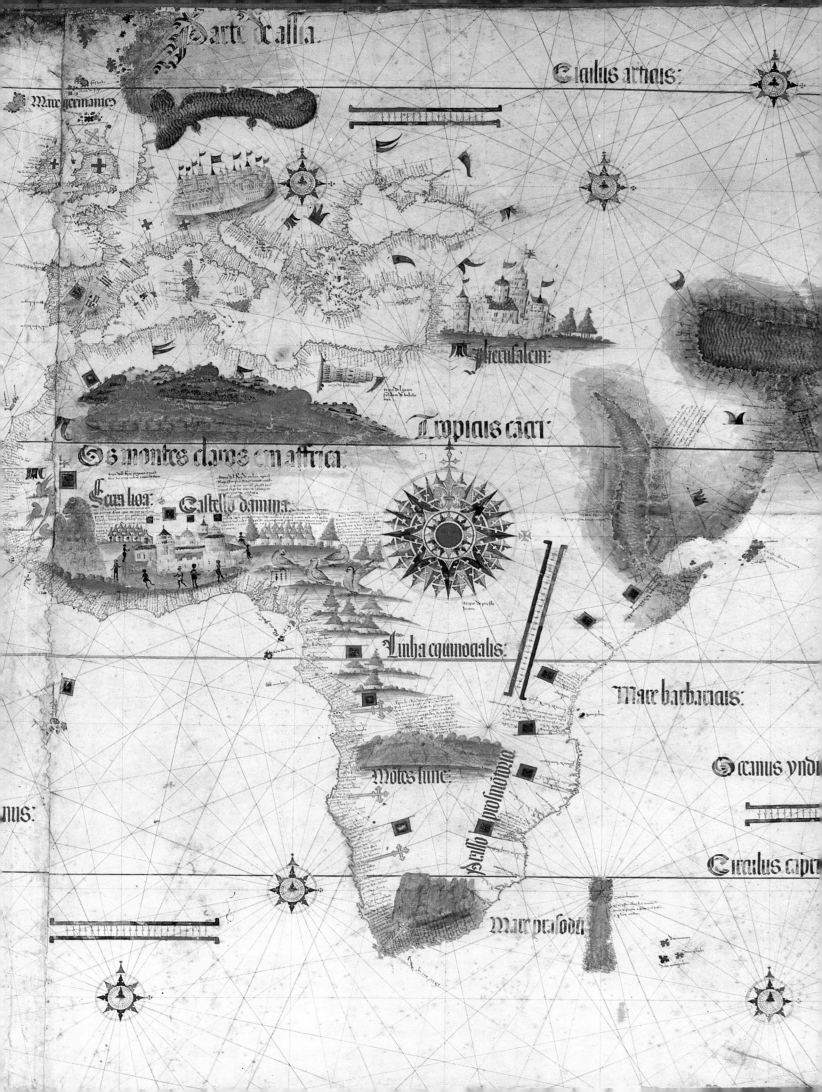

Parte de assia.

Circulus articus:

Mare germanico

Os montes claros en affrica

Sera lioa: Castello damina:

Jherusalem:

Tropicus caer:

Linha equinocialis:

Motes lune:

Mare barbaricis:

Oceanus yndi

Circulus capri

Mare prasodu

DOM MANVEL

per graça de dẽ Rey de portugall z dos algaruec, daquem z dalẽ mar em africa, senõr de guinee z da conquista nauegacam z comercio dethiopia arabia persia, z da ĩdia zc. A quantos, esto aperpetua memoria feito buem fazemos saber que assi como oproprio z pncipall cuydado dos, q tem algũu cargo deue ser trabalhar como as cousas q lhes sam encarregadas seiam postas no mais prospero z melhorado estado que ser possa. assy tanto mais cabe ysto nos, reis, z pncepes, fazello, quanto com mais excellente preminença sam per dẽs postos na terra pera bem della z de seus bassalloc, z pa toda execuçam z exẽplo de virtude. E por que esta obligaçam tam deuida

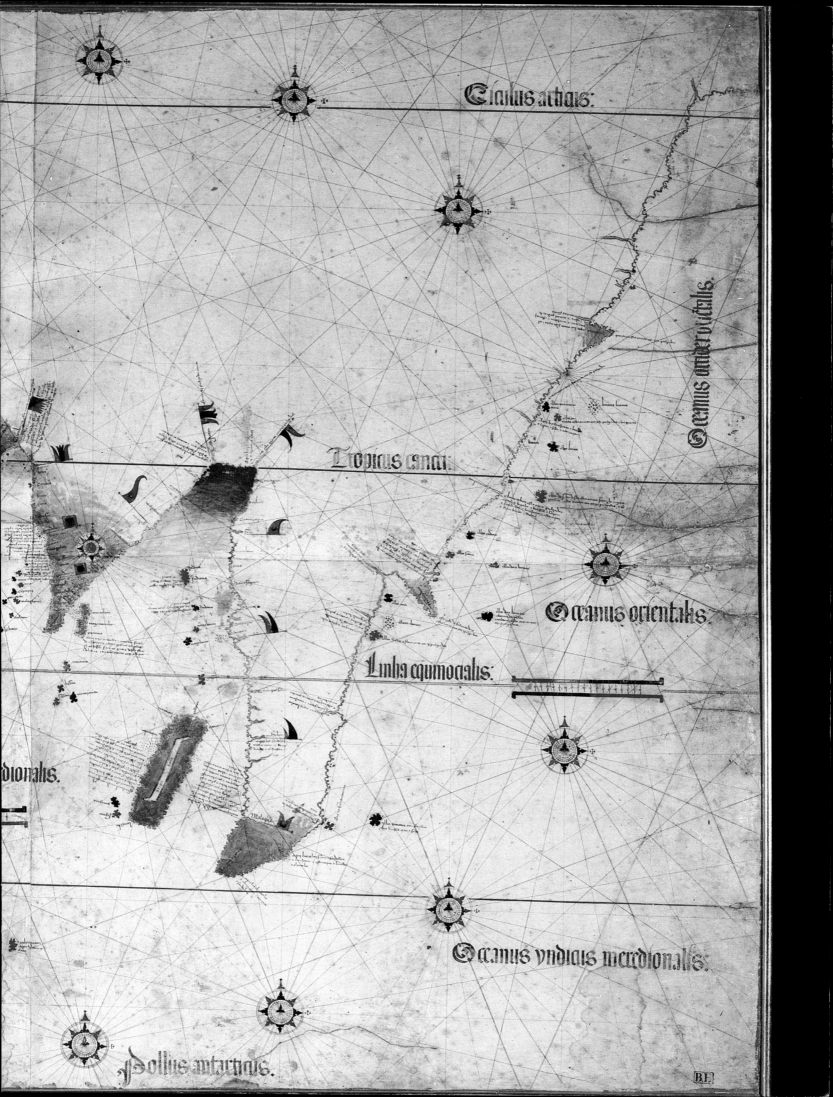

Circulus articus:

Oceanus amber occalis.

Tropicus cancri

Oceanus orientalis.

Linha equinocialis:

dionalis.

Oceanus yndicus meredionalis:

Pollus antarticus.

B.F.

TERA·D

Esta he a tera Dos
Corte. Reais ⁖

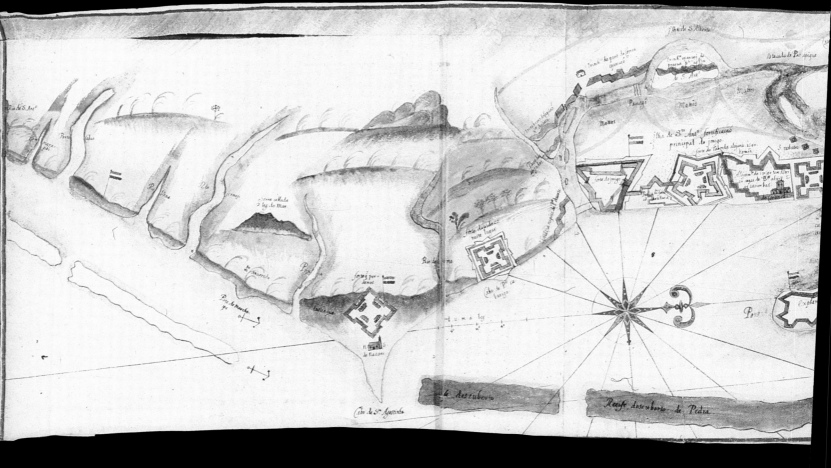

Rio do Varadouro

Perranil Trincheira do longo da Villa

Rio doce   2 leg   3 leg Pao A

collegio

5 b por Viuas Poso
3 b baix
4 b por Mortos
3 b baix   2½ pr
            1½ la Pua

Preamar 3½
Baix   2½
Barra

mea leg as trave desta Barra 6 bra limpo   Por aqui menos fundo 4 5 br

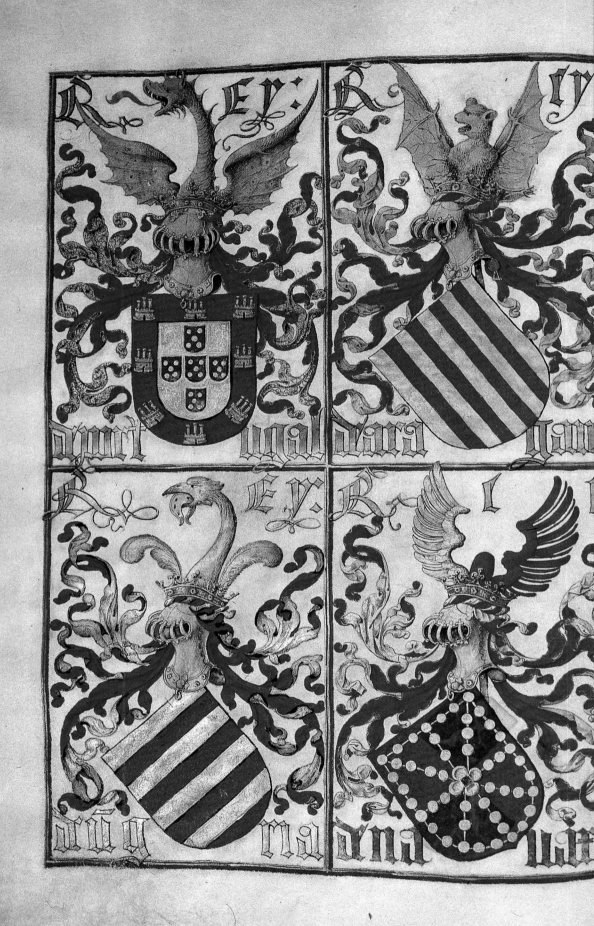

159-160

POLVS MVNDI ARCTICVS:

OCCEANVS SEPTETRIONA
.LIS.

MARE HYPERBOREV

TIERA DEL LABRADOR:

TIERA NOVA:
DE CORTEREAL:

TIERA DE ESTEVA GOMEZ:

GERMANIA
FLADRIA
POLONIA
FRANCIA V
TVMBAR HVGAR
GRETIA

TIERA DE AYLLON:

TIERA DE GARAY:

HISPAIA

OCCEANVS OCCIDENTALIS:

MAVRITANIA

SCITIFIESIS:— NVMIDIA

MARE ME

GETVLIA:

A F R I C A

MAR DEL SVR:

GVINEA: DESERTA LIBI

LIBIA INTERIOR ETHIOPIA

CASTILLA DELORO:

PERV.

MARE ETHIOPICVM:

MVNDVS
NOWS:—

TIERA BRASILIS:

TIERA DE SOLIS:

TIERA D' PATA
GONES:

POLVS MVNDI ATARCTICVS:—

PERBOREI
IONTES

SARMATIA EVROPÆ

SARMATIA ASIATICA

PONTVS EVXIVS   COLCHIS   MARECA
SPIV.

SCITHIA ITRA IMAV MOTE

SCITHIA EXTRA IMAV MOTE

MEDIA   HIRCANIA

ASIA MINOR   CARMAN   IA DESERTA

ARMENIA   CARMATIA   ARACHOSIA

DITERANEV   MESOPOTA   PAROPANISVS
SIRIA   MIA   PERSIA   M.   GEDROSIA

IVDEA   ARABIA DESERTA   INDIA ITRA GAGE   INDIA EXTRA GAGE

EGPTVS   ARABIA PETREA

ARABIA
FELIX

ETHIOPIA SVB EGIPTO

SINVS GAGETICVS   REGNO DE   MARE SINARV
ANSIAN

Rexbasar

REGIO ETHIOPV

SINVS
MAGN

CAMATRA

SINVS BARBARICVS

DAVAS

PALVDES NILI

MARE INDICVM

MOTES LVNÆ

OCCEANVS ORIENTALIS

INSVLA DIVI LAVRETIL

PROMOTORIVM BONÆ SPEI

OCCEANVS MERIDIONALIS

Section III

Max Justo Guedes
Portugal-Brazil:
The Encounter between
Two Worlds
Introduction by
Wilcomb E. Washburn

"They were dark and entirely naked, without anything to cover their shame. They carried in their hands bows with their arrows. All came boldly towards the boat, and Nicolau Coelho made a sign to them that they should lay down their bows, and they laid them down. He could not have any speech with them there, nor understanding which might be profitable, because of the breaking of the sea on the shore. He gave them only a red cap and a cap of linen, which he was wearing on his head, and a black hat. And one of them gave him a hat of long bird feathers with a little tuft of red and grey feathers like those of a parrot. And another gave him a large string of very small white beads which look like seed pearls . . . and with this he returned to the ships.

While we were at mass and at the sermon, about the same number of people were on the shore as yesterday with their bows and arrows, who were amusing themselves and watching us; and they sat down, and when the mass was finished and we were seated for the sermon, many of them arose and blew a horn or trumpet and began to leap and dance for a while, and some of them placed themselves in two or three canoes which they had there.

They seem to me people of such innocence that, if one could understand them and they us, they would soon be Christians, in accordance with the pious intent of Your Highness. . . . For it is certain this people is good and of pure simplicity, and there can easily be stamped upon them whatever belief we wish to give them; and furthermore, Our Lord gave them fine bodies and good faces as to good men; and He who brought us here,
I believe, did not do so without purpose."

From the letter of Pero Vaz de Caminha to King Manuel, written at Porto Seguro (Brazil), May 1, 1500 *(Item 90)*

Portuguese expansion into the Atlantic and its surrounding lands was not a one-sided entry into vacant territory, but a complex process involving African and American natives interacting in various ways with Portuguese explorers, traders, and settlers. The Age of Discoveries was truly an Age of Encounter. For Brazil, the inauguration of both ages was announced by the letter of Pero Vaz de Caminha, written on the shores of that land on May 1, 1500, describing the voyage in which Brazil was discovered. Sometimes the relationship between the Portuguese and the Indians was one of war; sometimes of trade; sometimes of missionary activity. European perceptions of the American natives focused on what Europeans saw as barbaric, exotic and uncivilized. Cannibalism particularly horrified the Portuguese, but at the same time, the notion that the Indians enjoyed complete freedom from the repressive mores of European society was powerfully attractive.
The Portuguese rapidly established control over the coastal portions of the new land, seeking to maintain the priority of their claim against intruders from other lands. Thus they began to build a vast continental power that would become the independent country of Brazil that we know today.
W.E.W.

The ocean voyages and discoveries of the Portuguese were *not* adventures: they were a state policy based, since the time of the Infante Dom Henrique, on a solid foundation of scientific and technical knowledge. These Portuguese navigations had acquired, by the end of the fifteenth century, a high degree of maturity, possessed of all the security the epoch allowed. When the second Armada to India *(Item 89)*, commanded by Pedro Álvares Cabral *(Items 88, 129)*, left the Restelo on March 9, 1500, they knew perfectly well the goal they intended to reach. Thus, it is irrelevant to recapitulate here the long-standing polemic to the effect that there were strong suspicions – if not widespread knowledge – in Portugal about the existence of lands or even a continent to the south of those that Christopher Columbus had discovered. And so, discussion about the intentionality of the discovery of Brazil is of little importance.
What *is* important was that morning of Thursday, April 23, 1500, when Nicolau Coelho, one of the captains of the Armada of Cabral, crashed through the waves in his small landing-boat, reached the mouth of the Rio do Frade, and convinced the 18 or 20 Indians he found there to put down their bows and arrows and exchange presents: a red beret, a linen cap and a black broad-brimmed hat in exchange for a

88. Draft of the letter of Dom Manuel naming Pedro Álvares de Gouveia (Cabral) captain-major of the armada being sent to India.
Lisbon, Feb. 15, 1500.

In this manuscript, the king Dom Manuel informs the captains, nobles, gentlemen, masters, pilots, sailors, crew, officers and other persons aboard the fleet and armada which he dispatched to India that, because of his great confidence in Cabral, a noble of his house, he had decided to appoint him captain-major. Accordingly, he granted him all powers to reward or punish persons on board. Exempt from punishment were noblemen in the fleet, against whom complaints could be asserted and brought to the attention of the monarch, who would pass judgment.

Arquivo Nacional da Torre do Tombo, Lisbon
(Below)

88

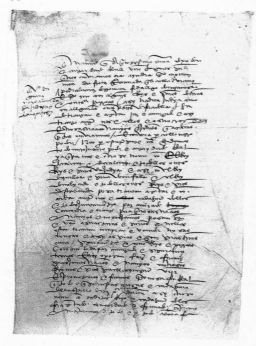

89. Fleet of Pedro Álvares Cabral.
In: "O Sucesso dos Visoreis"
Mid-16th c. Lizuarte de Abreu

The fleet of Pedro Álvares Cabral left Lisbon with thirteen vessels on March 9, 1500, discovered Brazil on April 22 and, in crossing toward the Cape of Good Hope, encountered a sudden storm which sank four ships, one of them with Bartholomeu Dias, the Cape's discoverer, aboard. This illustration notes the name of the captain of each vesesl, and its fate.

The manuscript from which the illustration is taken includes portraits of Portuguese governors and viceroys of India and depicts the India-bound fleets up to 1563, as well as two or three paintings, probably conventional, portraying naval engagements in the Orient.

Courtesy of The Pierpont Morgan Library, New York
Manuscript 525, Vol. II, fol. 16v - 17
(Pages 178, 179)

---

90. Letter to Dom Manuel giving notice of the voyage of Pedro Álvares Cabral and the discovery of Brazil.
Vera Cruz, May 1, 1500. Pero Vaz de Caminha

This is unquestionably the most important document on Brazil that exists today. The letter from Caminha, clerk to the factor of the armada of Pedro Álvares Cabral, is one of only three known first-hand accounts concerning the India-bound voyage during which Brazil was discovered. (The others are the letter of Master John, also shown in this catalogue, and an account by an anonymous pilot).

The first page tells of the ocean crossing from March 9 until April 21, when the fleet encountered signs of land, which was discovered the following day "at vesper time". In the remaining twenty-six pages Caminha recounts the daily events of the armada, which stayed in the "Porto Seguro da Vossa Ilha da Vera Cruz". (The Safe Harbour of Your Majesty's Isle of the True Cross). It gives a vivid, precise picture of the land and its inhabitants, their physical appearance, manners and customs.

Arquivo Nacional da Torre do Tombo, Lisbon
(Page 177)

feather headdress and a necklace of little white shells. Those were splendid days spent at the anchorage at Baia Cabrália (Cabralia Bay), the place these discoverers called Porto Seguro (Safe Harbour), when Portuguese and Indians lived together harmoniously, helped one another in the task of provisioning the ships, assisted at Mass together, innocently exchanged baubles and trinkets and together made music, danced, ate and enjoyed themselves.

At least, this is how it was all told to the king, Dom Manuel, by Pero Vaz de Caminha in a letter that he addressed from the Island of the True Cross — for thus they had baptized the discovered land, little knowing it was a vast continent. The letter is a veritable "birth certificate written on the shores of what would become the cradle of a future nationality", as it was put by Capistrano de Abreu, a master of Brazilian historiography. We note in this letter *(Item 90)* especially the description of the Indians, whose physical perfection and healthy appearance greatly surprised the writer; he found that the native women compared favourably with the patrician ladies of his native Portugal.

But the purpose of the voyage was to reach India, and to delay any longer would put the whole enterprise at risk; they had to get on course once again, and leave this pleasant stay behind them. While the armada set sail on its charted course, the supply ship made for Lisbon, with Captain Gaspar de Lemos charged with the task of bringing news to his monarch and carrying many letters to their various recipients. Of these letters, two remain: the one by Caminha already mentioned, and another by Master John, physician and surgeon to Dom Manuel, informing the king of the particulars of the voyage, the geographic position of the land they reached, the new skies they had observed *(Item 91)*. At Cabrália Bay, two *degredados* (Portuguese who had been banished from their homeland for various crimes) stayed behind to learn the language and customs of the indigenous people, an old Portuguese practice adopted now for the first time in Brazil.

It seems logical that Gaspar de Lemos, before crossing the Atlantic to return to the Tejo, should have sailed along the coast of the newly discovered land in order to assess, if only partially, its extent. Naturally, this was also the purpose of the exploratory expedition sent soon afterward in 1501, captained by Gonçalo Coelho to which participated the Florentine Amerigo Vespucci, though it is not certain in what capacity. He may have been captain of one of the ships of the merchants Sernigi or Marchione.

Between the middle of August and February/March of the following year (1502), the entire coast of Brazil was reconnoitred, from Rio Grande do Norte, where the first stone marker *(padrão)* was planted to claim possession of the land, to as far south as Cananéia in the present state of São Paulo. The results of this exploration were reflected shortly afterward in the celebrated Cantino Map *(Pages 147-149)*. The only extant documents from that period that go into detail about the events of that voyage are the letters of Vespucci, especially the one he wrote from Lisbon in 1502 (probably in

August) to Lorenzo di Pier Francesco de'Medici. This is the famous *Mundus Novus* whose numerous printed editions are discussed in the following section by Father Leite de Faria. An early manuscript copy is a treasure of the Biblioteca Riccardiana in Florence. A highly cultured man for that epoch, especially considering the nautical circles in which he made his way, Vespucci was able to make pertinent observations about the land and people of Brazil *(Items 93, 141)*. The possibility of contact with diverse tribes and cultural groups at the various stopping-points on the trip gave him and the other crew members a broader vision than that which had been permitted to the initial discoverers. Thus, the Florentine bragged about how he had eaten and slept for 27 days among the Indians; on the basis of this, he stated authoritatively that they possessed neither laws nor kings, and that holy faith, gratitude and friendship were unknown to them as well. They were a people most bestial and cruel, though Vespucci's logic failed to deduce the causes of their seemingly continuous wars: for since they held everything in common, they had no desire for material goods; and since they had no kingdoms or empires, they lacked a notion of territorial conquest; and lacking kings, there was no ambition to rule.

In combat they obeyed only the counsel of the elders; victors devoured the corpses of the vanquished and enslaved the survivors. Of these, men were well-treated for a while; the sisters and daughters of their masters would be given to them in marriage, until the day came for the men to be killed and eaten amid festivities. As for the women survivors, they were spared and taken as concubines. Such practices gave rise to a custom that the Portuguese adopted soon afterward: of buying war-prisoners in order to then enslave them. On that very voyage ten poor souls were bought in this manner, men and women alike.

When asked about the origin of their wars, therefore, the Indians could not explain it – they simply sought to avenge the death of those who came before them, and one confessed he had eaten the flesh of more than two hundred corpses.

Aside from these psychological observations, in which he was likely misled by his rudimentary knowledge of Indian languages, Vespucci has left us a decent description of the physical appearance of the indigenous peoples, though it is said to be inferior to Caminha's account; a description of their large collective dwellings, finely built, where the people slept in hammocks; and of their food, which consisted of wild game, roots, fruits, fish and shellfish. Much better still is his "explanation of the land": it was a very amenable place, with countless trees that never lose their foliage and have a suave and aromatic odour, producing a great variety of nutritious and pleasant-tasting fruits; the fields were full of herbs and flowers. Everything combined to make Vespucci imagine himself in the vicinity of a Paradise on Earth. Vespucci also was able to analyze the commercial possibilities of this vast territory. He had found Brazil-wood (*Caesalpina echinata* L., the most abundant, *C. brasiliensis* L., and other species), very useful in the textile industry because of its scarlet dye; he also found cassia (an

91. Letter to Dom Manuel.
Vera Cruz, May 1, 1500. Mestre João

Master John ("Mestre João", possibly João Faras, a Castilian), was Dom Manuel's physician and surgeon. He accompanied the voyage in order to make tests of the astrolabe as a latitude-measuring device. In the letter he seeks to fix the location of the discovered land in relation to those already known to Europeans, as during the crossing he had measured the ship's latitude daily at high noon. In his description of the southern heavens, of importance to future navigators, he highlights the beautiful Southern Cross, which today appears on the Brazilian flag. Master John also mentions a certain old map possessed by Pero Vaz Bisagudo. This passage has been interpreted by some scholars as evidence that Brazil's existence and location were already known, though there is still no additional evidence to confirm this. He states: "As regards the situation of this land, Senhor, Your Highness should order a mappa mundi to be brought which Pero Vaz Bisagudo has, and on it Your Highness will be able to see the location of this land. . . . It is an old mappa mundi, and there Your Highness will also find La Mina marked."

Arquivo Nacional da Torre do Tombo, Lisbon
(Below)

91

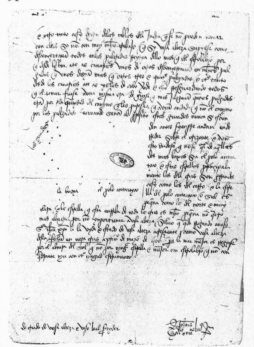

92

CHRONI

CA DO FELICISSIMO REI DOM EMA-
NVEL, COMPOSTA PER DAMIAM DE
GOES, DIVIDIDA EM QVATRO PARTES,
das quaes esta he ha primeira.

¶Foi vista, & approuada per ho R. P. F. Emanuel da veiga examinador dos liuros.

¶Em Lisboa em casa de Francisco correa, impressor do sereníssi-
mo Cardeal Infante, ahos xvij dias do mes de Iulho de 1566.

¶Esta taxada esta primeira parte no regno em papel a duzentos, & çinquoenta reaes, & fora delle
segundo ha distançia dos lugares onde se vender, & has outras tres partes pelo mesmo
modo naquillo em que forem taxadas.

Com priuilegio Real.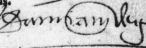

evergreen plant capable of yielding a mild laxative drug) in great quantity, and innumerable other spices previously unknown. In short, the land could possibly produce all types of riches, and not many years would pass before Portugal had indeed profited mightily by her. The economic results that Vespucci correctly predicted soon appeared and continually increased, accelerating throughout the period encompassed by this exhibition, a period that ended with the coronation of Philip II of Spain as king of Portugal in 1581. Three stages, relatively well-defined in political, social and economic terms, can be discerned within this period:
1) Utilization of the land: human contacts, generally friendly, resulting in collaborations to extract Brazil-wood and some other exotic products, and to transport and load them aboard ships (1503-1534);
2) The hereditary captaincies: antagonism and confrontation resulting from the beginnings of the implantation of the sugar industry, which required ample land and cheap labour, both to be obtained at the expense of the Indians (1534-1549);
3) The Governorship-General: compulsory pacification and religious conversion of the Indians, an indispensible step in the creation of a State and the expansion of the sugar industry, and obliging an increasing introduction of African slaves (from 1549 onward).

Occupation of the Land: 1503-1534

As soon as the squadron of Gonçalo Coelho returned to Lisbon, the Portuguese Crown understood that the possibility of immediate economic results in the "Land of Parrots" was limited, especially compared with those that were already being achieved in commerce with Asia. So, following an old and well-established custom, Dom Manuel resolved to rent the land for three-year periods to a consortium of "New Christians" (Jews who had been forced under penalty of exile to convert – superficially at least – to Christianity) led by Fernão de Loronha (sometimes spelled Noronha). The obligations of the participants would be to annually discover 300 additional leagues of coastline, erect and maintain a fort and pay the Crown 4,000 cruzados per year, a modest sum under the circumstances.

The contract was immediately fulfilled, except for the provision about increasing the discovered coastline; in July 1503, word had already reached Seville concerning the arrival of four ships at Lisbon, loaded with Indians and Brazil-wood. The following year, again under the command of Gonçalo Coelho, another armada set sail, this time with six ships.

It is only through the *Lettera di Amerigo Vespucci delle isole nuovamente trovate in quattro suoi viaggi,* (printed in 1505 or 1506, probably in Florence, and known as the "Letter to Soderini"), that something is known of the itinerary of this voyage. Its original destination was to be Malacca, in Asia; unaware of how far south the continent extended, they had probably intended to sail around its southern extremity and continue westward until reaching their destination. But the flagship foundered near the island that today is named after Fernando de Noronha, it having been ceded to this wealthy

92. Chronica do felicissimo rei Dom Emanuel.
Chronicle of most felicitous King Dom Manuel.
1556. Damião de Góes

This chronicle makes detailed reference to Pedro Álvares Cabral's discovery of Brazil, the most momentous event in the reign of Dom Manuel.
Damião de Góes was a humanist, a friend of Erasmus of Rotterdam, and knew Martin Luther and Melanchton. In 1548 he was appointed chief guardian of the Archives in the Torre do Tombo and in 1558 was assigned to chronicle the reign of Dom Manuel I. Publication of the first part roused the displeasure of many noblemen, and Góes became the target of criticism. The edition was recalled and redone; only three examples of the first printing are known to have survived, including this one.

The New York Public Library
(Facing page)

93. Dise figur anzaigt uns das folck und insel die gefunden ist durch den christenlichen Kunig zu Portigal oder von seinen underthonen.
This figure represents the people and the islands found by the Christian King of Portugal or his subjects.
Augsburg, 1505. Johann Froschauer Handcolored woodblock print

This broadside is probably the first printed picture of Brazilian natives. On the seashore, with ships in the distance, some Indians dressed in feather skirts and headdresses, with feather necklaces and armbands, the men bearing weapons, are gathered near a shelter fashioned from tree trunks, from which hang dismembered human limbs; one woman is devouring an arm, while another grasps a leg.

The caption, borrowed from Vespucci's Mundus Novus *letter (Page 238), states: "This image shows us the people and island discovered by the Christian King of Portugal or by his subjects. These people are naked, beautiful and brown of colour, well built in body. Their heads, necks, arms, intimate parts, and the feet of the men and women, are slightly covered by feathers. The men also wear on their faces and chests many precious stones. No one owns anything, but all things are communal. And the men take for wife those that please them, be it their mothers, sisters or friends, for they make no distinction. They fight among themselves and eat each other, even those they massacre, and hang the flesh over smoke. They live one hundred and fifty years. And they have no government."*

The New York Public Library (Pages 180-181)

merchant in 1504. This modified the initial plan: Vespucci's ship, with another in reserve, sailed southward after a long layover in the Baía de Todos os Santos. At or near a place known as Cabo Frio, a fort was erected and Brazil-wood collected; the work lasted five months, at the end of which time the ships returned to Lisbon, leaving twenty-four Christians in the fortification they had built. Thus was born the first *feitoria*, or permanent trading post, on Brazilian territory. This was indispensible to the traffic in Brazil-wood, given the delay in cutting and hauling it to the place of embarkation – tasks that obviously were left to Indians, and which were portrayed for the first time on a map of Brazil, in the Lopo Homen - Reineis atlas of 1519, now in the Bibliothèque Nationale de Paris. From this fort, we are led to believe from Vespucci's letter, the first expedition into the Brazilian interior set forth; 30 men reconnoitred some 40 leagues, thus opening quite early the cycle of expeditions which would continue until the eighteenth century, slowly revealing the extent of Brazilian territory and pushing westward the Line of Tordesillas. Concerning one of the twenty-four Christians at this fort, Sir Thomas More fantasized in 1516 in his book, *Utopia (Item 153)*. Thus began, at the dawn of the sixteenth century, what is known as "the Brazil-wood cycle". The wood was named *ibirapitanga* in the Tupi language, and it didn't take long to provoke a change in the country's name from "Land of the Holy Cross" to "Land of Brazil-wood" *(Terra do Brasil)*, as it was called by Duarte Pacheco Pereira in his *Esmeraldo de Situ Orbis*, written

between 1505 and 1508 *(Item 4)*. It is a fortunate circumstance that we still have the log-book of the *Bretoa (Item 94)*, a *nau* – a kind of large-bellied ship with fortified constructions at the bow and stern – which was plying the Brazil-wood trade in 1511. This log-book provides us with a very clear picture of the earliest days of that traffic: fitted out by the merchants Bartolomeu Marchione and Benedetto Morelli (both Florentines), and by Fernão de Loronha and Francisco Martins. The ship departed Lisbon on February 22, 1511, and reached Cabo Frio on May 22; it stayed there taking on cargo for one month and two days, loading a total of 5,008 Brazil-wood logs, thirty-five slaves, jaguariticas (a kind of small, spotted leopard), some parrots and long-tailed monkeys of the species *Midas ursulus*. From this log-book we can confirm the importance of the *feitorias*, the trading posts where wood was collected prior to the arrival of the ships: for during the first thirteen days of the *Bretoa*'s stay, 4,692 logs were loaded on board (daily average of 361), whereas it took another eleven days to get an additional 1,140 logs loaded, and twelve more days after that to obtain the final 176 logs, since these had to be cut and hauled while the ship was waiting to embark. Let it be noted that the rules laid down for the ship's captain prohibited, under severe penalty, any wrongdoing or injury to the land's inhabitants, even if there were some Indians among them who voluntarily wanted to go to Portugal and were taken there, because if they were to die – so the king warned – those left behind in Brazil would think their compatriots had been killed in order to be eaten, as was usual among the Indians themselves. . . .

But we know for a fact that despite such prohibitions, by 1511 the movement of Brazil-wood went hand-in-hand with the traffic in Indian slaves, the result of that arrangement whereby tribes friendly to the Portuguese would sell off their captives from the never-ending wars. For the Portuguese to release them from their fate as victims of cannibalism, only to then transform them into slaves, seemed absolutely natural in light of the moral code of the day; meanwhile, this practice resulted from the outset in the Portuguese's favouring certain tribes in detriment of others, a practice that would soon turn risky, when the French entered upon the scene.

French Invasion

Given the importance of the French textile trade in that epoch, it is easy to comprehend the attraction that the Brazil-wood traffic exerted upon Gallic mariners, as soon as they came to know the coast of Brazil. A pioneer in this was a certain Binot Paulmier de Gonneville, in the ship, *L'Éspoir*. Failing in his attempt to reach India, he made three landfalls along Brazilian shores (1504-1505), took on a load of Brazil-wood and brought an Indian named Essomeric back to France with him. Essomeric was the son of Aruoca, a *cacique*, or native chieftain, and in France he sired an illustrious line of descendants. But the French invasion would give rise to a widespread and bloody competition between factions of the *caraíbas* (an Indian word meaning "supernatural" and applied, not always as a compliment, to Whites because of their strange appearance,

customs and technology). It was a struggle of the *mair* and the *perós*, as the Indians called the French and Portuguese respectively.

By this point, both French and Portuguese were already aware of an implacable hatred that separated the Tupiniquín and the Tupinambá *(Item 135)*, even though both were of the same Tupi-Guaraní ethnic group, spoke similar languages and warred against the Tapyyas *(Items 133, 134)*. *Tapyya* means "barbarians" in the Tupi language (the word was *Tapuya* in the *língua geral*, an unwritten pidgin that settlers and their descendents invented by combining various Indian dialects). The Tupi and Guaraní dialects, by the way, were later combined by Jesuit missionaries into a language called Brasilic *(Item 107)* in conformance with the grammatical rules that governed European tongues.

At any rate, the Tupiniquín and Tupinambá, besides fighting the Tapyyas, were also enemies of tribes belonging to the *Gés*-speaking group (Aimorés, Botocudos and Apinayés), and of other groups whose relationship to one another is not known (Cariris and Tremembés), but who spoke languages different from Tupi-Guaraní, languages that were pejoratively called "stutter-talk" in Portuguese. If we wish to explain why the Tupi-Guaraní used a term that means something like our word "barbarian" to refer to other Indians whose languages were not intelligible, it helps perhaps to recall Ovid's words on the subject: *"Barbarus hic ego sum quia non intelligor ulli"* ("Here I am a barbarian, for here no one understands me").

Predictably, in order to hasten their occupation of the land,

94. **Llyuro da náoo bertoa que vay pera a Terra do brazyll de que som armadores bartolameu marchone e benadyto morelle e fernã de lloronha e francisco miz que partio deste porto de Lixª a xxij de feureiro de 1511.**
Book of the ship Bretoa which is going to Brazil, of which the sponsoring merchants are Bartolomeu Marchione and Benedetto Morelli and Fernando de Noronha . . . . *1511. Anonymous*

Commercial exploitation of Brazil began in 1502 under a consortium of "new Christians," Jews who had converted to Christianity. The primary source for information on these voyages is the Book of the Ship Bretoa (the vessel's name is spelled incorrectly by the writer himself). She sailed in 1511 to a trading post at Cabo Frio (east of Rio de Janeiro) to board a cargo of Brazil-wood. Besides a cargo list, the book records general directions to the trading post and back to Lisbon, information on the crew, and the captain's instructions.

*Arquivo Nacional da Torre do Tombo, Lisbon
(Below)*

94

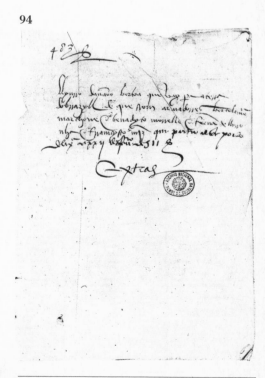

95. Copia der Newen Zeytung auss Presillg Landt.
Copy of the New Account of the Land of Brazil.
c. 1514. Anonymous

The source of this pamphlet was found in the Fugger archive in Augsburg: a handwritten copy of a letter written in 1514 on the Island of Madeira, informing the powerful banking family about the arrival of a ship from the Land of Brazil. The ship and its companion vessel had explored the coast some 600 or 700 miles beyond its previously-known limit, reaching a gulf or strait which we now identify as the estuary of the Rio da Prata (Rio de la Plata).

Besides a lucrative cargo of Brazil-wood and slaves, the voyage also garnered information that the interior of the country held an abundance of silver, copper and gold. This prompted a series of nautical expeditions to the southern part of the continent.

The John Carter Brown Library at Brown University, Providence RI
(Below)

95

Whites deliberately aggravated these intertribal rivalries, and forged alliances with one side or another (though many historians, less attentive to the question of the mentality of the age, have failed to comprehend this). At first, the Tupiniquín generally befriended the Portuguese, while the Tupinambá accepted material goods and engaged in commerce with the French *(Item 130)*. The Portuguese Crown would have none of this French interference, since it considered Portugal's jurisdiction to have been unjustifiably invaded. And at that very moment Castilians were beginning to cross the Atlantic, their first expedition to Brazil being that of João Dias de Solis, a Portuguese sailing for Castile, who was killed by Indians at the Rio da Prata (the "Silver River"). The Portuguese reaction was violent; Cristóvão Jacques, in three long voyages in the years 1516-1519, 1521-1522 (when he reached the estuary of the Rio da Prata) and 1527-1528, attacked ships found plying the Brazil trade and subjected their crews to dire punishments.

If the complaints of the French king, François I, were of little avail, then these armed coast-guarding expeditions also had minimal effect, and they failed to dampen the spirits of the interlopers, attracted by the prospect of easy wealth. The coastline was vast and it seemed there was room enough for everyone – especially for Jean Ango, the most outstanding of the merchant shipowners from the French port of Dieppe. He became exceedingly rich thanks to the traffic that he commanded, and the palace he built for himself would, in the next century, leave a strong impression upon no less a personage than the celebrated Cardinal Barberini.

First Settlements
Aside from those who worked the trading posts, both temporary and permanent, which were needed to supply the Brazil-wood ships, other people gradually found themselves washed up on Brazil's shores. Ignorance of the coastline, poorly maintained vessels, unfavourable weather conditions – these all contributed to the many shipwrecks that tossed Portuguese, Spaniards, French and other Europeans onto the beaches. Emerging from the ocean waves, they almost always made some kind of accommodation with the natives, finding it easy enough to obtain Indian women – whose nakedness and seemingly provocative behaviour the Whites took as a sign of natural lasciviousness, and who were thought to consider it an honour to lay down beside a White man. Soon there appeared the first generation of *mamelucos*, the children of these relationships *(Item 136)*. Among these early castaways are Diogo Álvares Correia, nicknamed "Caramurú" (an Indian name that means "moray eel"), who was in Bahia from 1509 onward; João Ramalho, who lived in Campos de Piratininga (circa 1510); and the survivors of one of the caravels of Solis, wrecked off Santa Catarina. Among these survivors were Melchor Ramires, Henrique Montes, and Aleixo Garcia, who perhaps in 1523, with four or five companions and some 2,000 Indians, set off from the coast in search of the "White King", the Inca Empire. He did manage to reach the region of Potosi, where he attacked a number of Indian settlements.

He then retreated, carrying valuable spoils with him, but was killed along with his men in Paraguay. Only the echoes of his adventure ever reached Santa Catarina. If it was good for anything, this early example of marching the flag into the hinterland showed that Garcia was a persuasive man; that Whites and Indians can form a potent alliance, able to face the most difficult challenge; and that the Andes (known as the Silver Mountains) could be reached from the Brazilian coastline. Aside from the shipwrecks, there were also the deserters and *degredados* who from the first moment of discovery were thrown up on the coastline by fleets and armadas. Attesting that the number of such people was considerable, and that their unfortunate destiny was well-known, we have the words of Gil Vicente. In his 1518 play, *Auto da Barca do Purgatório (Pageant of the The Ferry to Purgatory)*, the pioneer of Portuguese theatre has a simple fishwife respond in the following manner to the Devil, who is attempting to convince her to board his boat to Hell, after cleverly revealing that he already knows her by name:

"E marinheiro sodes vós?
Ora assi me salve Deus
e me livre do Brazil . . .
que estais sotil! . . ."

("And would you be a sailor, sir?
Then God save me
and take me not to Brazil . . .
How clever you are!")

One is not to wonder here, either at the fear of being carried off to Brazil, or at its implicit characterization as a kind of Hell. Under the Laws of Dom Manuel, one could be banished – *degredado* – to Brazil for infractions which today are considered insignificant, barely worth mention in the penal codes or deserving only of minor punishment. Such crimes included playing prohibited games, offenses against customs and morals, refusing to cooperate with the judiciary, and the like.

As with those who survived shipwrecks, there are few *degredados* whose stories have passed into the annals of history. We can cite the so-called *Bacharel* of Cananéia, his nickname ("the Bachelor") suggesting that he held a university degree, but who is still not known by his proper name. There is also João Lopes de Carvalho, first mate of the *Bretoa*, who later became pilot aboard the *Concepción* of the armada of Fernão de Magalhães (Ferdinand Magellan), who harboured in Rio de Janeiro in December 1519, while on his way to the Moluccas, and eventually around the world *(Item 96)*. Around these individuals were formed the first nuclei of White settlement in Brazil. In Pernambuco, they settled around the *feitoria* built by Cristóvão Jacques, and probably also at a sugar-mill for which a royal authorization had been granted in 1516, mandating that "a practical and capable man" be put in charge; another one provided for the donation of "axes and ploughs and all other tools for those persons who would go off to populate Brazil". In Bahia, the first settlement was that of Diogo Álvares, his progeny and some other shipwreck survivors. In Cabo Frio (or perhaps Rio de Janeiro, according to a recent hypothesis), it was the *feitoria* of João de Braga, where the *Bretoa* had picked up its cargo, and where Lopes de Carvalho found

96. Le voyage et navigation faict par les Espaignolz es Isles de Mollucques.
The voyage and navigation made by the Spanish to the Moluccas.
c. 1525-1536. Antonio Pigafetta

Little data on Antonio Pigafetta exist until he joined Fernão de Magalhães' attempt to reach the Moluccas in 1519 by sailing west, around the southern tip of the New World. Enroute, they explored portions of the Brazilian coastline and the estuary of the Rio de la Plata. A supernumerary on the flagship Trinidad, *Pigafetta kept a journal and notes. His account is our most important source on what became the first circumnavigation of the globe. Pigafetta was among the eighteen survivors who returned to Seville in 1522 aboard the ship* Victoria, *the only vessel (out of five) to return. The date of this first edition of the account is unknown, but is generally placed at 1526-1536. It was published in Paris by Simon de Colines, translated from a handwritten Italian copy.*

The Beineke Rare Book and Manuscript Library, Yale University
(Below)

96

97. Navegaçam q fez p° lopez de sousa no descobrimento da costado brasil militando na capitania de marti a° de sousa seu irmão na era da emcarnaçam de 1530.

Navigation made by Pero Lopes de Sousa in the discovery of the coast of Brazil. *c.1530. Pero Lopes de Sousa*

This incomplete handwritten copy from the second half of the 17th century recounts the voyage of the five-ship armada that was to secure dominion over Brazilian territory being threatened by French interlopers. It is valuable as a source of information on navigation along the Brazilian coast and on early colonization. Dom João de Castro, another great Portuguese navigator of the time, described the author in these words: "Pero Lopes de Sousa, whom all we Portuguese should recognize and revere as our master in the seafaring art and profession . . .".

Biblioteca da Ajuda, Lisbon (Below)

97

himself exiled. In São Vicente and Cananéia, it was the *Bacharel*, along with Antônio Rodrigues and Francisco de Chaves. Finally, in Porto dos Patos (Duck Port), in the vicinity of Santa Catarina Island, there were several survivors from the wrecks of the squadron of Solis.

In this initial phase of settlement, one of the greatest attractions for Europeans was undoubtedly the prospect of living a free life, in the broadest sense of the term. They came from societies that were highly repressive: to give just two examples from the Manueline Ordinances already cited, the theft of property valued at one silver mark was punishable by death, and counterfeiters were burned alive.

This led many of the earliest settlers, especially the deserters, to quickly adopt many habits of the Indians with whom they came to coexist: the native foods, the custom of polygamy, the use of native weapons. Some even shed their clothes, put on Indian adornments and participated (we suspect) in the rites of cannibalism. Concerning the behaviour of such men, there is an extremely interesting testimony by the Bavarian Utz Schmidl (*Item 112*), who served in the armada of Adelantado Don Pedro de Mendoza, founder in 1536 of Buenos Aires. From Buenos Aires Schmidl went to Paraguay, and after many adventures he made his way back to Europe. Along the way, he passed through Santo André da Borda do Campo (St. Andrew by-the-Fields) in 1553; this was a town that had just been built, with João Ramalho as its head. Schmidl relates:

"This João Ramalho does not want to be submissive to the king of Portugal or to his representative here, for he states and declares that for forty years he has been in this land of the Indies, he has lived in it and made it his own; why can't he govern it like any other? For this reason they make war among themselves, and if this João Ramalho wanted to bring together a force of 50,000 Indians, he could get them in one day – such is the power he has in this land. But neither the king nor his lieutenant would be able to gather together even 2,000 Indians.

I should say at this point that his sons, those of the above-named João Ramalho, received our Christians well; nonetheless, we felt much more apprehensive while among them than we did when we were among the Indians."

Search for the Silver Mountain Range; Settlement of the Southern Shore

The supposed Portuguese discovery in 1501-1502 of the Rio da Prata – better known to Americans as the Rio de la Plata – is narrated in a very confusing fashion in two printed works, the *Mundus Novus (New World)* and the *Lettera al Soderini,* composed haphazardly on the basis of texts by Vespucci. Dr. Leite de Faria, in his essay in this catalogue on the literary impact of the Portuguese Atlantic discoveries, explains some of the doubts that scholars have about the authenticity of these tales, and of the voyages Vespucci claimed to have made. Modern critics admit that the first real account of the Rio da Prata is in the *Copia der Newen Zeytung auss Presillg Landt,* which exists today in two versions: a handwritten copy of the original, dated October 12, 1514, and made on the island of Madeira, and a printed leaflet version with no date or place of publication (Item 95). It describes the voyage of two Portuguese ships to the Land of Brazil, where another 600 or 700 miles of coastline were discovered to the south of that already known, reaching a cape which marked the end of the territory. Curving around this cape, the explorers navigated 60 more miles through a gulf that ran in an east-west direction, keeping the other shore in sight, by which they came to believe they were in a strait. Then, with bad weather threatening, they were obliged to retreat.

The geographical data mentioned in the account permit us to identify this gulf or strait as the mouth of the Rio da Prata; the explorers heard news there that inland there were great mountains, covered in perpetual snow.

The pilot aboard one of the ships, described as "the most famous pilot that the king of Portugal had", and thus possibly identifiable as João de Lisboa (Item 121), had judged that from this cape westward to Malacca couldn't be more than 600 miles, a fact that would make for a much shorter trip to this important Asian outpost than was originally surmised. This gazette registers, furthermore, that at a certain port on Brazilian territory 200 miles from the cape, there had been information to the effect that inland there was much silver, copper and gold. The ship returned laden not with precious metal but with Brazil-wood and slaves – both male and female, and bought by the Portuguese for a pittance.

Considering that the Portuguese had already reached Malacca by sailing eastward around Africa's Cape of Good Hope, news of yet another cape at the apparent southern end of Brazil had great repercussions in Castilian nautical circles. They surmised this would be an ideal route to the Southern Sea (the Pacific Ocean) and thence to Asia, for the route would be on their own territory according to the Treaty of Tordesillas.

João Dias de Solis attempted this route for Castile in 1515, with the unfortunate results already mentioned. Soon afterward, in 1519, Fernão de Magalhães went in search of the passage, followed by Garcia Jofre de Loaysa in 1525, Sebastian Cabot in 1526, and Diogo Garcia de Moguer in 1527. According to his agreement with Emperor Carlos V, this latter explorer specifically went in search of "certain lands and islands that are called Silver and lie within our Ocean Sea" (that is, the Atlantic Ocean), where silver was supposed to be abundant. This very same Garcia de Moguer even presented his monarch with a lovely piece of silver that came from there.

Of this sequence of expeditions, that of Fernão de Magalhães was the only one that did not make any noticeable contribution to the settlement of Brazil's southern coast and to an intensification of the traffic in slaves, which was already centred in the southern ports of São Vicente and Cananéia. These expeditions also served to send a warning to the Portuguese Crown, which until then had its attention fixed on the spiceries of Asia, leaving the New World to its own devices: *"Com ilhas mil Deixai a terra do Brasil"* ("With your thousand isles, You ignore the land of Brazil") sang the poet

100. Record of the *foral* (statute) of the captaincies given to Pero Lopes de Sousa. Oct. 6, 1534.

Once a grant of hereditary captaincy had been issued by a charter of donation (carta de doação), there followed a foral, a statute which established the "fees, rents, taxes and things" which the colonists would be obliged to pay to the king and to the grantee; in a wider sense, it was a pact that set down the donatary's obligations to both the crown and the colonists.
To reward Pero Lopes de Sousa for his services during his expedition to Brazil, with his brother Martim Afonso de Sousa, Dom João III granted him three excellent parcels along the Brazilian coast. The charter of donation was signed on September 1, 1534, and the foral shown here followed soon after, on October 6.

Arquivo Nacional da Torre do Tombo, Lisbon
(Pages 184-185)

---

101. Sugar Mill in Brazil. 1640. *Frans Post*
Drawing; brown pen and grey wash on paper

Only eight drawings by Frans Post (1612-1680) are known today. Three portray sugar mills; the one shown here has an enormous waterwheel that turns the mill rollers via a large gear system. The works are protected by a vast shed roof.
The sugar cane is transported in oxcarts like the one shown at left in the drawing; African slaves then feed it into the mill, where it is crushed to extract the juice from which sugar is produced. From this product also came wealth for mill-owners and for the Portuguese Crown, and a change in European dietary habits.

Musées Royaux des Beaux-Arts de Belgique, Brussels
(Pages 186-187)

---

102. The Regulations of Tomé de Sousa, First Governor General of Brazil. Dec. 17, 1548.

The failure of several captaincies led Dom João III to reformulate the system by which Brazil was governed. The monarch decided to erect a city and fort in Bahia.

Tomé de Sousa, a well-reputed nobleman, was chosen governor; these regulations set down the provisions to be implemented, especially for pacification of Indians, distribution of land, propagation of the faith, contact with the captains-major, defence against corsairs and exploration of the interior. Highly detailed, the regulations were practically a constitution for the new state.

Arquivo Histórico Ultramarino, Lisbon
(Facing page)

Gil Vicente in 1510, in his *Auto da fama (The Pageant of Fame)*.

Expedition of Martim Afonso de Sousa

Adding together the growing French presence in Brazil and the Castilian invasions in the Rio da Prata, which Portugal considered its own, Dom João III deemed it necessary to take action. Diogo Álvares, the so-called "Caramurú," had wound up in the French seaport of St. Malo along with his Indian wife, Katherine du Brésil (Catarina Álvares), and she was baptized there on July 28, 1528. The godmother was Catherine de Granches, wife of the famous French explorer, Jacques Cartier. Given such threatening portents, Dom João put Martim Afonso de Sousa *(Item 98)* in command of an armada and charged him with a quadruple mission:
1) scatter the French interlopers and push them off the Brazilian coast;
2) take possession of the Rio da Prata once and for all;
3) grant territories to *donatários* (private individuals who would develop the land for their own profit) in order to create pockets of population;
4) improve knowledge of the Brazilian coastline, from Paraíba to the so-called East-West Coast in the north.
Although the royal orders given to Captain-Major Martim Afonso have been lost, there exists one document of the voyage, a shipboard diary by his brother, Pero Lopes de Sousa *(Item 97)*, who was second in command. This allows us to follow along with the adventures of this lengthy voyage.
The five ships included two caravels, and had a crew of 400,

including: Pero Anes, a pilot and interpreter; Henrique Montes, who had gone on to Spain with Caboto, returned eventually to Portugal, and whose contacts with settlers on the southern coast qualified him for the job of provisioning the expedition en route; and Pero Cápico, who also had lived in Brazil.
On December 31, 1530, the squadron departed Lisbon and, by the normal route that passed by the Canaries and Cape Verde, came within sight of Brazil somewhere near Pernambuco. At that time, a French vessel was spied, trafficking nearby. Panicked by the memory of the inflexible Cristóvão Jacques, the Gallic crew abandoned ship, made for shore and hid in the forest; their vessel was captured. This was only the first in a long series of reverses that French traffickers would suffer at the hands of the pitiless de Sousa brothers, whose reaction turned heavier still when they learned that the *feitoria* at Pernambuco had been sacked two months earlier by another French ship. In what was left of the aforementioned *feitoria*, Martim Afonso sheltered some ailing individuals among his contingent, and soon afterward dispatched the caravels *Rosa* and *Princesa* to perform a reconnaissance of the northern coast. The cartographic results promptly appeared on the Atlantic map of Gaspar Viegas in 1534, and in the so-called Luso-French Atlas *(Items 119, 120)*.
On March 1, 1531, Afonso's armada headed south, in a trip that took them as far as the Rio da Prata and didn't end until they reached Lisbon in August 1533. In the interval, besides combatting French traffickers and destroying a fort they had built in Pernambuco, Martim

Afonso sent two expeditions inland. The first, from Rio de Janeiro, marched 115 leagues and took two months; the other left Cananéia, attempting to find the "mountains of silver and gold", as long-time resident Francisco Chaves promised they would. There were 40 crossbowmen and as many musketeers; unfortunately, they wound up in the hands of Indians of the Paraná-Iguassu tribes, the same ones who had captured Aleixo Garcia and his companions.

But more important than all this expeditioning were the two towns founded by Martim Afonso, both magnificently situated: São Vicente, on the island of the same name; and Piratininga, on the high plateau of the present state of São Paulo, connected to the Rio da Prata basin by the Tietê river. Thus began what Pero Lopes ingenuously but quite properly termed the "secure and sociable life" in Brazil. That is, a life ruled by the civil authority, justice, morality and religion of Europe. Furthermore, by this expedition the Portuguese Crown took possession of the vast territory encompassed at one end by the estuary of the Rio da Prata and at the other by the Amazon delta. These two gigantic rivers would mark the boundaries of the lands claimed by Dom João III.

The Hereditary Captaincies: 1534-1549

The experience was not a novel one: in the settlement of the Atlantic islands of Madeira, Porto Santo and the Azores archipelago, the system had been tested and found to work well. It had worked for the Italians, who used it to settle the eastern Mediterranean and the Black Sea during the Middle Ages. We speak here of the system which entailed inheritable donations of territory, fiscal exemptions and the use of slave labour and *degredados*, which had always been the basis for primitive colonial establishments.

In Brazil itself, the island of São João (Fernando de Noronha) was the site of the first donation, four years after the arrival of Cabral at Porto Seguro. The Charter of Donation *(Item 99)* and the *Foral*, a statute granting certain rights to the donatary, were the cornerstones of the system *(Items 68, 100)*, widely utilized even within Portugal itself, as motivation and reward for those who distinguished themselves in the struggle to reconquer their land from the Muslims.

Thus, it required no great stroke of genius on the part of Dr. Diogo de Gouveia when, in 1532, he counselled Dom João III to donate Brazilian lands to his vassals, as guarantee of their settlement and defence. Indeed, this solution must have been ripe for implementation at the Portuguese court, for on September 28 of that year Dom João III wrote to Martim Afonso, who was still in Brazil, and announced that some individuals had asked for captaincies along the coast. The monarch's intention had been to await the return of his captain-major and learn what he could from the information brought back; but meanwhile, the threat had arisen that "certain parties were making preparations to populate the land called Brazil". That is, Spaniards and French were getting ready to occupy the place, which would make it all the more difficult to expel them afterward.

And besides, the Crown was facing financial difficulties, provoked by the cost of

103. Recording of letter of appointment of Tomé de Sousa as first governor-general of Brazil.
Jan. 7, 1549.

Issuance of the regulations to guide Tomé de Sousa in his administration was followed by his formal appointment. On January 7, 1549, this letter was issued, appointing Sousa to "the duties of captain of the town and lands of the so-called Baia de Todos os Santos and as governor-general of said captaincy (Bahia) and of the other captaincies and lands of the coast of Brazil, for a period of three years with remuneration of 400,000 reals each year."

The letter stipulated that the governor was to give aid to the other Brazilian settlements, administer justice (he was empowered to condemn peons, slaves and natives to death, and to sentence persons "of higher quality" to up to 10 years of banishment), and look after the royal exchequer.

Arquivo Nacional da Torre do Tombo, Lisbon
(Page 194)

102

Amdre — guoncaluez

Diguo — Diaz

Vasquo de Taidé

Nuno — Leytad

Ráis dem jraō Bo

Luis Pixis

Sancho de Touar
Daxou E puserad lho fogo

VARES·CAbRAL·ANO·DE·ſOO·

Nicolao coelho

Jaº frz

Pedraluez cabral·

Symao demjraodo

Dioguo de figueiro

Bertolameu Diaz

Sije figur anzaigt vns das volck vnd insel die gefunden ist durch den christenlichen künig zů
halß. arm. scham. füß. frawen vnd mann ain wenig mit federn bedeckt. Auch haben die mann
Vnd die mann habendt weyber welche in gefallen. es sey mütter. schwester oder freiundt. darst
werden. vnd hencken das selbig fleisch in den rauch. Sy werden alt hundert vnd fünfftzig iar. V

r von feinen vnderthonen. Die leüt find alfo nacket hübfch, braun wolgeftalt von leib, ir heübter,
efichten vnd bruft vñ edel geftain. Es hat auch nyemantz nichts fünder find alle ding gemain,
kain vnderfchayd. Sy ftreyten auch mit einander. Sy effen auch ainander felbs die erfchlagen
ein regiment.

MARTIA FO DE SOVSA GOV ERNADOR

jn auff das fewer/kratzen jm die haut alle ab/machen jn gant
weis/stopfen jm den hindersten mit eynem holtz zů/auf
das jm nichts entgehet.

Wann jm dann die haut ab gefeget ist/nimpt jn eyn man
person/schneidet jm die beyne ober den knihen ab/vnnd die
arme an dem leibe/dann kommen die vier weiber vnd nem
die vier stücke/vnnd lauffen mit vmb die hütten her/machen
ey

ß geſchrey/von freuden/darnach ſchneiden ſie jm den
t dem hinderſten von dem vortheyl ab/ daſſelbige
ſie dann vnter ſich/aber das ingeweyd behalten die
ſieden/vnd in der brůe machen ſie eynen brei/mingau
/den drincken ſie vnd die kinder/das ingeweyd eſſen
auch das fleyſch vmb das haubtßher/das hirn in
bt/die zungen/ vnnd weß ſie ſunſt daran genieſſen

EQVI

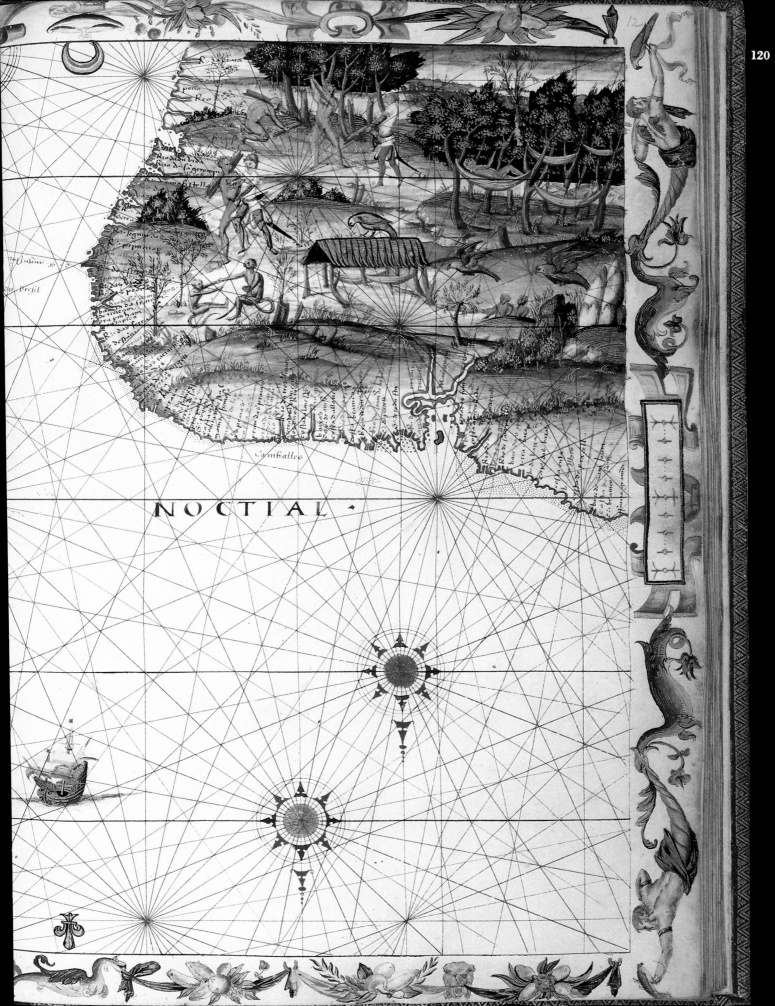

NOCTIAL ·

Camballes

GASPAR · VIEGAS ·

defending its vast territory; the famous Cruzados, which even Shakespeare's Desdemona possessed in great quantity ("Believe me, I had rather lost my purse/ Full of cruzadoes" – *Othello*, III: iv), were running scarce. The monarch quickly ordered the division of the coast from Pernambuco to Rio da Prata into captaincies, with 50 leagues of coastline for each one, reserving 100 leagues for Martim Afonso de Sousa and 50 for Pero Lopes de Sousa along the best stretches. The rest was to be donated, with the obligation that the fortunate recipients should populate them (supplying both ships and people) and defend them, at their own cost. In the end, twelve donataries received fifteen allotments, demarcated by parallel lines running inland from the shore to the Tordesillas Line. These were enormous plots of land: Pernambuco, now under the responsibility of Duarte Coelho, was several times larger than all of Portugal. The same was true of several other captaincies, such as the 225 leagues donated to João de Barros, Fernão Álvares de Andrade and Aires da Cunha, which began near the mouth of the Amazon river and ended in present-day Rio Grande do Norte (roughly a thousand miles), with a piece carved out for the enclave of Ceará, donated to Antônio Cardoso de Barros. The initial idea of simply using Pernambuco and Rio da Prata as the northern and southern borders of the territory had become more elaborate, after Martim Afonso had ordered Diogo Leite to make his exploratory voyage in the caravels *Rosa* and *Princesa*.

Except for Pernambuco and São Vicente, the captaincies enjoyed only fair success. Some, such as Ceará, under Antônio Cardoso de Barros, hardly experienced any colonization attempts at all; others, such as Maranhão, found their efforts aborted at the outset. A few, after auspicious beginnings, slid backward when the Indians broke off relations with the colonists and began terrible wars, upon realizing that the new system would deprive them of land and liberty. This occurred, for instance, in Espírito Santo, under Vasco Fernandes Coutinho; Porto Seguro, under Pero do Campo Tourinho; and Bahia, under Francisco Pereira Coutinho. Historian Bailey Diffie explains what happened: "The most important discovery made by the Indians was that the newcomers had come to take their lands. Lacking any sense of personal property ownership in a culture where all land belonged to the group – whether clan or tribe – for fishing, hunting, and cultivating small fields, they did not understand, at first, why the Europeans staked out boundaries, cut down their forests, claimed exclusive rights of fishing and hunting, took their wives and daughters when not offered, and enslaved them in ways contrary to their own rules of slavery. Soon Indian tribes turned on the colonists and fought them as long and hard, and as intermittently, as they had their local enemies . . . . Even temporarily 'friendly' Indians turned on the Portuguese. Indeed, the Indians considered the Europeans treacherous. Blood feuds became the rule on both sides. An offense against one white by an Indian could start a war; and one white injuring an Indian could likewise initiate conflict". São Vicente's local economy,

104. Excellentissimo, singvlarisque fidei ac pietatis viro Mendo de Saa, Avstralis, sev Brasilicae Indiae praesidi praestantissimo.
1563. Anonymous, attributed to Luís de Carvalho

This Latin poem of 2,463 lines is currently ascribed to Fr. Luís de Carvalho, a Latinist who taught at the College of Bahia, though scholars once thought it had been written by José de Anchieta, Brazil's most illustrious Jesuit missionary.

This copy is the only one known to exist in the world; the work recounts the exploits of the third governor-general of Brazil, Mem de Sá, against the French, who had attempted to establish a colony in Rio de Janeiro. The governor's son, who lived in Portugal, had the poem printed mainly to persuade the authorities to send aid to his father's threatened colony.

Biblioteca Pública e Arquivo Distrital de Évora
(Below)

104

Pub.º

(+ preto ...

Dom Johão etc. Quantos esta minha carta virem faço saber que vendo eu quanto
cumpre a serviço de ds. e meu conservar e ennobrecer as capitanias e povoações
que tenho nas minhas terras do brasil ordeney ora de mandar fazer hũa fortaleza
grande e forte na baya de todos os Santos por ser pera iso o mais
conveniente lugar que ha nas ditas terras do brasil pera dasy se dem favor e ajuda
as outras povoações e de minha Justiça e prover nas cousas que cumprem
a meu Serviço e aos negocios de minha fazenda e bem das partes e pela
muita confiança que tenho em tome de Sousa fidalgo de minha casa que nas
cousas de que o encarreguey me Servira bem Sam e como o ouue e da experiencia
que delle espero e como o ate agui tem feito nas cousas de meu Serviço de que
foy encarreguado ey por bem e me praz de lhe fazer mercê dos carregos de
capitão da povoação e terras da dita baya de todos os Santos e de gouernador
geral da dita capitania e das outras capitanias e terras acubde do dito brasil
por tempo de tres anos e com quatrocentos mil rs. de ordenado em cada hũ ano pagos
a custa de minha fazenda no tº.... de minhas rendas e dtos. que hade ter na
povoação da dita baya por esta carta somtr. que Sera registada no livro de
sua despa. ... de Sem corpus e pello tresledo della e conhecimento
do dito tome de Sousa mando que lhe sejão leuados em conta os ditos quatrocentos
mil rs. que lhe asy paguar em cada hũ ano. E notefico a todos os
capitais e gouernadores das ditas terras do brasil ou a quem seus carregos
tiuerem e aos officiais da Justiça e de minha fazenda em ellas e aos moradores
das ditas terras e a todos em geral e a cada hũ em especial mando que ajão
ao dito tome de Sousa por capitão da dita povoação e terras da baya e por
gouernador geral da dita capitania e das outras capitanias e terras da dita cobta como dito
he. E lhe obedeção e cumprão e fação o que elles o dito tome de Sousa
de minha parte lhe manda e mandar seg.do a forma dos regimentos e prouisões
minhas que pera iso leua. E se ao diante lhe forem enviadas. Sem embargo
de pellas doações por my feitas aos capitais das ditas terras do brasil lhes ter
concedido que nas terras das ditas capitanias nom entrem em tempo algũ
nem alçada nem outras algũas Justiças pera nellas usar jurdição a qual por
nhũa via nem modo que seja nem menos sejão os ditos capitais soospensos de
suas capitanias e ouuidores dellas. E asy sem embargo de pellas ditas doações
lhes ter concedido alçada nos casos ciuis asy pera auaçõ noua como p capillação
e agrauo ate contia de decem mil rs. E nos casos crimes ate morte natural
Incluindo em escrauos e gentios e em piães e cristãos homes liures em todolos
casos asy pera absoluer como pera condenar. E nas pessoas de mais calidade
ate diz anos de degredo e em tª.... de pena sem apelaçõ nem agrauo. Por
quanto por algũas justas causas e respeitos que me a iso moue uy ou e
por bem de minha certa ciencia por esta vez pera estes casos. E pera todo o q.
nos regimentos que o dito tome de Sousa leua derogar as ditas doações. E todo
o nellas conteudo emquanto forem contra o que se contem nesta carta. E nos
ditos regimentos e prouisões. Posto que nas ditas doações aja algũas clau-
sulas derogatorias ou outras quaisquer. De que pudera e minhas ordenações
se deuesse de fazer expressa e especial menção e derogação. As quais
uy agui por expressas e declaradas como se de uerbo ad uerbum fosem

based on the rapid installation of sugar mills, managed to maintain some equilibrium, thanks to three things: the presence of Europeans well before the beginning of the captaincy system; the family-based alliances of João Ramalho with the powerful chieftain Tibiriçá, alliances that translated into numerous mixed-blood progeny; and the energetic leadership left behind by Martim Afonso. Later, this leadership was consolidated when Brás Cubas (1544-1549) *(Item 109)* founded the village of Santos, an excellent seaport – to this day it is the principal outflow point for Brazilian exports – and also promoted the penetration of the interior, making possible the raising of cattle and the cultivation of cereals, which would complement the sugar-based agro-industry.

In Brazil's northeastern bulge, a privileged position for links with Europe, there would arise the second exception to the apparent non-success of the captaincy system: Nova Lusitânia, the name that its donatary, Duarte Coelho, gave to the present state of Pernambuco. Contrary to what happened in other parts, the opposition of Indian groups in Nova Lusitânia moved in step with the arrival of colonizers; as the 17th-century historian Sebastião da Rocha Pitta put it, "Duarte Coelho had to gain inch by inch what had been donated to him league by league."

Igaraçu, among the first villages to be created there, found itself surrounded for quite some time by the Potiguares tribe. Once, when the situation had turned particularly difficult, a relief expedition arrived; one of the participants was the German mercenary Hans Staden, who later gained undying fame as author of a book about his adventures in Brazil *(Item 113)*, especially his long captivity among the Tupinambá, by whom he was almost eaten.

Aside from Igaraçu, Duarte Coelho founded four more villages, one of them called Olinda *(Item 138)*. Its name is of uncertain origin, but has romantically been attributed to the exclamation its founder is said to have made upon seeing the locale: *"Oh! Linda!"* ("Oh, how beautiful!"). As in São Vicente, what guaranteed the success of this captaincy was not only the qualities of the soil for sugar cultivation, and the establishment of sugar mills *(Item 101)*, but also the leadership of Duarte Coelho and the help of various Whites and their mixed-blood children already living in the region before the arrival of the captaincy's founders. Their example quickly bore results among the new arrivals, and "marriages" were numerous among them, resulting in valuable alliances with the Indians. Another factor contributing to these alliances was the donatary's intransigent defence of the population, and the confidence the people consequently had in him. He vigorously punished adventurers who travelled up and down the coast assaulting Indians indiscriminately, appealing to the king to mete out exemplary punishment to such wrongdoers.

Governorship-General: 1549 onward

Contrary to the rule in the Western world in almost every field in which it is applied, private enterprise did not achieve the great success desired by the Portuguese Crown in the early colonization of Brazil. The

105. Copia de vnas cartas embiadas del Brasil por el padre Nobrega dela companhia de Jesus: y otros padres que estan debaxo de su obediẽcia . . . Tresladadas de Portugues en Castellano. Copies of some letters sent from Brazil by Father Nobrega of the Society of Jesus: and others who are under his obedience . . . Translated from Portuguese to Castilian. *1551.*

On their arrival in Bahia with the first governor-general, the Jesuits set out to minister the Christian faith in the main Portuguese settlements. To keep their superiors and companions abreast of their activities, the priests and brothers corresponded intensively. The great interest in these letters, coupled with the meagre knowledge of the Portuguese language in the rest of Europe, led to some of their being translated into Spanish, as in this edition. The following year, they appeared in Italian.

Biblioteca Nacional, Lisbon (Below)

105

106. Avisi particolari delle Indie di Portugallo Ricevuti in questi doi Anni del 1551 e 1552, da li Reverendi Padri de la compagnia de Iesu. . . .
Private Notices from the Portuguese Indies received in these two Years of 1551 and 1552 from the Reverend Fathers of the Society of Jesus. . . .
Rome, 1552.

In these letters, the Jesuit priests kept their superiors informed with regard to two major tasks: indoctrination of the Indians, and difficulties in correcting the licentious behaviour of the white colonists.
This volume contains letters from Brazil, Africa and the Orient. The letter shown here is a "copy of a letter from Fr. Manuel da Nóbrega... sent from Brazil to Doctor [Fr. Aspilcueta] Navarro, his teacher in Coimbra, received in 1552".

The John Carter Brown Library at Brown University, Providence RI (Below)

106

fault resided most likely not in the system but in those who attempted to apply it: precarious leadership; lack of necessary means; a human element that for the most part was not greatly to be trusted, consisting largely of deserters and *degredados*, clearly maladapted even to the environment from which they had come. Even those men who freely joined up with the donataries to cross the Atlantic made the trip, most of them, without their wives and children, tearing asunder the always health-giving ties of family life. It was necessary to reformulate the system or else the land would be lost; thus affirmed, in 1546, Pero de Góis, donatary of the Captaincy of São Tomé.
The occasion arose with the problems of Porto Seguro, whose donatary had gotten in trouble with the Inquisition, and also with the murder of Francisco Pereira Coutinho by Indians on the Island of Itaparica, in the Bay of All Saints (Bahia). In that Captaincy would be established the seat of the first governor-general mandated by the king, thus bringing political statehood to Brazil and specifying its manner of organization.

From Captaincy to Colony: The Government of Tomé de Sousa

Tomé de Sousa, a nobleman of great renown, was named to the post by a letter dated January 7, 1549 *(Item 103)*. A highly detailed set of instructions – practically a constitution for the new state, in the eyes of Brazilian writer Afrânio Peixoto – was handed over to him on the occasion *(Item 102)*. Its intent was to orient the new governor, and specifically to ensure the following: that he build a fort and city both large and strong on the Bay of All Saints; that he punish the Tupinambá who were guilty of rising up against Francisco Pereira Coutinho and favour those who were at peace; that he administer justice, direct royal business affairs, promote the defence of the colony, stimulate the conversion of the natives to Catholicism, oversee naval construction and stop the flow of arms to the Indians.
The royal instructions took special care to see that previously unused lands were parcelled out; some parcels were earmarked for sugar mills, and would be allotted only to those who could afford to undertake the necessary construction work. These future sugar-mill masters – who "live like barons, for all their wealth", according to a Jesuit writing some years later – must be acknowledged as the driving force behind the restructuring of an economy that had faltered under the hereditary captaincy system. It fell to them to advance from simple resource-extractive activities to a colonial plantation system, a change that would tie men to the soil and encourage population. The basis would continue to be sugar production, which had already proved itself well-adapted to tropical ecosystems. Sugar-production methods, financing and commercialization were matters that had already been fully perfected back in the homeland (the business was dominated by Italians: the Affeitati, Marchione, Morelli and others). This was thanks to successful prior stages of development on Madeira and São Tomé, and after the industry had already begun to flourish in Pernambuco.
Simultaneously with the appointment of Tomé de Sousa, a

chief magistrate (Pedro Borges) was chosen to administer justice, and a treasurer (Antônio Cardoso de Barros) was appointed; both had their respective instructions. Aside from these men, 300 more people would be paid by the royal purse: men at arms, physicians, architects, carpenters, ironsmiths and other workers needed for the establishment and operation of government. Colonists and *degredados*, numbering 600 in all, completed the group of settlers.

More important than all these, for the primary role they would play in the early formation of the country, were the six Jesuits who came with Tomé de Sousa, led by Father Manuel da Nóbrega. Despite the presence of the priests, the first measure taken by the governor, after being duly installed, was to attack – at the least possible risk to colonists – the Tupinambá who had risen against Pereira Coutinho, destroy their settlements and kill, or else capture and punish, some of the survivors as an example to other Indians. Tomé de Sousa's instructions further specified that when the Indians begged for peace, the governor should first demand that some of their leaders be handed over, so that they could be hung by the neck in their respective villages. In this war, the Portuguese would ally themselves with the Tupiniquín, promising them land.

As a counterpart to what present-day standards would call extremely harsh treatment of the hostile Indians, there was an equally forceful effort to convert them to Christianity *(Item 108)*. Those who made peace were to be well-treated and favoured, the governor prohibiting anyone from subjecting them to offence or oppression, and punishing any Whites who did so. Under penalties of death and confiscation of property, he thwarted and punished those Whites who, in ships and caravels, travelled among the Captaincies assaulting and robbing natives and capturing them for sale, which was a principal reason for the uprisings and wars they made against the Christians. Thus affirmed the treasurer Pedro Borges in a letter to the king shortly after assuming his post. He related the following dramatic case:

"The principal cause that makes these indigenous people wage war on the Christians was the assaults that the ships were making, sailing up and down this coast. And in this business they have done things so far beyond the pale that assaulting the Indians was only the least of it, because there was one man whom an Indian chief freed from some other Indians, he having been badly wounded and mistreated by them, and he took this White man into his home and cured him. . . . This man later came back in a ship and demanded to talk to this Indian, who had kept him in his own house, and said that he should go see the ship, the Indian imagining that this White man was coming back to thank him for the kindness he had shown. As soon as he had the Indian on the ship the White man captured him along with the others that had come aboard, and he went and sold them all somewhere in these captaincies."

Thus it became perfectly well known in Portugal exactly what it was that led the Indians to rise up in revolt, and who was provoking them. . . .

107. Arte de grammatica da lingoa mais usada na costa do Brasil. pelo padre Ioseph de Anchieta da Cõpanhia de Iesv. The Art of Grammar of the language most used on the coast of Brazil, by Father José de Anchieta of the Society of Jesus. *1595. José de Anchieta*

José de Anchieta was born in La Laguna, Tenerife (Canary Islands) in 1534 and joined the Society of Jesus at an early age. He went to Brazil in 1553; he learned the Tupi language fluently, which proved enormously useful in converting the Indians, for whom he wrote the Devocionário Brasílico, *many religious hymns, plays to be performed by the natives and a number of poems. According to historian Charles Boxer, 19th- and 20th-century efforts to reconstruct the basic language of the extinct Tupi tribes took this grammar as their point of departure. Anchieta died in an Indian village in the Captaincy of Espírito Santo in June 1597.*

Biblioteca Nacional, Rio de Janeiro (Below)

107

108. Our Lady of the Immaculate Conception.

c.1560. Attributed to João Gonçalo Fernandes
Polychromed terracotta sculpture

It is believed that, after the construction of the new mother church in São Vicente (State of São Paulo) in 1559, the inhabitants ordered terracotta images of Our Lady of the Rosary and of Saint Anthony from João Gonçalo Fernandes, a Portuguese sculptor. About the same time, the inhabitants of Itanhaém (a settlement in the same captaincy) ordered an image of Our Lady of the Conception, patroness of their mother church.

Chronicles state, however, that the residents of Itanhaém, through rudeness or ignorance, took a liking to the image of Our Lady of the Rosary instead of the one they had ordered, and carried it back to their settlement; the other two statues, including the one shown here, remained in São Vicente. All three pieces are considered to be the oldest of their genre in Brazil.

Museu de Arte Sacra de Santos
(Below)

108

On March 29, 1549, the governor and his six ships arrived in the Bay of All Saints. Dom João III had already written to Diogo Álvares (the so-called "Caramurú") begging his collaboration; this, plus the actions of the fathers of the Society of Jesus, was essential in order for them to get on good terms with the Indians, who helped greatly in the construction of a fort, a new city and its defensive wall "all around the city perimeter". A little more than one year later, the settlement was almost complete and ready to receive more colonists, as many as 300 more, preferably married couples, whom the king had ordered to be recruited on the Azores with offers of free transportation, supplies and land for cultivation.
Considered diligent and just, the governor soon managed a reversal of the colony's situation and put the Land of Brazil on the road to progress, with sugar leading the way economically and the cattle herds multiplying rapidly. In large measure, this reversal was due to the voyage the governor made with the coastguard armada of Pero de Góis to the southern captaincies, passing through Ilhéus, Porto Seguro (where he ordered twelve men and a Jesuit to enter the "sertão", the hinterlands far from shore, in search of the "resplendent mountains" spoken of by the Indians), Espírito Santo and São Vicente; and passing also through Rio de Janeiro, which he found enchanting to his eyes, for everything there was lovely and deserving to be inhabited, so that it's no wonder that later the place would be called "the marvellous city". Of course, a settlement there would also check the incursions of the French, who were already accustomed to gathering pepper and Brazil-wood in the area.
In the captaincy of Martim Afonso de Sousa the governor-general founded two more towns, Santo André da Borda do Campo, today a great centre of the car industry, and Nossa Senhora da Conceição de Itanhaém; he also had the Fortress of Bertioga built, where Hans Staden had some of his adventures as an artilleryman staving off frequent attacks by the Tamoios from Ubatuba *(Item 113)*.
When Tomé de Sousa returned to Bahia on May 1, 1553, having completed this important mission, Lisbon had already prepared for the departure of his recently named successor, Dom Duarte da Costa.

The Second Governor-General: Dom Duarte da Costa

The new governor arrived in Bahia on July 13 of the same year, bringing with him the third Jesuit mission, among whom was Brother José de Anchieta, a young man from the Canary Islands who had led an exemplary life, and who in Brazil would achieve fame as a miracle-worker and would have tremendous impact on colonial life. Also, there arrived some orphan girls of marrying age; these had been called for by the Jesuit fathers in order to quiet those who justified their sexual promiscuity with Indians on the grounds that there were no white women to be had.
Dom Duarte da Costa would not enjoy the same success as his predecessor because, although "clean of hand" and "mild of character" in the words of historian Pedro Calmon (a great specialist in this period), he was also "weak in punishing the

conhecimento pertençer, que aſsi o cum-
pram, & façam inteyramente cumprir,
& guardar. E ey por bem que eſte valha,
& tenha força & vigor como ſe foſſe carta feyta em meu nome, & paſſada pella
Chancelaria, ſem embargo da ordenaçam
do ſegundo liuro, Tit. 20. que o contrairo
diſpoem. Lopo ſoarez o fez em Euora, a
tres de Ianeyro, de Quinhentos, & ſetẽta,
& eu Miguel de Moura, o fiz eſcreuer.

LEY SOBRE A LI-
BERDADE DOS GENTIOS
das terras do Braſil: & em que ca-
ſos ſe podem, ou nam po-
dem catiuar.

OM SEBASTIAM
per graça de Deos Rey
de Portugal, & dos Al-
garues daquem & dalem
mar em Africa, ſenhor de
Guinè, & da conquiſta,
Nauegaçam, & Comerciò de Ethiopia,
Arabia, Perſia, & da India, &c. Faço ſaber

aos que eſta Ley virem, que ſendo eu in-
formado dos modos illicitos, que ſe tem
nas partes do Braſil em catiuar os gentios
das ditas partes, & dos grandes inconuenientes que diſſo naçem, aſsi per as con-
ſeiencias das peſſoas, que os catiuam pellos ditos modos, como pera o que toca a
meu ſeruiço, & bem, & conſeruaçam do
eſtado das ditas partes: & parecendome
que couuinha muito a ſeruiço de noſſo
Senhor prouer niſſo, em maneyra que ſe
atalhaſſe aos ditos inconuenientes, man-
dey ver o caſo na meſa da Conſciencia,
pellos deputados do deſpacho della, &
per outros letrados: & conformandome
niſſo com ſua determinaçam, & parecer.
Defendo, & mãdo, que daqui em diante
ſe nam vſe nas ditas partes do Braſil dos
modos que ſe atè ora vſou em fazer cati-
uos os ditos gentios, nem ſe poſſam catiuar per modo nem maneyra algũa, ſaluo
aquelles que forem tomados em guerra
juſta, que os portugueſes fezerem aos ditos gentios com autoridade & liçéça minha, ou do meu Gouernador das ditas
partes, ou aquelles que cuſtumam ſaltear

109. Letter from Brás Cubas, Examiner of the Captaincy of São Vicente, to King João III.
April 25, 1562.

From the time Cabral's fleet arrived in 1500, there was much interest in finding gold in Brazil. Brás Cubas was "purser and accountant", from 1551, of income and royal taxes in the captaincy of São Vicente. Aided by the expertise of a miner whom the king had sent from Lisbon, he financed two expeditions in search of mineral wealth. On the second, gold was found, "as good as that of the mines of Africa and of the same assay". in six different places.

Cubas hastened to dispatch the good news to the king in this letter, and at the same time requested means to defend the region, which was being threatened by Indians allied with the French.

Arquivo Nacional da Torre do Tombo, Lisbon
(Below)

109

abuses" of that undisciplined population, especially certain of them who were better-off and not inclined to give up their privileges.

Soon he found himself in conflict with the first bishop of Brazil, Dom Pero Fernandes Sardinha, who had arrived in June 1552, after Pope Julius III had proclaimed the Diocese of Bahia in a papal Bull entitled *Super specula militantes ecclesiae.* Energetic and stern, Sardinha was ever ready to pressure the governor, for the poor example the governor set for the people began with his preferential treatment of his own son, Dom Álvaro da Costa. The sympathies of the citizenry became divided, the situation turned insupportable, and neighbouring Indians began to take advantage of the confusion by rising up violently in rebellion.

This latter threat was quelled only thanks to the prowess of the turbulent Dom Álvaro as a warmaker; he meted out exemplary punishment to the rebels, tearing down and burning up their villages.

Echoes of the dissension between the two principal figures in the colony reached Lisbon, and Dom João III recalled the bishop, thus provoking one of the great tragedies of the period. The bishop embarked along with a hundred others, including leading members of the colony, on the ship *Nossa Senhora da Ajuda.* Passing through the River São Francisco, the ship touched shore near Cururipe (in present-day Alagoas), where the crew and passengers were attacked by Indians of the Caeté tribe, killed and devoured. To this day, Brazilian schoolchildren joke that it was only natural that Bishop Sardine *(Sardinha)* was eaten . . . .

Antarctic France

Adding to the various unfortunate experiences of Dom Duarte da Costa, there was the French attempt to colonize Rio de Janeiro.

The French initiative was assigned to Nicolas Durand de Villegagnon, Vice-Admiral of Brittany. No longer was there to be only the commercial contacts that the French – almost indifferent to Portuguese reaction – maintained with the Indians, who were fleeing in increasing numbers to French-dominated Rio de Janeiro and Paraíba as a result of the growth of the captaincies elsewhere. Instead, this time there would be real colonization; it even had the support and official incentive of King Henri II, who early in his reign had been vividly impressed by a Brazilian Fête offered to him at Rouen, on October 1, 1550 *(Items 154, 155)*. No less than fifty real Tupinambá Indians participated in this pageant, which featured an Indian village built in the middle of a mock Brazilian jungle on the banks of the Seine, replete with parrots, araras (a large fruit-eating bird) and monkeys.

In order to report on the country's prospects, deemed necessary despite much prior contact, the king sent to Brazil in 1551 the pilot and cartographer Guillaume Le Testu, accompanied by the Capuchin friar André Thevet, who would return later with Villegagnon. They sailed the whole length of the coast from Paraíba to São Paulo, producing copious geographic, economic and ethnographic data, as well as an atlas, *La Cosmographie Universelle*, consisting of 56 maps, now in the Ministry of the Army in Paris.

Rio de Janeiro received special

attention and would be the preferred site for the enterprise being prepared. Support came from many quarters: the noblemen Chantillons and Guise, Admiral Coligny and the Cardinal of Lorraine were among the enthusiasts; Henri II furnished the sum of ten thousand pounds and two excellent ships; merchants from Brittany and Normandy supplied the third.

On June 12, 1555, the colonizing expedition departed Havre de Grâce, commanded by Villegagnon and carrying a motley collection of some 600 would-be colonists, both Catholic and Protestant. Notable among them were the noblemen La Chappelle and Boissy, the pilot Nicolas Barre, and Thoret, all Protestants; and the Catholics Bois-le-Conte, a nephew of the admiral, the staunch patriot Cointra and the friar Thevet, who later wrote about his adventure in *Les singularités de la France Antarctique (The Wonders of Antarctic France) (Item 115)*, a fundamental work for those who would know the Brazil of the sixteenth century, its people, fauna and flora.

In November the squadron approached the Bay of Guanabara, and on the Island of Serigipe (today called Villegagnon Island and headquarters of the Brazilian Naval Academy) the admiral began construction of Fort Coligny *(Item 114)*.

Just as had befallen the Portuguese in some captaincies, there were problems: the intransigence of the leader, political dissension, social differences, problems with the Indians and principally with the French who were already living among the natives – all these things contributed to the failure of the enterprise. Bois-le-Conte and Thevet returned to France in search of help from various sources (and on this voyage Thevet may have introduced tobacco to Europe, although this is also attributed widely to his fellow Frenchman, Jean Nicot). They appealed to the French Protestant reformer John Calvin, who soon sent a substantial group of colonists led by Phillippe de Corgilleray du Pont. Among them was the shoe-maker Jean de Léry, who authored the celebrated *Histoire d'un voyage fait en la terre du Brésil (History of a voyage made to the land of Brazil) (Item 118)*, which follows the example of Thevet and is likewise an inestimable source of knowledge on the earliest days of Brazil. With this support, Villegagnon managed to reorganize the colony for awhile, but the problems soon reappeared, aggravated above all by the fact that the colonists were permanently confined to a tiny island, and also by Villegagnon's own rigidity. By the end of 1559 there was no alternative left to the admiral except to go himself in search of new and effective support, and so he returned to Paris. He did this at the worst possible moment, for the Portuguese were just beginning to react to this colonization attempt. That course could only end with the expulsion of the invaders, an achievement which the Jesuit fathers – fearful of Protestant infiltration – had been demanding incessantly.

The Jesuits in Portuguese America

Diogo Gouveia, the same man who had argued that Dom João III should institute the captaincy system by distributing Brazilian lands to the king's vassals, was

110. Leys, e Provisões, que el Rey Dom Sebastião nosso senhor fez depois que começou a governar.
Laws and Provisions that King Sebastião our lord made after he began to govern. 1570.

This compilation covers a wide variety of subjects: extravagance, arms, vagrants and idlers, districts in Lisbon where unmarried women should live, pepper, etc. . . . Of interest to us is the law issued in Évora, March 20, 1570, on freedom for Indians, which came in response to the oppression and abuses to which the colonists subjected the Brazilian natives.

Deriving from the indigenist policies of the governor, Mem de Sá, and of leading Jesuits, the law permitted enslavement only of Indians captured in "just warfare"; moreover, only those Indians could be enslaved who habitually attacked Portuguese or other natives in order to eat them. This was a progressive policy, in an epoch when scholarly debate raged over whether or not Indians were human beings.

The law caused outcries in Brazil and was consistently flouted, which obliged Dom Sebastião's successors to clarify or reaffirm it several times. Abuses continued, however, forcing the issue in repeated legislative measures during the colonial period.

Biblioteca Nacional, Lisbon (Page 199)

111. Enformação da missão do p.e Christovão de Gouueia as partes do Brasil no anno de 83.
Do clima e terra do Brasil e de alg.as cousas notaueis que se achão assi na terra como no mar.
Information on the mission of Father Christóvão de Gouveia to Brazil in the year 1583.
On the climate and land of Brazil and notable things that one finds on the land as well as in the sea.
1583. Fernão Cardim

These two manuscripts, together with a third, constitute what is called Treatises on the land and people of Brazil. *Their author, a Jesuit, sailed to Brazil in 1583. The first treatise consists of two letters to the Society's provincial, describing trips in which Cardim inspected the Jesuit colleges and residences. The second treatise focuses on the country's peculiar flora and fauna.*

His third work, not bound together with those shown here, is titled On the origin of the Indians of Brazil and their worship and ceremonies, *and is an insightful study of the Brazilian natives.*

Biblioteca Pública e Arquivo Distrital de Évora
(Below)

111

also responsible years later for reminding his monarch how convenient and useful it would be to engage Ignatius de Loyola and his companions in the Society of Jesus in the work of spreading the faith overseas (Gouveia had been Loyola's professor at the celebrated College of Saint Barbara in Paris). Obtaining a papal authorization, the Jesuit Father Simão Rodrigues set off for Lisbon in 1540, and the following year Francis Xavier departed for the East, marking the beginning of his far-flung apostolate. Coimbra, Évora and Lisbon soon had Jesuit colleges, such was the favour that the religious order received from the Portuguese monarch and the fame it so quickly accumulated. The logical consequence of this was that such colleges should be established in Brazil, so that when Tomé de Sousa arrived there, he brought with him the Jesuit mission mentioned previously, which included – besides Manuel da Nóbrega – Aspilcueta Navarro, Leonardo Nunes, Antônio Pires, Diogo Jacome and Vicente Rodrigues. Five years later, with the Jesuit Province of Brazil already a reality, and with Nóbrega as its head, the number of missionaries was 26, distributed as follows: Bahia - 4, Porto Seguro - 2, Espírito Santo - 2, São Vicente - 5, and Piratininga - 13. In this latter locale resided the greatest hope for the conversion of the Indians since there was much more interchange with them there, despite the negative side of this interchange, namely, the problem of the mixed-blood children, so refractory to discipline of any kind . . . . As if in compensation, the faith had reaped there a great harvest: the fiirst local white inhabitants to

enter the Society as "tongues", that is, as interpreters, and with them it was possible to begin to teach the faith in the interior of what is now the state of São Paulo, following an example already established in the interior of Bahia.
To correct the loose morals of the Whites, to convert the Indians and thus pluck them from the "barbarity" in which they had been born and raised, especially to abolish cannibalism, to stimulate and aid the Portuguese in their combat against the French invaders and to cure the sick: these were some of the many tasks of the Society of Jesus. An attentive reading of some of the fathers' correspondence, a part of which was printed as early as 1551 and 1552 *(Items 105, 106)*, one finds evidence there of the ardour and self-abnegation with which they dedicated themselves to their work; and one can weigh the enormous sacrifices they made. The letters serve also to acquaint us better with the land, the customs and habits of its inhabitants, and – most interesting to us today – to help us comprehend the differing world-views of Indians and Whites, the reasons why they sometimes managed to get along with each other and sometimes didn't, their oppressions and reactions, their collaborations and antagonisms: factors which sometimes would allow the land to develop rapidly under the Portuguese and at other times would place the settlers at dire risk.
Good examples of Jesuit thinking are the letters Nóbrega wrote to Father Ignatius Loyola in 1555: "The reason why our work will bear little fruit, at present, is that all these Indians along the coast where the Portuguese

inhabit are still undominated, and because so far only *degredados* have come here, the vilest and most perverse element of all the realm." Or, as Nóbrega affirmed to Tomé de Sousa in 1559, when the latter had already left Brazil: "Another sin springs up from this infernal source, namely that the Christians have taught the natives to steal each other and sell each other into slavery . . . In São Vicente those Tupinichin (i.e., Tupiniquín) peoples don't do this; but the Christians of São Vicente have taken many females from the Gato tribe (i.e, the Temiminó), to have as their wives, and they've given their fathers some payment in exchange, but the women are enslaved forever." This latter quote also suggests that European men had made some accommodation to the Indian custom of rendering goods in exchange for a wife, but without any recognition of the reciprocal rights and duties entailed by such an act. Unlike the Indian men, for whom exchange of women was – for better or worse – a means of creating mutual social responsibilites, for the Europeans it was a cash transaction resulting in simple ownership.

Also illuminating is this excerpt from Anchieta on the problem of the *mamelucos*: It would be "of very great service to God to have them and raise them on the same basis as the Indians and when they reach the age of reason, to send them off to Spain [i.e., to the Iberian peninsula], where there are fewer inconveniences and dangers that would lead them to ruin than there are here, where the women walk around naked and don't know how to refuse themselves to anyone, in fact they themselves importune

the men, throwing themselves into their hammocks because it gives honour to sleep with Christians."
And as if all these tribulations weren't enough for the fathers, Villegagnon was still in Rio de Janeiro with his Calvinists . . . .

Expulsion of the French by Mem de Sá

In December 1557, a new governor-general, Mem de Sá, arrived in Bahia, chosen by Dom João III shortly before the latter's death on June 11, 1557, at which time the monarch's widow, Dona Catarina, assumed the throne as regent for her grandson Dom Sebastião, a child of little more than three years. Also deceased was the French king, Henri II, he who had encouraged the creation of Antarctic France, a fact which would prove Dom João's choice a providential one.

A good politican and excellent administrator, Mem de Sá would transform himself in Brazil into a competent and valorous soldier as well. Fundamental for his success as governor was the clear perception he had of the important role already assumed by the Society of Jesus, and the advantages of allying himself with it in order for them to jointly consolidate Brazil's budding statehood.

Hardly had he disembarked in Bahia than the new governor undertook to restore internal order, seriously affected by the conflicts between his predecessor and the late Bishop Sardinha. Land disputes among colonists were resolved, while the completion of the royal mill at Itapagipe settled the problem of what to do with the poorer farmers, and also stimulated sugar production.
But there was the still larger

112. Itinerary and Travels of Utz Schmidl of Straubing, from Antwerp to Cadiz and the Indies.
c. 1554-55.

Schmidl, a Bavarian, embarked as a soldier on the expedition of Dom Pedro de Mendoza in August 1535 to the Rio de la Plata. After sixteen years of adventures, he began his return to Europe through Brazilian territory. In the captaincy of São Vicente, he observed relations between colonists and Indians, problems with the Jesuits, the Brazil-wood trade, the enslavement of the forest Indians and the development of the sugar industry. All of this he duly reported in this manuscript chronicle.

Württembergische Landesbibliothek, Stuttgart
(Below)

112

113. Wahraftige Historia und beschreibung einer Landtschaft der Wilden Nacketen Grimmigen Menschenfresser Leuthen in der Newenwelt America gelegen.
Truthful History and description of a Country of Wild, Naked, Cruel Man–Eating People in the New World called America.
Marburg, 1557. Hans Staden

Hans Staden was born in the Prussian city of Homburg around 1520. On the second of his two voyages to the New World, he was shipwrecked, washed ashore and wound up as an artilleryman at a Portuguese fort. While hunting one day, he was captured by Indians. Staden then spent nine and one-half months among his captors, under constant threat of being killed and eaten, until he was finally ransomed. His account, written in a simple and unpretentious style, was enormously popular in Europe. The illustration depicts cannibalism in detail.

*The New York Public Library
(Pages 188-189)*

problem of rebellious Indians. After gathering and resettling the peaceful ones in villages, which facilitated both religious instruction and the provisioning of the Whites' city with needed products, the governor went after those who refused to submit.

Intitially he met with no success. He sent his son, Fernão de Sá, to Espírito Santo, only to see him killed while covering the retreat of his soldiers from an unexpected Indian attack. Mem de Sá then decided to take personal control of the repression in Ilhéus, which was also at war with Indians who wouldn't accept the encroachment of sugar plantations and mills onto the best lands in the region. In two months' time the Indians were vanquished, obliged to abjure cannibalism and compelled to rebuild the sugar mills they had destroyed. In Paraguaçu he was even harsher in his repression: villages burned and resisters killed, perhaps to quench any thought of rebellion closer to the city of Salvador.

In short, it was a strong-arm policy of compulsory pacification, followed by resettlement in new villages – this being the task of the Jesuits, who could thus convert their flock even with few available priests.

For the French, the hour of truth came when the first contingent of requested reinforcements arrived from Portugal. In February 1560, Mem de Sá entered Rio de Janeiro and in the month that followed he attacked and destroyed Fort Coligny, which the French hastily abandoned just as the Portuguese forces, low on ammunition, had themselves begun to lose their fighting spirit.

But the governor's troops, being so few in number, actually impeded a real settlement of the region; Mem de Sá could only write to Lisbon, recommending that it be populated. In spite of this campaign's only partial success, it was highly praised in a lengthy Latin poem of 2,463 verses entitled *Excellentissimo singularisque fidei ac pietatis viro Mendo de Saa, Australis seu Brasilicae India praesidi praestantissimo*, printed in Coimbra in 1563 *(Item 104)*. First attributed to José de Anchieta, it is today credited to Father Luis de Carvalho, a Latinist who taught at the College of Bahia; this change in attribution came about largely because of a certain anti-Indian tone one detects in the poem, a tendency utterly contrary to all of Anchieta's sermons.

So once again, Mem de Sá appealed to the kingdom, seeking to obtain reinforcements to dislodge the French from their Guanabara stronghold. Estácio de Sá, his nephew, was charged with this mission, at the same time that the missionaries Nóbrega and Anchieta were trying something even more difficult: to break the alliance of the Tamoios, who occupied the shore from Rio de Janeiro to the vicinity of São Vicente, and who were the principal lifeline for the French.

Estácio de Sá returned with aid, and a partial armistice with the Indians was concluded in Iperoig, where Anchieta spent a long time as a hostage. On March 1, 1565, the Portuguese returned to Rio de Janeiro, where they simultaneously began work on a fortification, a village and their hostilities against the French. Important allies had been secured in Espírito Santo: the leader Araribóia (baptized

Martim Afonso) and his temiminós.

For almost two years the battles and skirmishes went on; on January 20, 1567, with reinforcements brought by Mem de Sá, a final attack became possible, followed by the downfall and flight of the French, with the survivors and their Indian allies retreating to Cabo Frio. Although marked by the lamentable death of Estácio de Sá, killed by an arrow wound, the victory was fundamental to the destiny of Brazil: it eliminated the French enclave, which had threatened to split the Portuguese colony across the middle.

More than ten years of tensions, struggles and hard sacrifices had left the fine old governor weary, and he pled ever more forcefully to be replaced. But destiny didn't want this to happen, for twice the newly chosen governor, Dom Luis Fernandes Vasconcelos, tried to get to Brazil. The first time, his squadron was dispersed by a storm, and one of the supply ships fell into the hands of the corsair Jacques Sore – the very ship that carried Father Inácio de Azevedo and thirty-nine Jesuit companions. All of them were thrown overboard to their deaths, and today they are revered as the "forty martyrs of Brazil". On the second attempt, Vasconcelos himself was killed in combat against French Protestant corsairs.

These unfortunate events permitted Mem de Sá one final happiness, however: to see the king, Dom Sebastião, recognize the Indian policy that he, Nóbrega and Anchieta had championed for so long. The law of March 20, 1570 *(Item 110)*, prohibited the capture of Indians for whatever reason, except in a "just war", the latter to be defined and defended by local authority, which included fathers of the Society of Jesus, the parochial vicar, and the treasurer of the colony.

Mem de Sá passed away in March 1572, as Nóbrega had done two years earlier. Thus, neither had to suffer the disgust of seeing this Indian policy systematically mocked by the colonists, to such an extent that Philip II was obliged to revoke it and pass another, on November 11, 1595, giving himself the power to declare war, and proclaiming all Indians to be free and posessed of "natural liberty", and that for this reason their labour was to be justly remunerated.

Daily Life in the Colony of Brazil

After the disaster of Alcácer Quibir, when their king was killed by Muslims in a senseless battle, Portugal succumbed to the forces of the Duke of Alba and handed over the Crown to the Castilian Philip II in April 1581. But by then, the Brazilian state was already consolidated. All rebellion had been broken, excluding small pockets of indigenous resistance principally inspired by the French who, with their Tamoio allies in Cabo Frio and their Potiguares allies in Paraíba, persisted in the Brazil-wood traffic. Pushed back into the hinterlands, the Indians who were not resettled in Christian villages or enslaved were on the defensive. The exception to this was perhaps the "plague" of the Aimorés – as Anchieta, otherwise willing to condone the Indians' behaviour, called these terrible Tapuyas – who inhabited the vicinities of Porto Seguro, Ilhéus, and even approached the

114. Letter from Nicolas Durand de Villegagnon to the Duke of Guise, peer of France.
Nov. 30, 1557.

On November 10, 1555, three ships arrived at Rio de Janeiro with about 200 colonists to establish Antarctic France, a colonial experiment that would give concrete form to French interest in Brazil. Among the supporters of the enterprise were the powerful Guise family. On November 30, 1557, from the fortress of Coligny in Antarctic France, the colony's leader, Nicolas Durand de Villegagnon, wrote this brief letter to the Duc de Guise, reporting that he had completed the fortress, redeemed slaves, persuaded the natives to rebel against the Portuguese and forged an alliance with more than 3,000 Indians.

Serviço de Documentação Geral da Marinha, Rio de Janeiro
(Below)

114

115. Les singularitez de la France Antarctique, avtrement nommée Amerique.
The wonders of Antarctic France, otherwise known as America.
Paris, 1557. André Thevet

Thevet was a Franciscan monk and native of Angoulême. During his two sojourns in Brazil, he closely observed the land, its inhabitants, their customs and ways, flora and fauna, especially those in the environs of the Bay of Guanabara, where the French settlement was located. Some of the book's illustrations are by the renowned engraver Jean Cousin, based, according to Thevet, on crayon drawings he himself made on the spot.

The one shown here depicts the Indians' manner of making fire, and includes one of the earliest portrayals of the use of tobacco.

*The New York Public Library
(Below)*

115

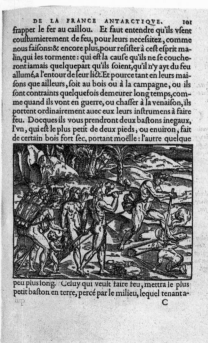

governor-general's capital of Bahia via the Camamu River. There were two extremely important factors contributing to this result, so auspicious for the Portuguese: first, the centralization of power and the new indigenist policy that Tomé de Sousa and, even more so, Mem de Sá implanted by listening to the wise admonitions of Father Nóbrega and his Jesuits. Still more relevant was the adoption of African slave labour, which started to be imported on a regular basis as of 1550, replacing – at an enormous advantage to the Portuguese – the former lords of the land in the work of tilling the soil.

In 1559 each sugar mill was authorized to import 100 more Africans, and in the three decades between 1550 and 1580, no less than 10,000 of them were brought into Brazil, destined for the sugar mills *(Item 101)*.

To the delight of historians, between the final years of Mem de Sá's office and the first years of Spanish domination, some magnificent pieces were written about the land and people of Brazil; and whether in manuscript or printed form, they have survived to our day. Thus, in sequence:

The writings of Pero de Magalhães de Gândavo, a great humanist, distinguished Latinist and friend of the poet Luis de Camões. These begin around 1570 with the *Treatise on the province of Brazil*, soon afterward rewritten as the *Treatise on the land of Brazil* and printed in 1576, with a somewhat different focus, under the title *History of the province of Sancta Cruz (Item 124)*.
Next, the *Information on Brazil and its captaincies* (1584), by Father José de Anchieta, and almost at the same time, the three works of the Jesuit Father Fernão Cardim, *On the climate and land of Brazil*, *On the origins of the Brazilian Indians*, and most important, *Information on the mission of Father Cristóvão de Gouveia to Brazil in the year 1583 (Item 111)*.

And finally, the *News of Brazil, and truthful description of the coast of that State (Item 126)*, authored by the sugar-mill owner Gabriel Soares de Sousa, without a doubt the most important work written in the 16th century about Brazil.

By comparing this notable group of works, we can get a bird's-eye view, from territorial, political, economic and social angles, of the evolution of the land discovered by Pedro Álvares Cabral. That gigantic and unknown territory, at first seen only as a possible resting-place on the route to India, had been transformed into an important jewel in the Portuguese Crown, which by then was lord over 350 leagues of fertile coastline blessed with excellent climate, many good ports and long, meandering rivers.

From Itamaracá to São Vicente, Portuguese sovereignty was incontestable, and Pernambuco and Piratininga already were assuming important roles as launching-points for expansion towards the natural borders, the rivers Amazon and Prata *(Items 125, 127)*. Gone was the old paradise of shipwrecked sailors, *degredados*, interlopers and their half-Indian children, hoping to find, in the Indians with whom they intermixed, a way to live "without God or laws or king". Brazil had evolved into a State, with the central government compelling obedience to the ordinances and rules in effect. And to these ordinances the colonists, nearly always against their inclination, had to bend themselves, ever fearful of the exemplary punishments that could befall transgressors.

Also, the French threat had been pushed back, whether this be the colonizing attempt of Villegagnon or the frequent attempts of the interlopers, attracted by lucrative commerce with the Indians.

The land's initially insignificant economic value, which had led to its being rented out for a meagre 4,000 cruzados per annum, had transformed itself completely. After "the Indian problem" was solved and sufficient manual labour brought in the form of African slaves, the development of the sugar industry, notably in Pernambuco and Bahia, was explosive. Around 1570, Gândavo calculated that there were 60 mills in seven captaincies, with annual production of 70,000 *arrobas* (2.24 million pounds) *(Item 124)*, figures which less than fifteen years later would rise to 112 sugar mills, quintupling annual production to 350,000 *arrobas* (10.5 million pounds) according to Father Cardim, or 466,000 *arrobas* according to the estimate of Gabriel Soares de Sousa. In parallel, although its numbers are not quite so expressive in terms of the overall economy, Brazil-wood continued to weigh heavily; cattle herds had multiplied; cotton production was already sufficient to clothe almost the entire Christian population; and as for *farinha de pau* (manioc flour), besides being a staple in the local diet, there was enough left over for it to figure in the trade with Africa.

Social life was already established in two cities (Salvador and Rio de Janeiro) and at least eleven towns, around which the sugar mills, plantations and farms of the Portuguese were spread, along with numerous villages of converted Indians, all of them with churches, kitchen-gardens and cattle.

The capital had 3,000 Portuguese, 8,000 Catholicized Indians and 4,000 African slaves. Olinda was not far behind, with its 2,000 inhabitants and an unspecified number of "slaves from Guinea", as the Africans were indiscriminately called. Colleges and Jesuit houses provided teaching in its various modalities and served as watchdogs for the rights of Indians and the maintenance of good behaviour. "This Brazil is already another Portugal, for the many amenities that come from the homeland" affirmed Father Cardim, referring naturally to the habits of those Whites in Pernambuco and Bahia who were better-off. In his opinion, they were more vain than the wealthy of Lisbon, and some had already amassed sizeable fortunes.

Sugar production was inherently elitist, tending towards concentration of wealth, a creator of enormous private landholdings and a stimulant to social disparity. Aside from the lands themselves, it demanded mills, stills, clay sugarloaf molds, warehouses, ox-carts and transport barges, at a cost of 50,000 cruzados for an average-sized mill, one capable of generating annual income on investment in the range of ten percent. This was more than enough to permit the happy proprietors to have houses in the city, silver utensils, stylish furniture, silks and linens, imported foodstuffs from the

116. Histoire des choses memorables advenues en la terre du Bresil.
History of memorable things encountered in the land of Brazil.
1561. Jean de Léry (?)

This extremely rare book is ascribed to Jean de Léry, who accompanied the reinforcements brought to the Bay of Guanabara in 1557 to aid the French colony. Léry was a shoe-maker and Calvinist theology student, and would become one of the colony's chroniclers.

The History *was intended as an attack against Nicolas Durand de Villegagnon, whose leadership of the French effort was controversial. The book transcended this minor objective, and is now a fundamental source of information on the earliest days of Brazil.*

The New York Public Library (Below)

116

Following pages

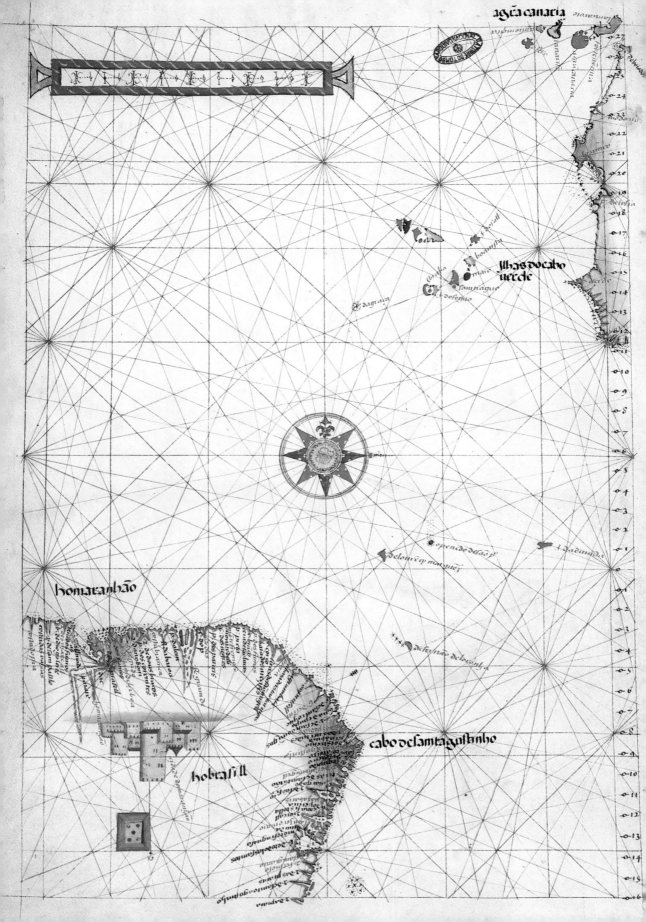

ÆQVINOCTIAL

BRASIL

T CAPRICORNII

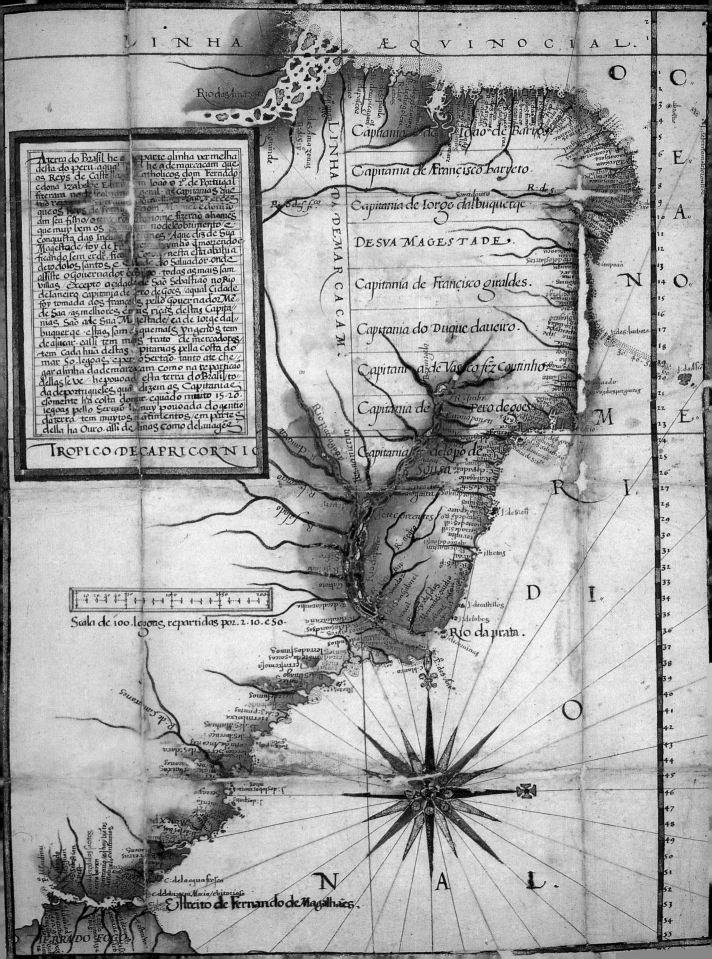

LINHA ÆQVINOCIAL.

Rio das Amazonas

LINHA DA DEMARCACAM

Capitania de Ioão de Barros.

Capitania de Francisco barreto.

Capitania de Iorge dalbuquerqe.

DE SVA MAGESTADE.

Capitania de Francisco giraldes.

Capitania do Duque claueiro.

Capitania de Vasco frz Coutinho.

Capitania de Pero de goes

Capitania de lopo de Souſa

TROPICO DE CAPRICORNIO

Scala de 100 legoas, repartidas por 2. 10. e 50.

Rio da prata.

Estreito de Fernando de Magalhães.

TERRA DO FOGO.

OCEANO MERIDIONAL.

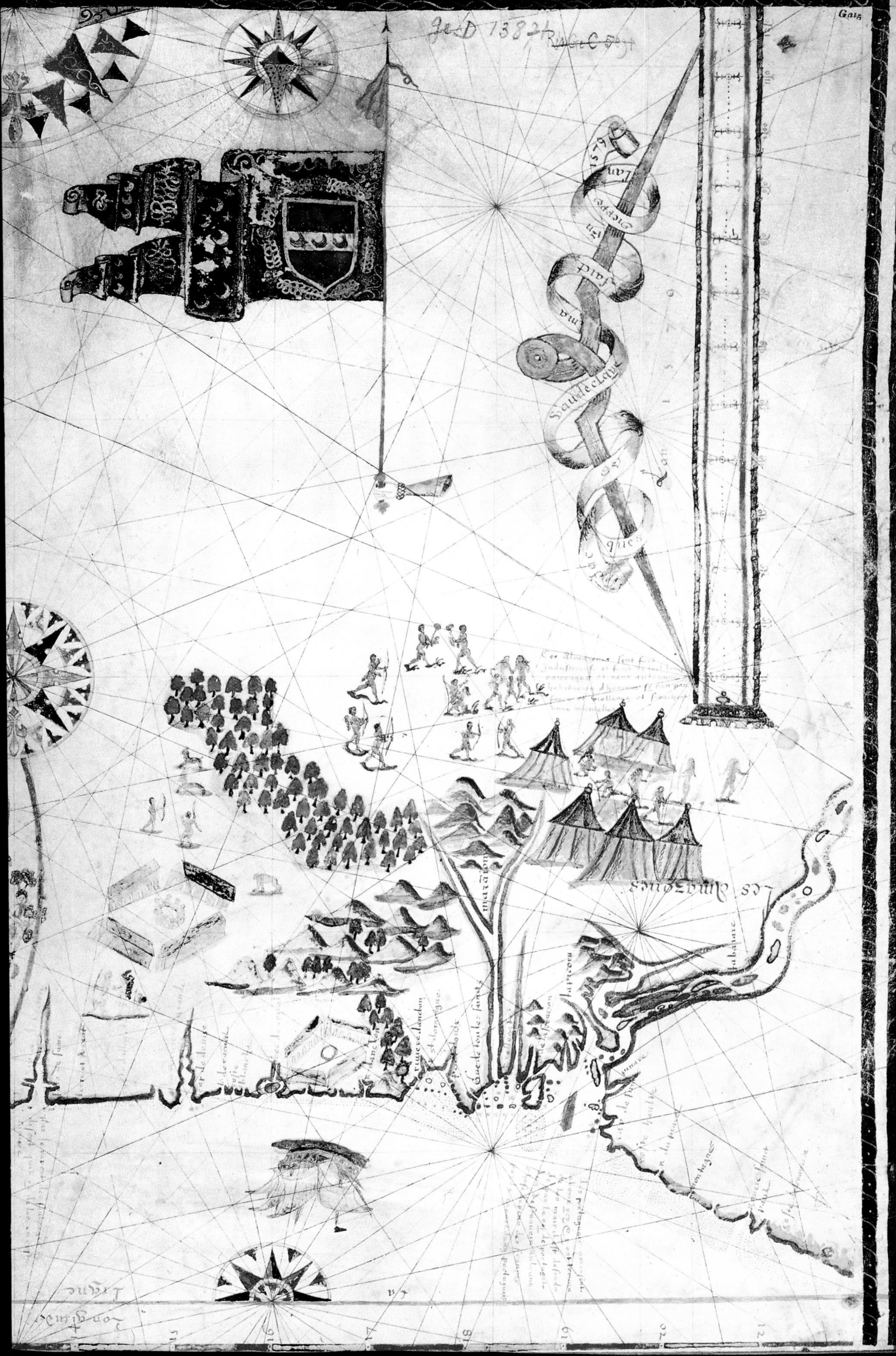

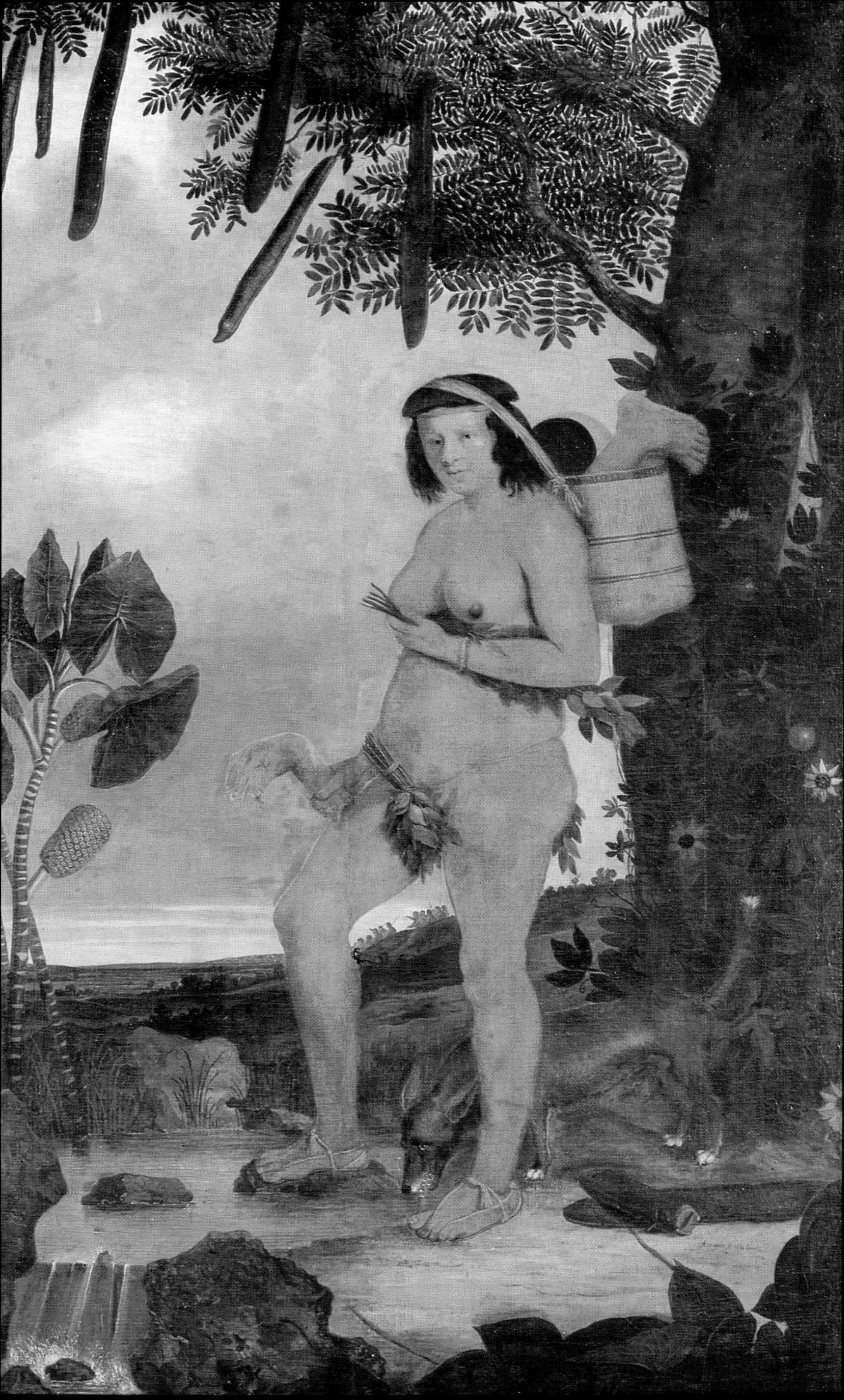

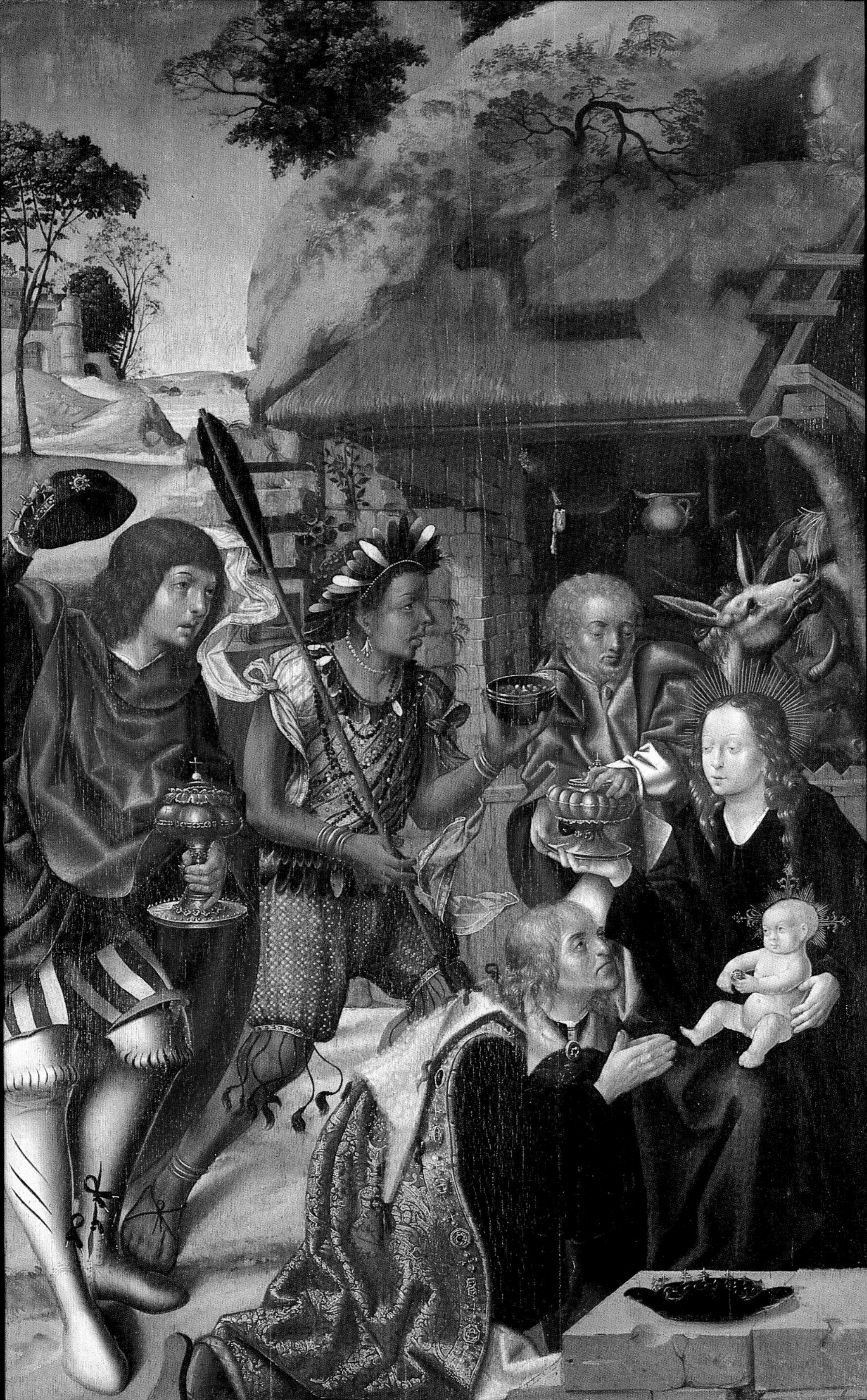

Cusco

16

Havana

15

Mexico

14

ning.

PARA

Porto Bello

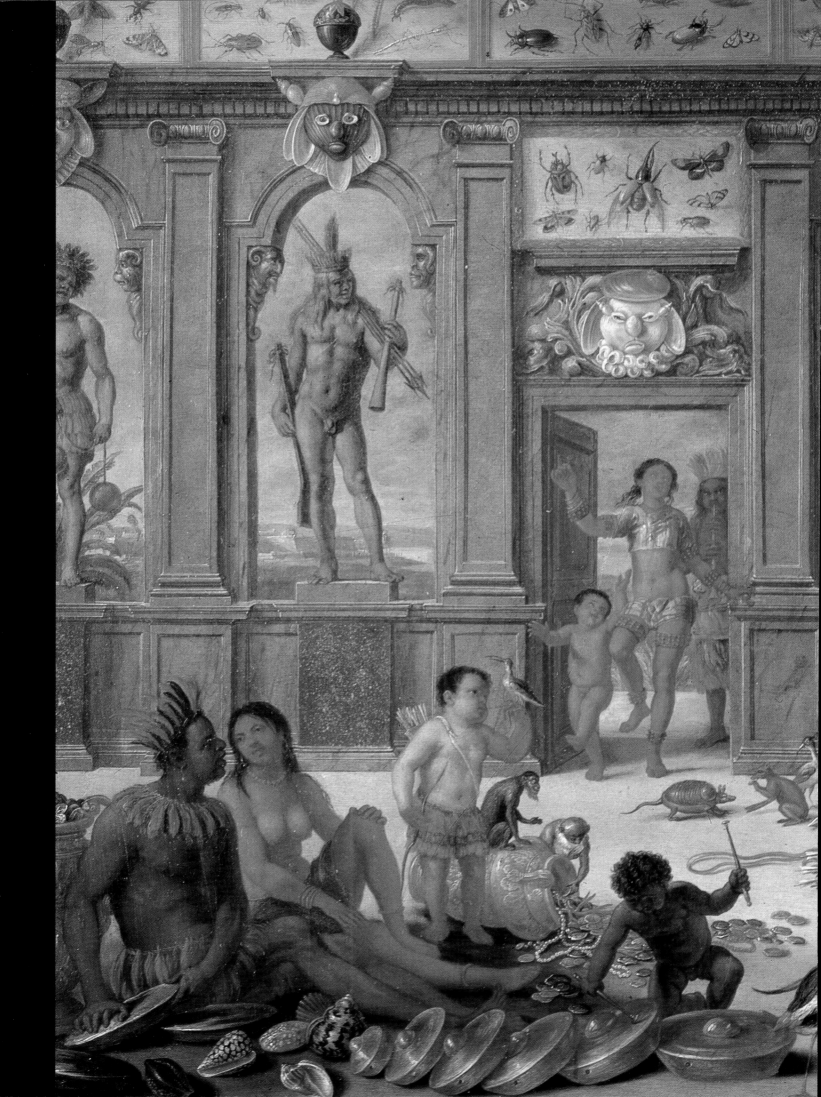

kingdom and a growing tendency toward a caste-like social system and interlocking marriages.

Evidently, this was not the general situation of the colonists (and still less so of their *mameluco* descendants); circumstances obliged them to rapidly adapt to their surroundings, giving up the habits they had brought from Europe, which only the lords of the sugar-mills could continue to cultivate. Marriage with Indian women was almost the only option available to new colonists, who for the most part were single and poor, and the same was true of the *degredados*, whose situation was certainly no better. As a result of these marriages, they came to adopt houses of wattle-and-daub and straw, domestic utensils of clay, with a hammock to sleep in and a leather trunk for storage. Clothing was of cotton; meals were basically cakes and porridges of manioc flour, plus wild game and fruits; and they also learned the necessity of constantly bathing themselves, something that European notions of hygiene prevented the elite from doing. . . .

Thus there arose with notable rapidity a peculiar kind of society, a Portuguese way of colonizing in tropical latitudes which the Brazilian sociologist Gilberto Freyre, in his genial and ground-breaking fashion, labelled "Luso-Tropical", and of which the equilibrating elements that inhibited a total assimilation of Indian ways were the Catholic religion and, principally, the unflagging work of the Jesuit fathers.

By the close of the first century of colonization, Brazil's destiny was already sealed: the country had affirmed its Luso-indigenous character, despite the growing desire that other Europeans demonstrated for it, first by multiple incursions of pirates and corsairs, and soon afterward by repeated attempts at occupation and conquest by the French, English and Dutch. With a growing and captivating African influence that accompanied the increase in the slave trade, this Brazilian national character would become Luso-Indian-African, and in this form would reach the twentieth century, a social experiment whose result is without equal on the planet.

117

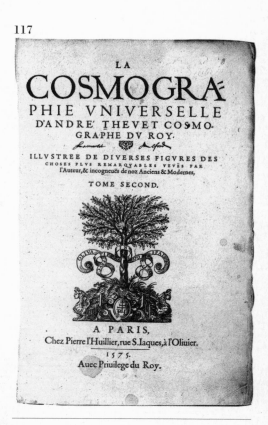

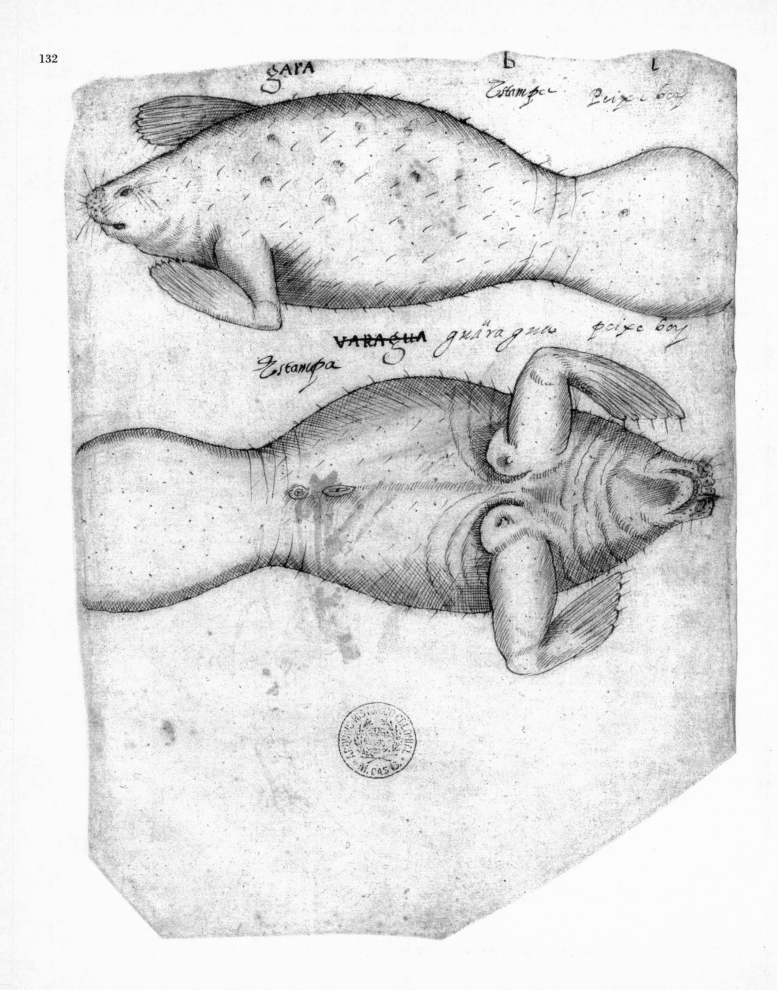

gara b l

Estampa Peixe boy

VARAGUA guaragua peixe boy

Estampa

118. Histoire d'un voyage fait en la terre du Brésil, autrement dit Amerique.
History of a voyage made to the land of Brazil, otherwise known as America.
1578. Jean de Léry

When he returned from his stay in the colony of Antarctic France, Léry was motivated to write the History of a Voyage by friends eager to know of his adventures, and by the desire to comment on Thevet's The Wonders of Antarctic France. Illustrated with six full-page engravings, the work also contains a dialogue between a Frenchman and a Tupi Indian, and three songs (lyrics and music) used in the Indians' festivities.

The illustration shown below is of a European man and an Indian woman engaging in the "greeting of tears", an Indian custom by which people who have been separated for some time recount the events of their lives in stylized form, accompanied by ritualized weeping. Shown opposite is a similar ceremony for a deceased.

The New York Public Library
(Below and opposite)

118

119. Atlantic Chart.
1534. Gaspar Viegas
Manuscript map on parchment

This map, by a Portuguese master, is based on the voyage of Martim Afonso de Sousa (1531-1533). It includes new plottings of Brazil's northern coast and of the Rio da Prata (Rio de la Plata) and its confluents, which sources are close to the São Paulo plateau. This would indicate that Martim Afonso had information that the Plata estuary could be reached from there, a plausible reason for his founding the settlement of Piratininga, precursor of present-day São Paulo, the largest city in South America.

Bibliothèque Nationale, Paris
(Page 192)

120. Luso-French Atlas.
c. 1538. Anonymous
Bound manuscript atlas on vellum

This atlas comprises fourteen charts of the Atlantic and the Mediterranean, followed by solar declination tables and solar and polar star rules. It was probably drawn by a Portuguese cartographer working in France, then illuminated by a French miniaturist.

Part of Brazil is shown on the Atlantic chart on display here. The illuminations show the cutting and transporting of Brazil-wood, battles between native tribes, incursions of whites into the interior, indigenous dwellings, natives sleeping in hammocks, local birds, animals and some flora.

Royal Library, The Hague
(Pages 190-191)

121. Livro de Marinharia, Tratado da Agulha de Marear.
Book of Seamanship and Treatise on the Mariner's Compass.
Handmade copy, with a universal atlas containing twenty nautical charts.
c. 1560. João de Lisboa

Books of seafaring (livros de marinharia) were, in the words of one authority, "heterogeneous compilations resulting from notes accumulated by pilots, to record all information which might be worthwhile in the practice of their profession". This one by João de Lisboa, a renowned chief pilot, contains information about explorations of the South American coast in the first years following the discovery of Brazil.

Arquivo Nacional da Torre do Tombo, Lisbon
(Page 209)

122. Map of Brazil and the South Atlantic.
1565. Sebastião Lopes
Manuscript atlas on paper

This is a beautiful specimen of Portuguese cartography, ascribed to Sebastião Lopes, who flourished from at least 1558 to circa 1595.

The map shown covers Brazilian territory from a point slightly beyond the Pará river to the island of Santa Catarina. The illumination, depicting an Indian man cutting Brazil-wood, with an Indian woman nearby holding a child on her lap, points up the importance which the harvesting of this dyewood held for Brazilian economy and Indian-European relations.

The Newberry Library, Chicago
(Page 210)

118

123. Tratado da Terra do Brasil.
Treatise on the Land of Brasil.
c.1572. Pero de Magalhães de Gândavo

Pero de Magalhães de Gândavo gathered the information for this book during the course of several years' residence in Brazil. It served as a basis for his later printed work, History of the province of Sancta Cruz. *This was published by António Gonsalves, the printer of the Lusíadas of Luís de Camões.*

Biblioteca Nacional, Lisbon
(Below)

124. Historia da provincia sãcta Cruz a que vulgarmente chamamos Brasil.
History of the Province of Sancta Cruz, which we popularly call Brazil.
Lisbon, 1576. Pero de Magalhães de Gândavo

During his residence in Brazil, Pero de Magalhães de Gândavo became conscious of the immense potential of the land, and of the fact that many foreigners (especially the French) wanted to possess it. News of Brazil was spreading throughout Europe, and Gândavo wished his fellow Portuguese to know that they could find haven there, regardless of how poor they were.

Based on two texts he had already written, Gândavo wrote the History of the province of Sancta Cruz, *in which he presented a historical sketch, as well as descriptions of the inhabitants, flora and fauna of the territory.*

Besides the title page, a dedicatory sonnet by Luis de Camões is shown from this book.

The New York Public Library
(Below and opposite)

125. Hand-drawn nautical chart of the northern coast of Brazil, from around the equator to the river São Francisco.
Signed and dated: "Jacques de Vau de Claye ma faict en Dieppe l'an 1579." ("Made by Jacques de Vau de Claye in Dieppe in the year 1579").

Little is known of this French map-maker, author of at least two nautical charts showing sections of the Brazilian coast. The one here was the result of exploratory missions prior to an attempted French colonization of the Brazilian coast above the Paraiba, after the adventure of Antarctic France had failed.

The drawings illustrate the everyday life of Indians and the transport of Brazil-wood; a pennant on a flagpole displays the coat of arms (with errors) of Philippe Strozzi, Lord Epernay, who had been secretly appointed French viceroy of Brazil, but died on his way there in a battle against Spaniards in the Azores.

Bibliothèque Nationale, Paris
(Pages 212-213)

123

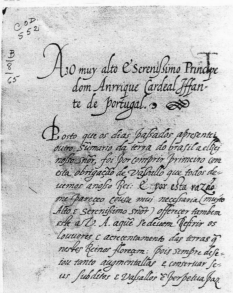

124

124

126. Roteiro geral com largas informações de toda a costa que pertence ao estado do Brasil e a descripçam de muitos lugares dela.
General pilot-book with much information on the entire coast of Brazil.
1587. Gabriel Soares de Sousa

Sugar-mill owner Gabriel Soares de Sousa resided for fifteen years in Bahia. He had started out to join in the conquest of the mines of the African kingdom of Monomotapa; however, when the ship on which he was travelling arrived at Bahia (1569), he decided to remain there and marry.

After inheriting from his brother the directions to certain mines in the interior, Gabriel Soares went to Lisbon and Madrid to petition for royal authorization to take possession of them. During a stay in the Spanish capital he made a copy of the directions and offered it to the minister Cristovão de Moura. It was printed in the 19th century, and since then has been considered the most complete overall study on Brazil produced during the Age of Discovery.

Biblioteca Pública e Arquivo Distrital de Évora
(Below)

127. Roteiro de todos os sinaes conhecimtos, fundos, baixos, Alturas e derrotas que ha na Costa do Brasil desdo cabo de Sãto Agostinho até o estreito de Fernão de Magalhães.
Pilot book showing all signs, landmarks, depths, shallows, altitudes and detours on the Coast of Brazil from Cape Santo Agostinho to the Straits of Magellan.
c. 1590. Ascribed to Luis Teixeira.

Popularly known as the "Ajuda Pilot Book", this book of sailing directions describes the east coast of South America from north of Olinda (Pernambuco) to the Straits of Magellan, and gives guidelines for navigating and reconnoitring the straits as far as their outlet to the "Southern Sea" (Pacific Ocean). The book also contains thirteen maps of the most important Brazilian harbours and coastlines at the end of the 16th century. The map shown here portrays the captaincies into which Brazil had been divided, with their territories extending from the Atlantic coast to the line established by the Treaty of Tordesillas.

Luis Teixeira, son of another map-maker, Pero Fernandes, later became cosmographer to the king of Portugal. Around 1573 he surveyed the Brazilian coast, which was probably the basis for this book.

Biblioteca da Ajuda, Lisbon
(Page 211)

128. Purchas His Pilgrims.
Part IV. 1625. Samuel Purchas

This is one of the first English-language compilations of voyages to include a first-hand account of Brazil, "written by a Portugall which had long lived there", namely Fr. Fernão Cardim. Purchas begins the account with Cardim's treatise "On the origin of the Indians of Brazil".

Noting his pleasure at having come by such a worthwhile manuscript, Purchas states a truth which, in an era of Iberian decline and North European ascent, was as much political and economic as it was literary: "England . . . hath reaped an English harvest of Spanish and Portugall seede". Later in the same preface, Purchas – a Protestant – cannot resist criticizing the Catholic Iberians for their "unchristian christianity" and "civil uncivil dealings . . with the Indians".

The New York Public Library
(Below)

126

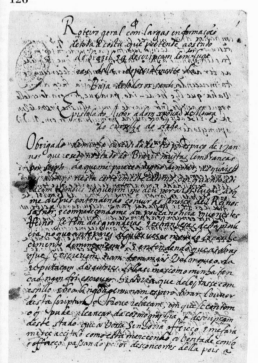

128

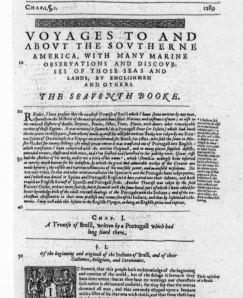

129. Adoration of the Magi.
Panel depicting the Epiphany, from the old retable of the cathedral of Viseu.
c. 1501-1505. Ascribed to Vasco Fernandes de Viseu
Oil on panel

Of particular note here is the presence of a Tupi Indian in place of the African king, making this perhaps the earliest European painting of a native Brazilian. The artist has attired the gift-bearer in shirt and breeches, to make him more presentable in church; however, the feather headdress, necklace and weapons are accurately copied from authentic Brazilian objects.

Also interesting is the strong resemblance of the face of the kneeling figure to the portrait on the medallion of the monastery of the Hieronymites, generally identified as Pedro Álvares Cabral.

Museu Grão Vasco, Viseu
(Page 219)

130. L'Ile du Brésil
The Island of Brazil.
c. 1550. Anonymous
Bas-relief sculpture on two wooden panels

The two bas-reliefs were removed from a house in Rouen that was demolished in 1837. The first depicts Brazilian Indians felling and transporting Brazil-wood – source of a red dye prized by Europeans. It was to be traded with French seafarers who gathered this dyestuff for France's flourishing textile industry. The second panel shows the logs being loaded into skiffs, while ships await the goods in the distance. The Portuguese responded to this Gallic trafficking by dispatching armadas to patrol the coast; to little avail, however, for the profits were enticing and, furthermore, King François I of France rejected Portuguese-Spanish hegemony in this part of the New World, uttering a famous dictum, "The sun shines for me as much as for anyone else; I should like to see that clause in Adam's testament which excludes me from the division of the world."

Musées Departementaux de la Seine Maritime, Rouen
(Pages 214-215)

131. Recueil da la diversité des habits qui sont a present en usaige tant es pays d'Europe, Asie d'Afrique ei Illes sauvages, le tout fait après le naturel.
A Compendium of the diversity of costumes that are presently in use in many countries of Europe, Asia, Africa and the savage Isles, all copied from life.
1562. François Descerpz

This book contains drawings of male and female types from many lands, accompanied by short descriptive captions in the form of quatrains. It juxtaposes fairly accurate depictions of Europeans and Asians with pictures of utterly fantastic creatures based on medieval legend. The Brazilian woman and man are rendered more or less correctly; the artist had as models the woodcuts from Staden's popular Truthful History and Description*. . . . and the engravings in Thevet's* Wonders of Antarctic France.

The New York Public Library
(Below)

131

132. Historia dos animais e arvores do Maranhão.
History of the Animals and Trees of Maranhão.
c. 1624-1635. Frei Cristóvão de Lisboa

The evangelization of northern Brazil was assigned to the clergy of the Province of Santo António (Portugal), and Fr. Cristóvão de Lisboa (1583-1652) volunteered to head the mission. He sailed for Brazil in 1624 and remained there until 1635, doing missionary work and gathering material for a four-volume Natural and moral history of Maranhão.

Those volumes have disappeared, but his descriptions of over 300 animals and plants of the region have survived, illustrated with somewhat crude but nonetheless valuable drawings, under the title History of the animals and trees of Maranhão.

Arquivo Histórico Ultramarino, Lisbon (Page 226)

133. Tarariu (Tapuia) Indian.
c. 1641. Albert Eckhout
Red, black and white chalk.

Very little is known about this Dutch artist – except that his parents were from Gröningen, where he must have been born c. 1610 – until his voyage to Brazil in 1637. His work is unsurpassed for its portrayal of the people, flora and fauna that the Europeans found in Brazil. He produced perfect depictions of Tupi and Tapuia Indians, as well as of mamelucos (Indian-Caucasian mestizos), mulattoes and blacks.
This study is one of a set of five, probably taken from the group presented by Count Johan Maurits to the Elector of Brandenburg in 1652, all of which portray Tapuias (their own name for themselves was Tarariu) of the Rio Grande do Norte.

Staatliche Museen Preussischer Kulturbesitz, Kupferstichkabinett,Berlin (Below)

134. Portrait of a Tapuia Indian Woman.
19th c. Neils Agaard Lytzen
Oil on wood panel, after an original by Albert Eckhout

After his return to Europe from Brazil, Count Johan Maurits made two large donations of artistic and scientific materials; one of these was to Frederick III of Denmark and included twenty-six life-size oil paintings; all are today part of the ethnographic collection of the National Museum in Copenhagen.

In August 1876, Brazilian Emperor Dom Pedro II visited the Danish capital and viewed the collection. Later, he commissioned Niels Agaard Lytzen (1826-1890), genre painter and miniaturist, to make copies of five portraits and a painting of a Tapuia dance scene. Painted in a vivid style with ethnographic precision, and placed in a natural setting valuable for botanical and zoological study, the Tapuia Indian Woman is a significant contribution to our knowledge of that ethnic group.

Instituto Histórico e Geográfico Brasileiro, Rio de Janeiro (Reproduction of the original by Albert Eckhout on page 216)

133

135. Portrait of Tupi Woman and Child.
19th c. Neils Agaard Lytzen
Oil on wood panel, after an original by
Albert Eckhout

Unlike the nomadic Tapuias, who shunned life in colonial communities, the Tupis rapidly became Christianized and integrated into the emerging social order. This painting graphically illustrates that process: the Indian woman is clad in a cotton skirt, and on her head she carries a rectangular basket (panacu) containing gourd vessels and a folded net; another vessel hangs from one arm. Her expression might suggest resignation to her lot as a domestic chorewoman, perhaps in the imposing plantation house, with its defence tower, which stands in the distance.

Instituto Histórico e Geográfico Brasileiro, Rio de Janeiro
(Reproduction of the original by Albert Eckhout on page 217)

136. Portrait of a Mameluke Woman.
19th c. Neils Agaard Lytzen
Oil on wood panel, after an original by
Albert Eckhout

The term mameluco was said to refer to the offspring of "indecent relations" between Indian women and Portuguese and Dutch men. However, these mestizo women were sometimes taken into formal wedlock by the Portuguese. One is not surprised, therefore, at the fine quality of this subject's white camisole, her pearl-trimmed headpiece, gold filigree earrings with pearl pendants, the necklace of gems and pearls and the ring on her left hand. All of this, plus her saucy pose, one hand holding aloft a basket of flowers while the other hitches up her camisole to reveal a portion of leg, display her confidence and heightened social status.

Instituto Histórico e Geográfico Brasileiro, Rio de Janeiro
(Reproduction of the original by Albert Eckhout on page 218)

137. Brasiliae Geographica & Hydrographica Tabula nova, continens Praefecturas de Ciriji, cum Itapuama de Paranambuca, Itamaraca, Paraiba & Potiji vel Rio Grande.
New Hydrographic and Geographic Map of Brazil, containing the Provinces of Ciriji, with Itapuama in Paranambuca, Itamaraca, Paraiba and Potigi to the Rio Grande.
1643. Georg Marcgraf
Printed map on 9 sheets

This remarkable cartographic item was engraved by Johan Blaeu in Amsterdam and dated 1643. It is generally agreed that its vignettes were the work of Frans Post. Though outside the period of this exhibit, it is presented here because of the extraordinary quality of these vignettes, many with informative captions. They portray the everyday life of Whites, Indians and Blacks. Besides the finest rendering of a sugar mill known to us today, the map also bears a rare depiction of a manioc mill (one of only two known to exist). The zoological and botanical illustrations are also valuable.

Map Collection of the Ministry of External Relations, Rio de Janeiro
(Facing page)

138. Olinda.
1652. Franz Post
Oil on canvas

In 1630, the Dutch invaded northeastern Brazil and attempted to establish a colony. The hilltop city of Olinda, former capital of the captaincy of Pernambuco, was judged indefensible by the Dutch against the guerrilla resistence of the Portuguese-Brazilian settlers. They decided to concentrate their forces in the nearby city of Recife. On November 24, 1631, Olinda was evacuated and the town was set afire. Post's painting depicts the ruins of the former capital.

Born in Haarlem in 1612, Frans Post went to Brazil in the service of the Dutch Count Johan Maurits, probably to document military and civil sites and structures in the newly claimed territory.

Museu Nacional de Belas Artes, Fundação Pró-Memória, Rio de Janeiro
(Page 224)

139. Americque.
1666. Jan van Kessel.
Oil on copper

These allegorical panels are loosely based on a seventeenth-century Wunderkammer, or cabinet of curiosities. According to specialists, the landscape and the fort shown are inspired by Brazilian works of Frans Post, while the two natives occupying the niches bordering the door are reminiscent of the Tapuias of Albert Eckhout. The twenty animals, live or stuffed, are based either on material brought from Brazil by the Dutch Count Johann Maurits of Nassau or on pictures by artists who accompanied him.
A personification of America sits on the floor, surrounded by symbols of the continent's mineral wealth. Meanwhile, the figures dancing through the door are Asian, as is the Japanese armour in one corner: a reminiscence, perhaps, of the early confusion between the "true" Indies and the new Indies of America.

Surrounding the central panel are sixteen fanciful wildlife studies, each identified with the name of a city of the New World, Africa or East Asia.

Bayerische Staatsgemäldesammlungen, Alte Pinakothek, Munich
(Pages 220-223)

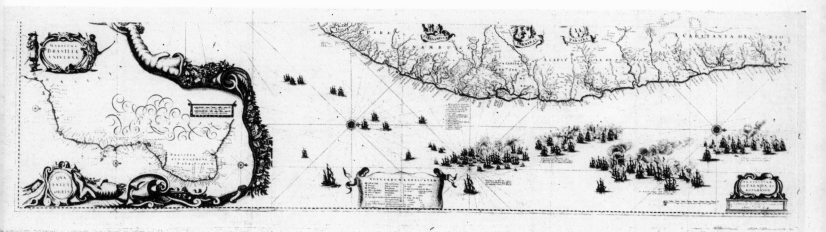

Section IV

Francisco Leite de Faria
Literary Echoes of the Portuguese Discoveries
Introduction by
Wilcomb E. Washburn

*The Portuguese arms and commemorative pillars placed in Africa
and Asia, and in so many thousand islands beyond the three
continents of the world, are material things, and Time may destroy
them. But Time will not destroy the religion, the customs, and the
language which the Portuguese have implanted
in these lands.*

From João de Barros, Grammatica, *1539-40. (Item 140)*

*. . . To tell thee all the dangers of the deep
(Which humane Judgment cannot comprehend)
Suddain and fearfull storms, the Ayre that sweep;
Lightnings, that with the Ayre the fire doe blend;
Black Hurracans; thick Nights; Thunders, that keep
The World alarm'd, and threaten the Last End:
Would be too tedious: indeed vain and mad,
though a brasse Tongue and Iron lungs I had. . . .*

*If old Philosophers (who travayld through
so many Lands, her secrets out to spye)
Had viewd the Miracles which I did view,
had sayled with so many winds as I;
What writings had they left behind! what new,
Both Starres and Signs, bequeath'd to Us! What high
and strong Influxes! What hid Qualities!
And all pure Truths, without allay of Lies!*

From Fanshawe's English translation of The Lusiads, *1655.
(Item 151)*

*I think there is nothing barbarous and savage in that nation, from
what I have been told, except that each man calls barbarism
whatever is not his own practice. . . .
The law of nature still rules them, very little corrupted by ours. . . .
it seems to me that what we actually see in these nations surpasses . . .
all the pictures in which poets have idealized the golden age . . .
no custom of servitude, no riches or poverty, no contracts, no
successions, no partitions, no occupations but leisure ones, no care
for any but common kinship, no clothes. . . .*

*The whole day is spent in dancing. . . . their whole ethical science
contains only these two articles: resoluteness in war and affection
for their wives.*

*From Michel de Montaigne, "Des Cannibales", Essais, 1580.
(Item 156)*

Literary Echoes of the Portuguese Discoveries

The cultural impact of Portuguese exploration and discovery is little understood by most Americans, but it is strongly felt by both the discoverers and "the discovered". The official language of six countries bordering on the Atlantic is Portuguese, and the language has more than 170 million native speakers, far more than the number who speak Italian, German or French.

As for the Portuguese and other Europeans, the very existence of the New World raised doubts about their own political and social systems. Were the harsh penal codes and rigid hierarchies of the Old World ordained from on high? To writers like Sir Thomas More, Michel de Montaigne and Daniel Defoe, the apparent freedom, ease and innocence of life among the "natural men" of the New World suggested that they were not. Thus, while the natives of the New World were required to accommodate themselves to European political, linguistic and religious values, the Old World experienced a cultural and intellectual shock that immediately challenged traditional social assumptions and, eventually, European political authority.

W.E.W.

This essay describes only printed works, since only such works could have had literary echoes or cultural impact. Thus, in this section we will not point out printed works which had only one edition, or which do not refer directly or indirectly, historically or literarily, to the Portuguese discoveries in the Atlantic. However, reference will be made, finally, to the first work printed and published in Brazil, which is still preserved in a booklet edition and which does not in fact mention the Portuguese discoveries in the Atlantic. Even though the previous reason may not be convincing, this first printed work from Brazil is pointed out because the press had literary echoes and cultural impact. It also stresses how that first printed work appeared very late, in 1747, and without the required licences, which soon prompted its prohibition and the consequent rarity of such work.

The oldest known printed work that refers to the Portuguese navigations of the Atlantic is a letter, translated into Latin, written by "Albericus Vesputius" to "Laurentio Petri de Medicis"; that is, written by Amerigo Vespucci to Lorenzo the son of Pier Francesco de Medici, in which the former relates the voyage which he is supposed to

Mundus nouus.
The New World.
1505. Amerigo Vespucci

This pamphlet, extremely rare, is the oldest known printed work that describes a voyage to Brazil. It is based on a letter Vespucci wrote in Lisbon in August 1502, addressed to Lorenzo de Pier Francesco de' Medici, the lord of his native city of Florence. As part of the expedition of Gonçalo Coelho to reconnoitre the Brazilian coast shortly after its discovery by Cabral, Vespucci brought his cultured sensibility to bear on the astonishing sights, people and phenomena of the New World. His engaging style and seemingly erudite descriptions made his letter a success as soon as it was published, and it went through numerous re-editions in many languages, helping establish Vespucci's fame. Prior to his voyages to the New World, Vespucci had been a merchant and provisioner of ships.

*The New York Public Library
(Page 238)*

Cosmographiae Introductio.
Introduction to Cosmography.
Saint-Dié, April 25, 1507.
Martin Waldseemüller

This work was of fundamental importance in the transformation of the accounts of Atlantic Discoveries into formal history. Published several times in the first half of the sixteenth century, the booklet states that the fourth part of the world (the other three parts being Europe, Asia and Africa), since it was discovered by Amerigo Vespucci, ought therefore to be called "America". The book is opened to the page (folio a5 v) on which this recommendation is made. This incorrect affirmation was gradually accepted and the name "America" came into general use as the designation first for Brazil, and then for all the New World.

*The New York Public Library
(Page 239)*

Mundus nouus.

Albericus Vesputius Laurentio Petri
de medicis Salutem plurimam dicit.

Vperioribus diebus satis ample tibi scripsi de reditu meo ab
nouis illis regionibus:q̃s z classe:z impẽsis: z mãdato istius
serenissimi Portugalie Regis pquesiuimus:z inuenimus: quasq̃
nouũ mundũ appellare licet. Q̃n apud maiores nr̃os nulla de ip̃is
fuerit habita cognitõ z audiẽtibus oĩbus sit nouissima res. Eteñ
hec opinionẽ nr̃oꝝ antiquoꝝ excedit: cum illoꝝ maioꝛ pars dicat
vltra lineã equinoctialem:z versus meridiẽ non esse ꝑtinentẽ: sed
mare tm̃ q̃ atlanticũ vocare: z siqui eaꝝ cõtinentẽ ibi esse affirma
uerũt.eam esse terrã habitabilẽ multis ratõnibus negauerũt. Sed
hanc eoꝝ opinionẽ esse falsam:z veritati oĩno ꝑtrariã hec mea vlti
ma nauigatõ declarauit: cũ in partibus illis meridianis ꝑtinentẽ
inuenerim frequẽtioꝛib° p̃plis:z aĩalibus habitatã:q̃ nr̃am Euro
pam.seu Asiam: vel Africam:z insup aerem magi tꝑatum z ame
nũ:q̃ in quauis alia regione nobis ꝑgnita. p̃ut inferius intelliges
vbi succincte tm̃ reꝝ capita scribemus. z res digniores annotatõe.
et memoꝛia.que a me vel vise.vel audite in hoc nouo mũdo fuere.
vt infra patebit.

℄ Prospero cursu q̃rtadecima mensis Maij Millesimoquingẽte
simoprimo recessimus ab Olysippo mãdãte p̃fato Rege cũ tribus
nauibus ad inqrendas nouas regiones ṽsus austrũ Viginti men
sibus ꝑtinẽter nauigauimus ad meridiẽ. Cuius nauigatõis oꝛdo
talis est.Nauigatio nr̃a fuit per insulas fortunatas.sic olim dictas
nũc aũt nũcupanꝶ insule magne canarie.que sunt in tercio climate
et in ꝑfinibus habitati occidẽtis. Jnde p occeanũ totũ littus Afri
cũ. et partẽ Ethiopici ꝑcurrimus vsq̃ ad promotoꝛiũ Ethiopum
sic a Ptolomeo dictũ.quod nũc a nr̃is appellaꝶ caput viride. z ab
Ethiopicis Geseghice.z regio illa mandinga gradibus q̃tuoꝛde
im intra toꝛridam zonã a linea equinoctiali ṽsus Septentrionẽ.
que a nigris gẽtibus z p̃plis habitaꝶ. Jbi resumptis viribus. z ne
cessariis nr̃e nauigatõni extulimus anchoꝛas. et expãdimus vela
ventis.et nr̃m iter per vastissimũ occeanũ dirigẽtes ṽsus Antarti
cum parumꝙ per occidentẽ infleximus per ventũ. qui Vulturus
diciꝶ.z a die qua recessimus a dicto promotoꝛio duũ mensũ.z triũ
dieꝝ spacio nauigauimus anteꝙ vlla terra nobis appareret. Jn ea
aũt maris vastitate quid passi fuerimus. q̃ naufragi picula.z que
coꝛpis incõmoda sustinuerimus. quibusꝙ anxietatibus animi la

COSMOGRPHIAE

Capadociam/Pamphiliam/Lidiam/Ciliciã/Armẽ
nias maiorẽ & minorẽ.Colchiden/Hircaniam/Hi
beriam/Albaniã:et prẹterea mltas quas singilatim
enumerare longa mora esset.Ita dicta ab eius nomi
nis regina.

Nũc ỷo & hẹ partes sunt latius lustratæ/& alia
quarta pars per Americũ Vesputiũ(vt in sequenti
bus audietur)inuenta est/quã non video cur quis
iure vetet ab Americo inuentore sagacis ingenij vi
Ameri‐ ro Amerigen quasi Americi terrã / siue Americam
ca dicendã:cũ & Europa & Asia a mulieribus sua sor
tita sint nomina.Eius situ & gentis mores ex bis bi
nis Americi nauigationibus quæ sequunt̃ liquide
intelligi datur.

Hunc in modũ terra iam quadripartita cogno‐
scit̃:et sunt tres primẹ partes cõtinentes/quarta est
insula:cũ omni quaqɜ mari circũdata conspiciat̃.Et
licet mare vnũ sit quẽadmodũ et ipsa tellus/multis
tamen sinibus distinctum / & innumeris replẹtum
Priscia insulis varia sibi noĩa assumit:quẹ et in Cosmogra
nus. phiæ tabulis cõspiciunt̃/& Priscianus in tralatione
Dionisij talibus enumerat versibus.
Circuit Oceani gurges tamen vndiqɜ vastus
Qui q̃uis vnus sit plurima nomina sumit.
Finibus Hesperijs Athlanticus ille vocatur
At Borẹɜ qua gens furit Armiaspa sub armis
Dicit̃ ille piger necnõ Satur,idẽ Mortuus est alijs.

140. Grammatica da lingua portuguesa com os mandamentos da santa madre igreja.
A Grammar of the Portuguese language, with the commandments of the Holy Mother Church.
Lisbon, 1539. João de Barros

João de Barros, besides being a notable historian (see Item 147), was one of the first Portuguese scholars to deal with linguistic and grammatical problems. Shown here is the world's only known copy of the first part of his grammar book, or primeira cartinha, as he called it, intended for the instruction of children from Africa and Asia at the Convent of St. Elói in Lisbon. The second part was published the following year.

This linguistic and religious instruction would prove more lasting than the stone padrões that the Portuguese left on the shores of the newly discovered lands, as Barros himself says in the book. In fact, the Portuguese language and the Catholic faith are, in Brazil as in the Lusophone countries of West Africa, eternal reminders of the Portuguese discoveries.

Biblioteca Nacional, Rio de Janeiro (Below)

140

have made along the coast of Brazil in service of the king of Portugal in 1501-1502. In various editions of this short work, it is known as the *Mundus Novus*, the "New World" *(Page 238)*, a designation that began to be applied to what was later called America. According to the bibliographer Borba de Moraes, twelve or thirteen editions of this work were published in Latin alone before Vespucci's death in 1512, in addition to several in German and French, one in Flemish and one in Czech. Volume 26 of the *Bibliotheca Americana* by J. Sabin, published in 1935, describes in fine and accurate detail twenty-six editions of the letter as a separate work, and points out many other editions of it as part of collections of accounts of voyages.

Oddly, not one edition of this work is known to have been printed in the nations which were most interested in its publication, namely, Portugal and Spain. This is quite symptomatic, and leads us to doubt the truthfulness of this voyage of Vespucci along the coast of Brazil. Although the noted bibliographer Borba de Moraes has affirmed it, no edition of this letter as a separate work is known to have been made in French, but four Latin editions were printed in Paris. The historicity of this voyage of Vespucci, between May of 1501 and September of 1502 and extending all along the coast of Brazil, has been doubted. It cannot be doubted, however, that the little book that narrates this voyage had, during the first two decades of the 16th century, a clamorous literary echo and great cultural impact. It is the first known printed work that refers exclusively to Brazil and

to the discoveries of the Portuguese in the Atlantic. This booklet was still to be published in its repeated German and French editions, when there appeared in Italy, most probably in Florence, another booklet with the title: *Lettera di Amerigo Vespucci delle isole nuouamente trouate in quattro suoi viaggi*; that is, "Letter of Amerigo Vespucci concerning the islands recently found in his four voyages". This letter, written from Lisbon on September 4, 1504, describes four voyages which Vespucci is supposed to have made to the new world: to wit, the first in 1497 to the coast of present-day Mexico and the United States; the second in 1499 under the direction of Alonso de Hojeda or of Vicente Pinzon to the coast of Guiana and Venezuela; a third to the coast of Brazil from 3 degrees to 50 degrees South Latitude, from May 14, 1501, until September 7, 1502, this being the same voyage about which the first booklet was published; and finally the fourth voyage, from May 10, 1503, until June 18, 1504, on which Vespucci is presumed to have voyaged from the Bay of All Saints in Brazil to a stopping-point situated 260 leagues to the south.

The "Lettera" must have been printed in 1506 since, as will be seen, its Latin translation was published in April 1507, in Saint Dié, France. The person to whom the letter was addressed, although not indicated in the printed versions, appears in two manuscripts preserved in Florentine libraries and was Piero Soderini, the "gonfaloniere" (supreme magistrate) of the Republic of Florence. Of that "Lettera" in Italian, only one separate edition is known, and today is extremely rare, existing in six or seven exemplars, one of which is at Princeton University in the United States. There was also a very rare German translation, which was printed in two different versions in Strasbourg by Johannes Grüniger on March 18, 1509, and in the opening mentions the names of the kings, Fernando of Castile and Manuel of Portugal. There were, moreover, eight published editions containing extracts from this letter, in German, Dutch, Latin, English and Czech, between 1505-1506 and 1510-1515. These editions are minutely described by Wilberforce Eames in the *Bibliotheca Americana of J. Sabin.*

Overall, then, the account of the supposed four voyages of Vespucci had 18 editions in the first half of the 16th century: seven as part of the Latin compilation entitled *Cosmographiæ Introductio* (Page 239), produced by Martin Waldseemüller, one separate edition in Italian, two separate editions in German, and eight consisting only of extracts in German (3), Flemish (2), Latin (1), English (1) and Czech (1). Although this account is not considered entirely truthful, there is no doubt that in the first half of the 16th century it had tremendous cultural impact. Aside from this, the *Cosmographiæ Introductio* of Waldseemüller had extraordinary importance of its own in the history of the Atlantic discoveries, for this booklet is the first to say that the fourth part of the globe, that is, the New World, should be called America, after its supposed discoverer, Amerigo Vespucci. The text reads as follows: "In the antarctic [i.e., southern] region there are situated the extreme portion of Africa, recently discovered, . . . and the fourth part of the world, which since it was discovered by Amerigo, ought to be called Amerigen, that is, the land of Amerigo, or America." In the same year of 1507 Waldseemüller, a professor of cosmography, published a series of maps for which the *Cosmographiæ Introductio* was to be the complement and on which the fourth part of the world is designated with the name "America". These maps were thought to have been lost, but were found at the beginning of this century in a private German library, and were brought to our attention in 1903 by the Jesuit, Joseph Fischer.

In 1509 in Strasbourg, there was published a booklet entitled *Globus mundi. Declaratio siue descriptio mundi . . . Et . . . de quarta orbis terrarum parte nuper ab Americo reperta*; that is, "Declaration and description of the world . . . And . . . concerning the fourth part of the world, of the lands recently discovered by Americo". On the frontispiece, below the title, a globe is reproduced with a representation of Europe, Africa, half of Asia and the extreme eastern part of Brazil, bearing the name "Nüwwelt", that is, New World. This globe is reproduced three times in the text, wherein on folio B[3] the recently discovered fourth part of the world is again called America. After 1509 the word "America" came into common use to designate the new world. We must note that even if one admits the truthfulness of the supposed four voyages of Vespucci, he actually discovered nothing, for those voyages were always as part of an armada commanded by someone else.

141. Paesi novamente retrovati et Novo Mondo de Alberico Vesputio Florentino intitulato.
Lands newly rediscovered and named the New World by Amerigo Vespucci of Florence.
1508. Fracanzano Montalboddo

This book deals almost entirely with the Portuguese discoveries, including the discovery of Guinea and Cape Verde, the anonymous account of the pilot on the voyage of Pedro Álvares Cabral, and the voyage of Corte-Real to North America. Most important in it, though, is the letter of Amerigo Vespucci, a merchant who accompanied three voyages to the New World. By the very popularity of his accounts (and a good amount of exaggeration) he became credited with discovering part of the New World, which came to be named after him, "America".

This work was published six times in Italian shortly after its first issue, and was the model for the various editions in Latin, German and French, also shown here.

The New York Public Library (Below)

141

Paesi nouamente retrouati, & Nouo Modo da Alberico Vespu tio Florentino intitulato.

142. Itinerarium Portugallensium e Lusitania in Indiam & inde in Occidentem & demum ad aquilonem.
Portuguese Voyages from Lusitania to India and from there to the West and finally to the north.
Milan, 1508. Fracanzano Montalboddo

This book is a Latin version of the "Countries newly rediscovered. . .", translated by the Cistercian monk Arcangelo Madrignano. It helped disseminate news of Portuguese-sponsored explorations among educated Latinists of the era. The title of this version, instead of referring only to Brazil, the land Vespucci named the "New World", refers also to the Portuguese voyages to India and to North America, which is more exact, since the voyages to those other parts occupy a large part of the book.

The New York Public Library (Below)

142

Who discovered the land would then have been the commanding officers of those armadas, whose names Vespucci never mentions, which is typical of him. On the third and fourth voyages, those which traversed only the coast of Brazil, the commanding officer would have probably been Gonçalo Coelho.

In the same year in which Waldseemüller's *Cosmographiae Introductio* was published, another work was published in Vicenza, near Venice, entitled *Paesi nouamente retrouati Et Nouo Mondo da Alberico Vesputio Florentino intitulato (Item 141)*, "Countries newly found and named the New World by Amerigo Vespucci of Florence". The printing of this work, precious and extremely valuable, compiled by Fracanzano Montalboddo was completed on November 3, 1507, and consists of six divisions called "books". In the first book is the account of a voyage by Cadamosto to Guinea on orders from the Infante, Prince Henry; in the second are the accounts of the voyages of Pedro de Sintra to Guinea, Vasco da Gama to India and Pedro Álvares Cabral to Brazil and India; and the third book continues the account of the voyage of Pedro Álvares Cabral. These three divisions occupy more than half the book, folios [1]^r to [77]^v and refer exclusively to the Portuguese navigations. The fourth book deals with the voyages of the Spaniards, and is a transcription of the booklet published shortly before and entitled *Libretto di tutta la nauigatione de Re de Spagna delle Isole et terreni nouamente trouati*, "Booklet about all the voyages of the King of Spain over the Isles and lands newly found". The fifth book

reproduces the *Mundus Novus* letter of Vespucci; that is, the account of the supposed third voyage of the Florentine; and the sixth book contains letters from Italians residing in Lisbon concerning voyages of the Portuguese to Asia and to present-day Canada, plus a narrative by Father José Indiano.

Except for the fourth book, all the rest of this work refers exclusively to the Portuguese navigations. This work published, for the first time, the accounts of Portuguese voyages to Guinea, India, Brazil and North America. The one that refers to Brazil is the account of an anonymous Portuguese pilot, concerning the voyage of Pedro Álvares Cabral. Thus, the *Paesi* are works of great importance for our understanding of the Portuguese discoveries. Aside from that, they had forceful cultural impact, for they quickly went through five re-editions in Italian (Milan: 1508, 1512 and 1519, and Venice: 1517 and 1521), one in Latin (Milan: 1508), two in German (Nuremberg: 1508) and seven in French (Paris: all undated but all prior to 1530). Before 1530 the *Paesi* had no less than 26 editions. A Spanish translation has been noted, published in 1521 in Venice, but this most likely never existed since no one has ever encountered a single exemplar, nor has anyone ever described it. An Italian edition of 1508, published in Venice, is also mentioned, but this likewise probably never existed for the same reason. After 1530 the work continued to be published, either in its entirety or in incomplete versions, to such an extent that the number of editions is quite high. It is strange, however, that in Spain and Portugal, the nations most interested in knowing about this work, it was not published until the 19th century, in editions that include only some of the treatises contained in the original.

On July 1, 1508, a Latin translation of the *Paesi* was published, without indication of the city or printer, though it was most certainly in Milan. It was made by the Milanese Cistercian monk Arcangelo Madrignano, who dedicated it to the Vice-Chancellor of the Senate of Milan. At that time, King Louis XII of France was the Lord of Milan and its surrounding territory, which he had conquered in 1500 and left to his successor François I, who in turn, after his defeat at Pavia in 1525, had renounced the possession of this city and its territory.

Of this Latin translation there are at least two versions, depending on whether the frontispiece map reads SINUS ARABICUS or SINUS PERSICUS to indicate the Red Sea. In my 1977 work entitled *Bibliographic Studies on Damião de Góis and his Epoch*, I managed to locate 39 exemplars of it, more than the 34 that I located of the first Italian edition. Of these 39 examples, three are in Portugal, two in Brazil, and twelve in the United States. In Portugal there is now one more example, that of the Biblioteca Dom Manuel II, at Vila Viçosa, which the Foundation of the House of Bragança acquired in 1988. The title of this Latin translation is *Itinerarium Portugallensium in Indiam & inde in Occidentem & demum ad aquilonem*, "Itinerary of the Portuguese from Lusitania to India and from there to the Occident and finally towards the north" (Item 142). This title better conveys the

contents of the *Paesi*, which for the most part deals with the Portuguese navigations to India, Guinea, Brazil and North America. The title of the Italian original, as we said, is *Countries newly found and named the New World by Amerigo Vespucci of Florence*, or in the editions of 1517 and 1521, *Countries newly found by the navigations of Spain to Calicut and named the New World by the Florentine Amerigo Vespucci*. This title is more misleading than that of the Latin translation, since it says that the lands recently discovered are the ones that Vespucci called the New World. This is not exactly true, since the New World is America, or originally just Brazil to be precise, as we can deduce from Vespucci's account of his supposed third voyage, published in the *Paesi*. But in fact, the newly discovered lands to which this work refers are not only America and Brazil, but also Guinea and Asia, which have nothing to do with the New World to which Vespucci referred.

On September 20, 1508, the printer Georg Stüchszen published in Nuremberg a German translation of the *Paesi*, done by Dr. Jobsten Ruchamer under the title *Newe vnbekanthe landte Und ein newe weldte in kurtz verganger zeythe erfunden*, "New Unknown Lands and a New World recently encountered" *(Item 143)*. To this edition there was added as a final chapter the German translation of the letter of King Dom Manuel to Pope Julius II, written from Alcochete on June 12, 1508, about the provinces, cities, lands and places of the Orient, conquered by Portugal and for the Christian faith.

On November 8, 1508, the same printer, Stüchszen, finished

143. Newe vnbekanthe landte Und ein newe weldte in kurtz verganger zeythe erfunden.
New Unknown Lands and a New World recently encountered.
Nuremberg, 1508.
Fracanzano Montalboddo

This German edition of the "Countries newly rediscovered . . ." was translated from the original by Dr. Jobsten Ruchamer. In addition to the accounts of the voyages included in the original work, this version contains a letter from Dom Manuel of Portugal to Pope Julius II, written on June 12, 1508.

The New York Public Library (Below)

143

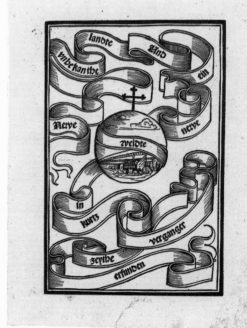

144. SEnsuyt le nouueau mõde et nauigations: faictes par Emeric de vespuce Florentin . . . .
What Follows is the New World and Navigations: made by Amerigo Vespucci the Florentine . . . .
1516(?) Fracanzano Montalboddo

This is one of the very rare French editions of the "Countries newly rediscovered . . ." translated by Mathurin du Redouer and published in Paris without any indication of the date of publication, except for the version shown here, printed by Galliot du Pré. In most of these editions, the text states somewhat exaggeratedly that all the navigations described therein were made by the King of Portugal, that is, in Portuguese ships, which is not exactly true. The occasional lapses from factuality in all these popular accounts suggests the degree to which the "history" of the voyages was already becoming a matter of public perception rather than of pure truth.

The New York Public Library (Below)

144

printing in Nuremberg the translation of the *Paesi* into the lower-Saxon dialect, based on Ruchamer's German version and translated by Henning Ghetelen of Lübeck, which today is in the Federal Republic of Germany. I have never seen this translation, entitled *Nye vnbekande lande Unde eine nye Verldt in korter vorgangener tyd gefunden*, and for my 1977 study I was able to locate only two examplars, both in the United States.

In a year that cannot be determined with certainty, in Paris, there was published the French translation of the *Paesi* by Mathurin du Redouer (*Item 144*), licensed in laws, under the title *Le nouveau monde et nauigations faictes par Emeric de Vespuce Florentin Des pays et isles nouuellement trouuez auparavant a nous incongneuz tant en lethiope que arabie, Calichut & aultres plusieurs regions estranges*; that is, "The new world and navigations made by Amerigo Vespucci the Florentine to the isles and lands recently encountered, previously unknown to us, in Ethiopia and in Arabia, Calicut and many other strange regions". As this edition is impressed with the royal privilege, it appears that it would be the first, and in 1977 I located eight exemplars of it, of which six are in the United States. There were three editions with a notice stating that they were for sale at the Rue neufue Nostre Dame on the emblematic shield of France, which means they were for sale at the bookseller who used that emblem, namely, Jean Trepperel and later his widow. There was one more edition printed by Philippe le Noir, another by Jean Janot, and another for sale by the bookseller Denis Janot. In sum, the *Paesi*, in its original

Italian version and in the other languages into which it was translated, was a veritable literary best-seller in the sixteenth century and had great cultural impact, as we can see from the sixteen editions mentioned here.

Late in the year 1516, there was published, under the supervision of Master Petrus Aegidius of Antwerp and by the artful printing of Theodoricus Martinus of Alost, typographers of the University of Louvain, the first and extremely rare edition of *Utopia*, by the famous English humanist Thomas More, now Saint Thomas More. This was a book that soon afterward was re-edited in Paris and Basel and went through dozens of editions, not only in its original Latin but also in English. It was also translated and published from early times in Dutch, French, German and Italian and more recently in Spanish and Portuguese. This famous work of fiction describes the imaginary voyage of a navigator who, having set sail probably from the coast of Brazil, reached and settled himself on an ideal island called Utopia. Thomas More based his book on the printed accounts of the supposed voyages of Vespucci, as found in the editions of the *Paesi*.

In March 1532, the Swiss humanist Simon Grynaeus published in Basel a collection of voyages, to which he gave the title, *Novus Orbis Regionvm ac Insvlarvm veteribvs incognitarvm (Item 145)*; that is, "New World of Regions and Isles unknown to the ancients". It is a thick volume that begins with a Latin translation (by Arcangelo Madrignano) of the *Paesi*, followed by a Latin translation of the account of the four supposed voyages of Vespucci as published by Waldseemüller. In 1977 I located 51 exemplars of this first edition of the collection of voyages published by Grynaeus, ten are in the United States, five in Portugal, and one in Brazil. There was soon a second edition, in October 1532, published in Paris by the printer Antoine Augereau in two versions, one sponsored by the bookseller Jean Petit and the other sponsored by the bookseller Galliot du Pré. Of this second edition, rarer than the first, I found 39 exemplars in 1977, of which six are in the United States, four in Portugal and one in Brazil. This compilation of voyages was then re-edited in Basel in 1555 and, translated into German, was published in Strasbourg in 1534, and then translated into Flemish at Antwerp in 1563.

The famous collection of navigations and voyages compiled by Giovanni Battista Ramusio, and published in Venice six times, to wit: 1550, 1554, 1563, 1588, 1606 and 1613, also included accounts from the *Paesi* in Italian, and after being translated into French was printed at Lyon in 1566. Thus, the *Paesi* was published an extremely large number of times throughout the 16th century, and propagated knowledge of the Portuguese discoveries far and wide.

When great Portuguese discoveries began to unfold during the reign of Dom João II (d. 1495), Rui de Pina, future chief-chronicler of the realm, had been in charge, since 1490, of writing and registering the famous deeds that were taking place. To carry out this task, he wrote an account of the voyage of Rui de Sousa to the Congo and

back in 1492. The original of this account has been lost, but a manuscript in the Biblioteca Riccardiana in Florence contains its Italian translation, which I brought to light in 1966. Later, in 1533, Garcia de Resende wrote the life of Dom João II, in which he practically copied what Rui de Pina had written concerning the Congo in the latter's own manuscript chronicle about the same king. That biography of Dom João II, together with other works by Garcia de Resende, was not published until eleven years after the author's death in 1545, and had some degree of literary and cultural impact, for it was re-edited eight times, in 1554, 1596, 1607, 1622, 1725, 1798, 1902 and 1973. It is true that it was never published in a foreign language, but the nine editions of this biography in Portuguese, of which three are of the 16th century, justify its claim to significance. The first edition, which was published in Lisbon in 1545, is a very rare work today; its very existence was doubted by some, and in 1977 I was able to locate only nine exemplars, all of them incomplete or imperfect. For this reason it couldn't be shown in this exhibition; but the second edition, published in Évora in 1554, is known through at least 24 exemplars, of which three are in the United States, another three in Brazil, and nine in Portugal.

In 1551 Fernão Lopes de Castanheda published in Coimbra the *Historia do descobrimento & conquista da Índia pelos Portugueses (Item 146)*, "History of the Discovery and conquest of India by the Portuguese". The first volume of this monumental work relates events up to 1504, and thus

145. Novvs orbis regionvm.
Basel, 1532. Simon Grynaeus

This collection of voyages, with a preface by the Swiss Simon Grynaeus, achieved wide diffusion, being published five times in Latin, once in German, and once in Flemish. In the Latin version shown here, Grynaeus reproduced the Latin translation of the "Countries newly rediscovered . . ." along with an account of four voyages of Vespucci, at least one of which is now doubted by historians.

Through such compilations, the Portuguese discoveries became much more widely known, and the name "America" came into widespread use to refer to the New World, even though its namesake – Amerigo Vespucci – was not a major explorer in his own right.

The Newberry Library, Chicago (Below)

145

Liuro quinto da primeira Decada da Asia

de Joam de Barros: dos feitos que os Portugueses fizeram no
descobrimento dos mares τ terras do Oriente: no qual se
contem o que Pedraluarez Cabral fez no anno de
quinhentos, q̃ deste reyno partio com hũa
grossa armada, τ o q̃ fez Joã da Noua
no anno seguinte de quinhẽtos τ hũ,
com outra de quatro naos.

¶ Capitulo. j. Como elrey por razam da nóua q̃ dom Vasco da Gama
troute da India: mandou fazer hũa armáda de treze vẽlas, da qual
foy por capitam mór Pedraluarez Cabral.

Lrey dom Manuel como éra principe cathólico τ q̃ todas suas coisas offe-
recia a deos, por esta merce q̃ delle tinha recebido, dáualhe muytos louuóres:
pois lhe aprouéra ser elle o jnstruméto per quẽ quiséra cõceder hũ bem tã vni-
uersal como éra abrir as pórtas doutro nóuo mũdo de jnfiẽes, onde o seu nome podia ser conhecido τ louuádo, τ as chágas de seu precióso filho Christo
Jesu recebidas per fẽ τ baptismo, pera redempçã de tãtas mil álmas como o
demónio naq̃llas pártes da jnfidelidade jmperáua. E era gratificaçã da qual merce q̃ tinha re-
cebida de deos, τ porq̃ o seu póuo se gloriásse nella, escreueo a todalas cidádes τ villas notáues
do reyno, notificádolhe a chegáda de dõ Vásco da Gáma, τ os grãdes trabalhos q̃ tinha passado, τ o q̃ aprouue a nósso senhor q̃ no fim delles descobrisse: encomédádolhe q̃ solẽnizássem
tamanha merce como este reyno tinha recebido de deos, cõ muytas procissões τ festas espiri-
tuáes em seu louuor. E como nos táes ajuntaméntos sempre concórrẽ diuérsos pareceres em tã
nóuos cásos, leixádo aq̃lles q̃ perderã pay, jrmão, filho, ou parẽte nésta viágẽ, cuja dór nã lei-
xáua julgar a verdáde do cáso: toda a outra gente a hũa vóz era no louuor deste descobrimento.
Quádo viã neste reyno pimẽta, cráuo, canella, aljófre, τ pedraria, q̃ os nóssos trouxerã, como
mostra das ríquezas daq̃lla oriental párte q̃ descobrirã: lembrandolhe quã espantádos ós fazia
algũa destas cousas, que as galées de Veneza traziam a este reyno. As quáes práticas todas
se conuertiã em louuóres delrey, dizẽdo q̃ elle éra o mais bem afortunádo rey da christandáde:
pois nos primeiros dous ánnos de seu reynádo descobrira mayór estádo á coróa deste reyno,
do q̃ éra o património q̃ cõ elle herdára. Cousa q̃ deos nam cõcedera a nenhũ principe de Es-
panha, nem a seus antecessóres q̃ nisso bem trabalhárã, per discurso de tãtos ánnos: nem se
achaua escriptura de Gregos, Romanos, ou dalgũa outra naçam, que contásse tamanho feito.
Cómo era tres nauios com óbra de cento τ sessenta hómeẽs, quasy todos doentes de nouas
doenças de que múytos falecerã, com a mudança de tam vários dimas per que passáram, diffe-
rença dos mántimentos que comiam, máres perigósos q̃ naueáuam, τ com fóme, sede, frio,
τ temor que mais a tormenta que todalas outras necessidádes: obrar nelles tanto a virtude da
constancia τ precepto de seu rey, que pospóstas todas estas cousas, nauegáram tres mil τ tan-
tas léguoas, τ contenderã com tres ou quátro reyes tam differentés em ley, costumes, τ lin-
guágem, sempre cõ victória de todalas jndustrias, τ engános da guérra que lhe fizéram. Por
razam das quáes cousas, posto q̃ muyto se deuesse ao esfórço de tal capitam, τ vassállos como
elrey mandára, mais se auia de atribuir á bóa fortuna deste seu rey: porque nam éra em poder ou saber de hómeẽs, tam grande τ tam nóua cousa como elles acabáram. Elrey de todas
estas praticas τ louuóres do cáso éra sabédor, porque naquelles dias nam se falaua em outra cousa: que éra parélle dobrádo contentamento, saber quam prompta estáua a vontáde de
seu pouo pera proseguir esta conquista. E porque pela jnformaçam que tinha da nauegaçam daquellas pártes, o principal tempo éra partir daquy em márço, τ por ser já muyto curto

includes the voyage of Pedro Álvares Cabral and the discovery of Brazil. It is the first book in Portuguese to describe this event, and it was re-edited in 1554, 1797, 1833 and 1924. Translated into French by Nicolas de Grouchy, it was published in Paris in 1553, a rare edition, of which I knew the location of only twelve exemplars in 1977. It was re-edited at Antwerp in 1554 and in Antwerp and Paris in 1576. The Spanish translation was also published at Antwerp in 1554, and the German translation in 1556, without mentioning Castanheda's name nor the place of its printing; of this one, I located six exemplars in 1977. It has been written that an Italian translation was done by A. de Cravaliz and published in Rome in 1556, but I was not able to locate any exemplar of it as it is extremely rare, if it existed at all. In 1577 and 1578 two Italian editions were published in Venice, and in 1582 the English translation of this important and famous work was published in London. Thus this work went through 13 editions in Portuguese, French, Spanish, German, Italian and English, producing notable literary and cultural impact.

In June 1552, the *Asia de João de Barros (Item 147)* was published in Lisbon. This was the first of his so-called "Decades", which recount the discoveries and conquests of the Portuguese in the Far East up to 1505. This monumental work, on which João de Barros laboured for many years, refers also to the Portuguese voyages along the coast of Africa and the discovery of Brazil by Pedro Álvares Cabral. The first edition of 1552, is an extremely valuable work. It

was re-edited in 1628, 1752, 1778, 1923, 1945 and 1973, and had two editions in Italian, published in Venice in 1561 and 1562, and two in German (although those were incomplete) edited in 1821 and 1844, in addition to French and Dutch versions consisting of lengthy extracts. I managed to locate 47 exemplars of this work in 1977, of which 5 are in the United States, another 5 in Brazil, and 13 in Portugal.

In Lisbon, toward the end of 1563, there was a posthumous work published of António Galvão, deceased in 1557, concerning the discoveries made up to 1550. This work, which in Portuguese was re-edited only in 1731 and 1944, speaks of the Portuguese discoveries in the Atlantic. Its first edition is rare and precious, for in 1977 I located only eight exemplars, of which there are two in the United States and four in Portugal. It would appear, then, that this work had no literary impact, for three editions in more than four centuries don't qualify a work for that honour. However, Richard Hakluyt, the famous compiler of narratives of discovery voyages and patron of the Hakluyt Society, translated it into English and published it in London in 1601. That translation was re-edited at least four more times in the 18th and 19th centuries, and the work achieved some impact in this way.

In September 1572, the Royal Privilege was given to the publication of *De Rebus Emmanuelis Regis Lusitaniae . . . Gestis Libri duodecim*, "Twelve Books about the activities of King Dom Manuel of Portugal", written by Dom Jeronimo Osório, who,

146. Historia do descobrimento & conquista da India pelos Portugueses.
History of the discovery and conquest of India by the Portuguese.
Coimbra, 1551. Fernão Lopes de Castanheda

In this work on the Portuguese voyages to India, Castanheda relates the story of the discovery of Brazil by Cabral, since this took place in connection with one such voyage. Although other printed references had already been made to Brazil, this is the first book printed in Portuguese which refers explicitly to this discovery. In the sixteenth century, the book went through editions in Portuguese, French, Spanish, German, Italian and English. The first Portuguese edition, shown here, is extremely rare, with only eight examples of it known to exist. The English version, translated by Nicholas Lichefield and dedicated to Admiral Drake, is the first book originally written in Portuguese and then translated into English.

The Newberry Library, Chicago (Below)

146

147. Asia de Ioam de Barros.
Asia.
Lisbon, 1552. João de Barros

This is the first edition of the first volume of a monumental work that contains much information about the Portuguese discoveries on both sides of the Atlantic. A classic writer of the Portuguese tongue; Superintendent of India House, where he had at his disposal many documents relating to the discoveries; donatary of a captaincy in Brazil; author of a now-lost work about the "Land of the Holy Cross", as Brazil was originally called: João de Barros still merits attentive reading by anyone who seeks to understand the history of the Portuguese discoveries.

The New York Public Library
(Page 246)

---

148. Os Lusíadas de Luis de Camões
The Lusiads.
First Portuguese edition, Lisbon, 1572.
Luís de Camões

There is some dispute over which edition of this work is truly the first: if it is this one, in which the frontispiece engraving shows the pelican's head turned to the reader's right, or if it is a slightly different one in which the head is turned to the left. Other copies exist in the New York Public Library, the Hispanic Society of America, and at Harvard University, as well as in some Portuguese libraries.

The John Carter Brown Library at Brown University, Providence, RI
(Below)

148

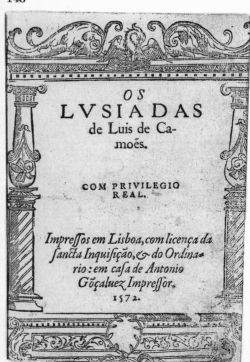

taking advantage of what Damião de Góis had published in 1566, narrated in scrupulous and methodical Latin the events of the reign of Dom Manuel "The Fortunate". Among these was the discovery of Brazil. Contrary to what happened with the work by Damião de Góis, which was published only in Portugal and almost exclusively in the twentieth century, the work of Osório was edited many times in foreign lands: in Cologne in 1574, 1575, 1576, 1580, 1581, 1586 and 1597; and in Rome in 1592. As for Portuguese versions, it was also printed at Coimbra in 1791, aside from the first edition, which was put on sale in Lisbon in 1572. There was, moreover, a Dutch translation in 1661, one in English in 1752, one in German in 1795, and Portuguese editions in 1804 and 1944.

Having just mentioned 25 editions of this work by Dom Jerónimo Osório concerning the reign of Dom Manuel, published in various languages, we can say that its literary echo and cultural impact were of great importance.

In 1572, sometime after September 24, the first edition of *The Lusiads (Item 148)* came off the press of António Gonçalves of Lisbon. The famous poem by Luís de Camões *(Item 152)* describes the voyage of Vasco da Gama to India, with brief references to the parts of the Atlantic coast discovered by the Portuguese: Cape Verde, the Senegal River, Congo, Brazil, and the Cape of Good Hope, where the giant Adamastor was enthroned. *The Lusiads* is not a historical work but poetic fiction imbued with and based upon historical events. Since the poem refers first and foremost to the Portuguese discoveries, not

excluding those in the Atlantic, and since it had tremendous literary and cultural impact, it must necessarily figure in this discussion.

Another and slightly different version of the poem was also published in Lisbon in 1572. Or rather, in another edition almost identical to the original there was imprinted in the frontispiece an indication of the year "1572", which normally would mean that the book was re-edited in that year. There has been discussion over which of these two editions is really the first. In the last century it was said the first edition was the one featuring, on the decoration that surrounds the words of the frontispiece, a pelican with its head turned to the reader's right; nowadays, the first edition is considered to be the one that features, besides a few other small differences, a frontispiece figure of a pelican with its head turned to the reader's left. The arguments mustered to prove that this is really the first edition are not convincing, and it is safer to affirm that we do not know which of these two editions is the first. I have prepared for publication in the *Annals* of the Portuguese Academy of History, to which I have delivered the original, a study of the first five editions of *The Lusiads*: the two of 1572; that of 1574, known as the "piscos" edition because it contains a typographical error in which the word "piscos" is used instead of "peixes" ("fishes"), in a phrase referring to the "piscosa Cizimbra" ("the port of Sesimbra, abundant in fishes"); and finally, the editions of 1591 and 1597. In this study I located the known exemplars of each edition. These were: 15 from 1572 with the pelican's head turned to the reader's right, 27

of the 1572 edition with the pelican's head turned to the left, 20 of the "piscos" edition, 12 from 1591, and 40 from 1597.
I said previously that the use of "piscos" instead of "peixes" in the 1584 edition is a typographical error. However, those who have dedicated themselves to the study of the first editions of *The Lusiads* affirm that this 1584 edition was the work of Jesuits who did not know the significance of the word "piscoso", i.e., abundant in fishes. They allegedly thought it meant "full of 'piscos' " (a type of small bird), and deliberately sent it to the printer in this way. Now, nobody could prove that the 1584 edition, although destined principally for students of the humanities, was in fact ordered by the Jesuits; furthermore, whoever it was who skilfully wrote all the notes for that edition must have also known what the word "piscoso" really meant.
In the 16th century, aside from the previously mentioned five editions of *The Lusiads* in Portuguese, there were three Spanish translations, of which two were published in 1580 *(Item 149)* and one in 1591; they, too, are rare books, but there are exemplars in the United States. In the 17th century *The Lusiads* was published eleven times in Portuguese *(Item 150)*; twice in English, in a translation by Richard Fanshawe, in 1655 *(Item 151)* and 1664, this latter one being extremely rare, since only two exemplars are known; twice in Italian, translated by Carlo Antonio Paggi and published in 1658 and 1659; and once in Latin, translated by Tomé de Faria and published in 1622. In the 18th century, there were ten Portuguese editions, six in French, four in English

following a translation by William Julius Mickle, and one each in Italian, Dutch and Polish.
In the 19th century, editions of *The Lusiads* became even more numerous. In Portuguese alone, there were 76, of which eleven were published either in Brazil or for distribution in Brazil: nine in Rio de Janeiro (1821, 1841, 1849, 1855, 1856, 1861, 1866, 1868 and 1899), one in Pernambuco (1843), and also one in Brussels (1879). In French, there were 16 editions; 13 in German; 11 in Italian; and another 11 in English, namely, the editions of 1807, 1809, 1809 and 1877 based on W. J. Mickle's translation, the 1826 printing of Thomas More Musgrave's translation, the 1853 edition of the Edward Killinan translation with notes by the Camões scholar John Adamson, the 1854 edition of the translation by Livingston Mitchell, the 1880 edition of the Robert French Duff translation, the 1880 edition of the Richard Francis Burton translation, and the editions of 1880 and 1884 of the J. J. Aubertin translation. There were a further five editions in Spanish, two in Swedish, two in Hungarian, one in Danish, one in Polish, and one in Latin. Aside from all these, there are many editions of the complete works of Camões that naturally include *The Lusiads*, dated 1815, 1834, 1843, 1852, 1860-1867, and 1873-1874. This brings the total number of 19th-century editions of this poem to not less than 145!
In our own century, there have likewise been many editions of the work. As of 1972, there were 33 Portuguese editions published in Portugal, aside from three editions of the complete works of Camões, and four editions printed in Brazil. That was how

149. La Lusíada.
The Lusiads.
First Spanish edition, Salamanca, 1580.
Luís de Camões

Proof of The Lusiads' *literary importance is the fact that it was translated into a foreign language only eight years after its original appearance – a major undertaking for such a lengthy work. This translation was by the Sevillian Luis Gomez de Tápia. The exemplar shown here is one of seven that the National Library of Madrid owns of this rare edition, represented in the United States by very few copies. In 1913 this edition was reissued in Barcelona with engravings and a lovely graphic presentation.*

Biblioteca Nacional, Madrid
(Below)

149

LA LVSIADA
DE EL FAMOSO POETA
Luys de Camões.

TRADVZIDA EN VERSO CA
stellano de Portugues, por el Ma-
estro Luys Gomez de Tapia,
vezino de Seuilla.

DIRIGIDA AL ILLVSTRISS.
mo Señor Ascanio Colona, Abbad
de Sancta Sophia.

Con priuilegio.

EN SALAMANCA,
En casa de Ioan Perier Impressor
de Libros . Año de
M.D.LXXX.

150. Os Lusíadas
The Lusiads.
First annotated Portuguese edition, 1613.
Luís de Camões

This edition is the seventh in its original language and exists in two forms: one showing the Portuguese royal crown on the title page, this being the more common variant; and another, quite rare, with the letters "D.F.D.F." in place of the royal crown. It is notable for including commentaries by Father Manuel Correia, a friend of Camões, and for being the first edition of the work to include biographical notes about the author, written by Pedro de Mariz.

Biblioteca Nacional, Lisbon
(Below)

---

151. The Lusiads.
First English edition, London, 1655.
Luís de Camões

This first English edition of The Lusiads *was translated by Sir Richard Fanshawe, who from 1661 to 1663 was English Ambassador in Lisbon. It is adorned with engravings of Camões, the Infante Dom Henrique and Vasco da Gama. This particular exemplar contains handwritten annotations by Fanshawe himself, and once belonged to eminent Luso-Brazilian historian Charles R. Boxer. This translation was reissued at least once in London (1664) and three times in the United States (1940, 1963 and 1969).*

Lilly Library, Indiana University
(Page 252)

150

many were to be found that year at the National Library in Lisbon, for the Exposition honoring the quarter-centenary of the publication of *The Lusiads*. Also at that exhibition were these other 20th-century editions: five in Spanish, four in Italian, three in French, one each in German, Czech, Romanian, Catalan and Latin, seven in English, the Hispanic Society of America's New York editions of 1903, 1940, 1946 and 1950, the 1952 edition at Harmondsworth, England, the 1963 Carbondale, Illinois edition, and the 1969 reprint by the New York bookdealer H.P. Kraus, to which we must add the Oxford edition of 1973. Since then, there have been further editions of *The Lusiads*, so that we must add several more to the 262 that figured in the National Library's exhibition in 1972. *The Lusiads*, in other words, produced extraordinary literary echoes and an enormous cultural impact, and stands as one of the greatest artistic legacies of the Portuguese discoveries.

In 1580, Michel de Montaigne's *Essais* were published at Bordeaux (Item 156). This classic philosophical work quickly gained wide diffusion, not only in France, where its editions continued practically without interruption, but also throughout the whole of Europe at that time. That book contains an essay entitled "Des Cannibales", which refers to the notion of the innate goodness of the Brazilian Indians encountered by the Portuguese. This idea was not directly based on what the Portuguese themselves had written, writings with which Montaigne may have had no familiarity. It is likewise not supported by what the

French Capuchin friars Claude de Abbeville and Yves de Evreux had published in 1614 and 1615 about the Indians of Maranhão. Nonetheless, the idea was adopted by thinkers like Voltaire and Rousseau in their own writings about the characteristics of primitive peoples. These clearly are not works that deal with the Portuguese discoveries, nor were these authors necessarily capable of writing on that subject. What Montaigne, Voltaire and Rousseau said about the innate goodness of primitive man, with speculative reference to the Indians of Brazil, demonstrates how they were influenced by the general atmosphere of ideas concerning the Portuguese discoveries in the Atlantic.

In 1591, in Rome, there was published the *Relatione del Reame di Congo et delle circonvicine contrade*; that is, "Report on the Kingdom of the Congo and the regions that form its frontiers". It was prepared by the Italian Filippo Pigafetta, based on writings and verbal accounts by the Portuguese Duarte Lopes, who had arrived at Rome as ambassador of the King of the Congo. This book, adorned with maps and engravings, describes the Congo and recounts its history, narrating how it was discovered by the Portuguese, who converted its chiefs to the Catholic faith. In 1728 and 1753 this first Italian edition was re-edited in Venice; the Dutch translation appeared in 1596 and had reissues in 1650, 1658, 1706, one edition without year, and again in 1727; in 1597 it was published in German, a language in which it had reissues in 1609, an abbreviated version in 1628 and one in 1791; also in 1597, it

Estampa 3ª. Retrato de Luis de Camões
o unico q dizem existir, e ser tirado do
natural. — Fernando Gomes fez em Lxª

152. Portrait of Luís de Camões.
19th c. Painting on paper, after a 16th-century original by Fernão Gomes

Judging from its style and size, the original of this portrait was intended as a model for a frontispiece illustration in an edition of Camões' works. It was the only existing picture of the poet known to have been drawn from life. Unfortunately, the original has disappeared, but this copy, faithfully reproducing even the damage and makeshift repairs that the original had suffered, was made in the nineteenth century. It became the model for most subsequent depictions of the Lusiads' author.

Comissão Nacional para as Comemorações dos Descobrimentos Portugueses, Lisbon (Page 251)

151

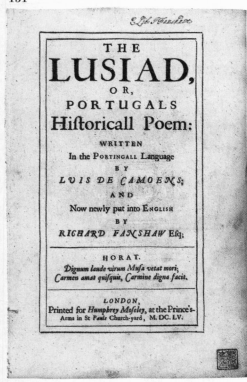

was published in English, in which language it was reissued in abbreviated form in 1625 and 1905 in the compilation of Samuel Purchas, then published in its entirety in 1745, 1747, 1752 and 1881. In 1598, it was published in Latin, and in 1624 it was re-edited in that language. In French, it only came to be published in 1883, 1963 and 1965 in Belgium, and the Portuguese translation appeared in 1951, made by Rosa Capeans, who in 1949 had published the facsimile edition of the Italian version of 1591.

1719 was the year of publication, in London, of the famous book by Daniel Defoe entitled, *The Life and Strange Surprizing Adventures of Robinson Crusoe (Item 157)*, a book that in various editions continues to be published up to the present day. In this classic of world literature, the strange and surprising adventures of its chief character begin at Bahia and end on Brazilian territory as well. The discovery and colonization of Brazil by the Portuguese impressed the imagination of Daniel Defoe and contributed to his idealization of the legendary figure of Crusoe.

In 1747, the Lisbon printer António Isidoro da Fonseca established in Rio de Janeiro his second typographical workshop. There he printed, with licence from the local bishop, the booklet entitled *Relação da Entrada que fez o . . . Senhor D.F. António do Desterro Malheyro Bispo do Rio de Janeiro . . . composta pelo Doutor Luiz Antonio Rosado da Cunha (Item 161)*, "A Report of the Arrival of Senhor Dom Frei António do Desterro Malheyro, Bishop of Rio de Janeiro . . .

composed by Dr. Luiz António Rosado da Cunha". The same printer also produced broadsides in Rio de Janeiro, of which some are preserved. As soon as this became known in Lisbon, it motivated the dissemination, on July 7, 1747, of a royal provision prohibiting any books, booklets or unbound sheets to be printed in Brazil, and also mandating that any typographical equipment found there was to be confiscated and sent back to Portugal. Thus António Isidoro da Fonseca returned to Lisbon and never again printed anything in Rio de Janeiro.

It seems strange that Portugal was opposed to the installation of a printing-press in Brazil, especially since in the 16th century it had already permitted, or at least was not opposed to, the presses that were printing books in the Portuguese outposts of Goa, Macau and Japan. In 1860 Inocêncio Francisco da Silva, who certainly did not read attentively the royal prohibition of 1747, printed in his *Diccionario Bibliographico Portuguez* a reference about Luis António Rosado da Cunha which states that the workshop of António Isidoro da Fonseca in Rio de Janeiro was abolished "doubtless because political considerations or reasons of state posed an obstacle to granting to the colonists permission to use the press, and thereby to spread enlightenment which at the time was judged inimical to the interests of the home country and perilous to its continued dominion". This opinion was accepted by other authors who dealt with the same subject: that is, Portugal prohibited the installation of printing presses in Brazil in order to impede the diffusion of the light of culture, and to preserve its colony in a state of ignorance and of obedience to orders from the government in Lisbon. Of course, this would also be a reason for prohibiting the installation of presses in Portuguese Africa, Madeira, the Azores in practically every tiny village presently in Portugal. If this were the motive for prohibiting printing-presses overseas, it would seem that the same reasoning might manifest itself in the form of Brazilian students' encountering difficulties in matriculating at the University of Coimbra, or in Brazilian authors' having difficulty arranging for their works to be printed in Portugal. Needless to say, none of this ever occurred. Many Brazilian students matriculated at the University of Coimbra, especially in the 18th century. Likewise, many books by Brazilian authors came off the printing-presses of Portugal. One need only look at Rubens Borba de Moraes' *Bibliografia Brasileira do Período Colonial.* That bibliographer, who attentively read the royal prohibition of July 7, 1747, affirmed that the printing-press of Rio de Janeiro was abolished because the licences required to print books could be given only in Portugal at the time. Located in Portugal were the commissions of the Holy Office and of the Palace High Court, to which anything to be printed had to be presented twice, both before and then after printing, to verify that it conformed with that which had been originally approved. Not only Portugal required licences from the authorities to print books; they were required in every European country. To avoid expenses and delays in the Portuguese overseas territories, printing-presses could only be

installed in the centre of the empire, where a good part of the readers lived. That was the principal reason, if not the only one, why books could not be printed in Brazil. But in 1808, the Portuguese royal family, fleeing from the Napoleonic Wars, established the imperial court temporarily in Rio de Janeiro. Soon after, the Royal Press was established there. It began to print books, leaflets and broadsides in relative abundance, and with the necessary licences, because the respective commissions had been installed there. To be sure, in some parts of Spanish America printing-presses were in operation in the 16th century; but in other nations of Spanish America, and they are not few, printing began only *after* it did so in Brazil. The same can be said of all the regions of West Africa, the Republic of South Africa, and in many regions of North America: the press commenced there only after it did so in Brazil.

One of the works published shortly after 1808 in Rio de Janeiro was the letter describing the discovery of Brazil, written by Pero Vaz de Caminha and published by Father Manuel Aires do Casal in the *Corographia Brazilica.* Since then, many works have been printed in Brazil about the Portuguese Atlantic discoveries, and although the 1747 *Relação da Entrada que fez o . . . bispo do Rio de Janeiro* does not in fact refer to those discoveries, that booklet is included in this exhibition because it was the first printed work published in Brazil. After all, only printed works can have literary echoes and cultural impact!

153. Utopia.
Louvain, 1516. Thomas More

This work was influenced by printed accounts of the Portuguese discoveries, especially by the letter of Vespucci entitled "The New World", and by the "Countries Newly Rediscovered" of Fracanzano Montalboddo. More used these accounts as the factual starting point for a purely fictional story. The book's principal character, a Portuguese adventurer, recounts his travels from the Brazilian trading post at Cabo Frio (which really existed) to an imaginary island called Utopia off the coast of Brazil, whose inhabitants enjoy a perfect society: ". . . where things are run so efficiently and with so few laws, and recognition of individual merit is combined with equal prosperity for all". It was, of course, an undisguised critique of the shortcomings of European civilization.
The volume was issued afterward in Paris in 1517, in Basel twice in 1518, in Florence in 1519, and then many times in Latin, English, German, Italian, and other languages down to the present day.

Houghton Library, Harvard University (Below)

153

Libellus vere aureus nec
MINVS SALVTARIS QVAM FESTI-
uus de optimo reip.ftatu,deq; noua Infula Vtopia
authore clariffimo viro Thoma Moro inclytæ
ciuitatis Londinenfis ciue & vicecomite cura M.Petri Aegidii Antuerpiéfis,& arte
Theodorici Martini Aluftenfis,Ty
pographi almæ Louanienfium
Académiæ nunc primum
accuratiffime edi
tus.:.

Cum gratia z priuilegio.

1516

Clark &c P

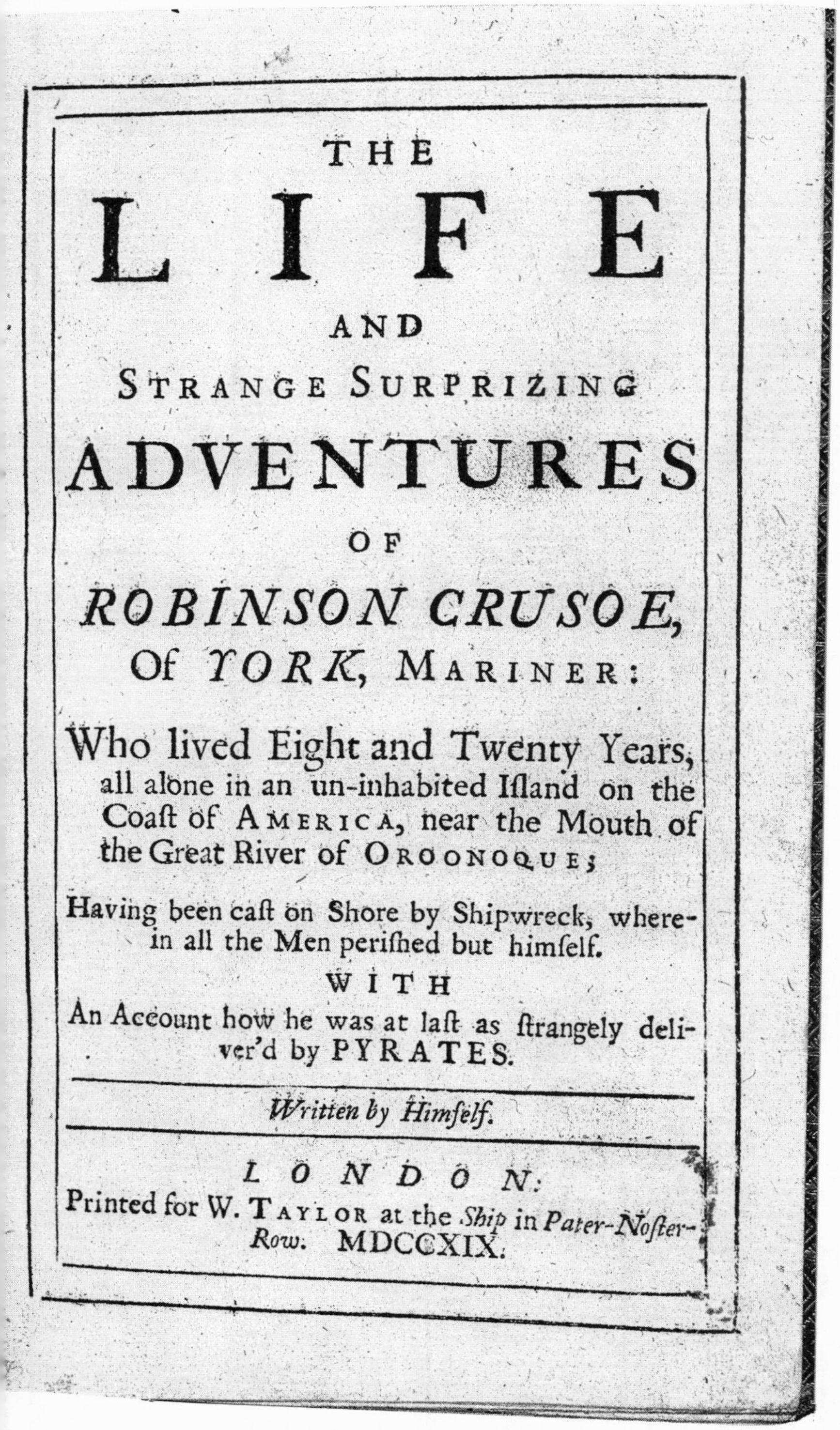

THE
LIFE
AND
STRANGE SURPRIZING
ADVENTURES
OF
ROBINSON CRUSOE,
Of *YORK,* MARINER:

Who lived Eight and Twenty Years,
all alone in an un-inhabited Island on the
Coast of AMERICA, near the Mouth of
the Great River of OROONOQUE;

Having been cast on Shore by Shipwreck, wherein all the Men perished but himself.
WITH
An Account how he was at last as strangely deli-
ver'd by PYRATES.

Written by Himself.

LONDON:
Printed for W. TAYLOR at the *Ship* in *Pater-Noster-
Row.* MDCCXIX.

154, 155. Brazilian Fête at Rouen.
Originally published in: "Cest la dedvction du sumptueux ordre plaisantz spectacles et magnifiqves theatres dresses, et exhibes par les citoiens de Rouen ville Metropolitaine du pays de Normandie."
This is a summation of the sumptuous orders, pleasing spectacles, and magnificent theatre displayed and presented by the citizens of Rouen.
Rouen, 1551.

This rare book, commemorating a visit by the French royal couple to Rouen, includes among its twenty-nine woodcuts one entitled "Figure des brisilians", which was also produced as a separate work, as shown here.

As evidence of the close ties between Normandy and Brazil during the Age of Discoveries, the high point of the royal festivities was the construction of a Brazilian Indian village (taba), and the use of local trees and plants to imitate tropical vegetation. About 50 Indians then living in Rouen populated the "forest", while, naked and painted in Indian fashion, about 150 seamen who were familiar with Brazil enlivened the scene. The climax was a mock battle between Tupinambás and Tabajaras, which ended with the burning of the fanciful taba.

Bibliothèque Nationale, Paris
(Below)

156. Essais.
Essays.
Second edition, Bordeaux, 1582.
Michel de Montaigne

Montaigne had not only spoken with Brazilian Indians living in Rouen, but also had a servant who had lived in Brazil for some ten or twelve years. Based partly on this, he wrote "Des Cannibales", ("On Cannibals"), in which he ventures some philosophical considerations about the apparently idyllic lives of the Brazilian Indians: "I think there is nothing barbarous and savage in that nation, from what I have been told, except that each man calls barbarism whatever is not his own practice. . . . for it seems to me that what we actually see in these nations surpasses . . . all the pictures in which poets have idealized the golden age."

Later in the essay, Montaigne contrasts the horrors of cannibalism with the religious torture and social injustice of European society: "I think there is more barbarity in eating a man alive than in eating him dead." From such works was born the prototype of the Indian as "Natural Man", a living reminder of a Golden Age when human society was at one with nature. The theme was picked up time and again, especially by other French writers like Rousseau.

The New York Public Library
(Below)

157. The Life and Strange Surprizing Adventures of Robinson Crusoe.
3 volumes, London, 1719-20. Daniel Defoe

This work, which served as a model for an entire genre of fictional adventures in tropical settings, does not deal expressly with the Portuguese discoveries, but the hero's voyage commences in Bahia, and after taking him through many other regions, it ends in Brazil as well. Thus it helped to establish the Brazilian milieu as one important element in the European notion of "the exotic".

The New York Public Library
(Pages 254-255)

156

158

154-155

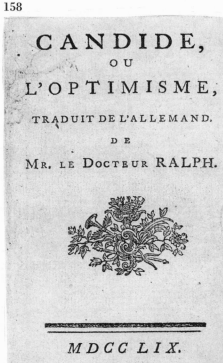

158. Candide, ou l'Optimisme.
Candide, or Optimism.
First Edition, Paris, 1759. François Marie Arouet de Voltaire

Though couched as a ribald phantasmagoria, Candide tackles – among many other things – two centuries of thought and writing based on the European experience in the New World. It pokes fun at simplistic dreams of Utopia; lampoons the exaggerated "travel literature" of Vespucci and others; speculates on the relative merits of the "natural" versus the "civilized" man; and in general, epitomizes the intellectual ferment of the mid-eighteenth century, when the accumulated results of the discoveries were helping to provoke revolutionary changes in the structure of European society.

Voltaire communicated, and frequently disagreed, with Rousseau, and participated in an intellectual lineage that dates back to Montaigne. Candide went through several editions in its first year of publication, and countless ones in the years that followed, not only in French but also in other languages.

Courtesy of The Pierpont Morgan Library, New York
acc. PML 66172
(Facing page)

159. History of Brazil.
Author's manuscript, 1801-1809.
Robert Southey

Southey was an English poet and writer with familial and intellectual links to Wordsworth and Coleridge. He first became interested in Brazil during a lengthy stay in Portugal; on returning to England in 1801, he dedicated years to writing this three-volume history, which is still considered ground-breaking in some ways.
The original manuscript of all three volumes, along with two more volumes of accessory information, was acquired by the National Library of Rio de Janeiro in the early twentieth century.

Biblioteca Nacional, Rio de Janeiro
(Opposite)

160. History of Brazil
3 volumes, London, 1810, 1817, 1819.
Robert Southey

A glance at the opening lines of this work reveals the excellence of Southey's prose, and his passion for his subject. His deep affection for Portugal and Brazil was lavished on this book, which became the great labour of his life. Though it was not possible, Southey intended to continually correct it and issue revised editions, stating that ". . . centuries hence, when Brazil shall have become the great and prosperous country which one day it must be, I shall be regarded as the first person who ever attempted to give a consistent form to its crude, unconnected and neglected history".

The New York Public Library
(Below)

161. Relação da entrada que fez o excellentíssimo, e reverendíssimo senhor D. Fr. Antonio do Desterro Malheyro Bispo de Rio de Janeiro, em o primeiro dia deste prezente Anno de 1747.
Report of the entry of the most excellent and reverend Senhor Dom Francisco Antonio do Desterro Malheyro, Bishop of Rio de Janeiro, on the first day of this present year of 1747.
Rio de Janeiro, 1747. Luis António Rosado da Cunha

This is the earliest extant work that is known to have been printed in Brazil. As soon as it was issued, the Portuguese Crown ordered the printer's equipment confiscated because the necessary royal licences had not been obtained.
The press began to spread freely in Brazil only in 1808, when the Portuguese Court, fleeing the Napoleonic Wars, took refuge temporarily in Rio de Janeiro, and established the Royal Press there. Soon, Brazilian presses began to produce editions of some of the works shown in this catalogue: the documents and records of its own discovery and settlement.

The John Carter Brown Library at Brown University, Providence, RI
(Below)

159

160

HISTORY OF BRAZIL.

The history of Brazil is less beautiful than that of the mother country, and less splendid than that of the Portuguese in Asia; but it is not less important than either. Its materials differ from those of other histories: here are no tangles of crooked policy to unravel, no mysteries of state iniquity to elucidate, no revolutions to record, nor victories to celebrate, the fame of which remains among us long after their effects have past away. . Discovered by chance, and long left to chance, it is by individual industry and enterprize, and by the operation of the common laws of nature and society, that this empire has risen and flourished, extensive as it now is, and mighty as it must one day become. In the course of its annals disgust and anger will oftener be felt than those exalted feelings which it is more grateful for the historian to excite. I have to speak of savages so barbarous that little sympathy can be felt for any sufferings which they endured, and of colonists in whose triumphs no joy will be taken, because they added avarice to barbarity;..ignoble men, carrying on an obscure warfare, the consequences of which have been greater than were produced by the conquests of Alexander

B

161

RELAÇAŌ
DA ENTRADA QUE FEZ
O EXCELLENTISSIMO, E REVEAENDISSIMO SENHOR
D. F. ANTONIO
DO DESTERRO MALHEYRO
Bispo do Rio de Janeiro , em o primeiro dia deste prezente Anno de 1747.
havendo sido seis Annos Bispo do Reyno de Angola , donde por admissaõ de Sua Magestade , e Bulla Pontificia , foy promovido para esta Diocesi.
COMPOSTA PELO DOUTOR
LUIZ ANTONIO ROSADO
DA CUNHA
Juiz de Fóra , e Provedor dos defuntos , e auzentes , Capellas , e Resíduos do Rio de Janeiro.

✳

RIO DE JANEIRO
Na Segunda Officina de ANTONIO ISIDORO DA FONCECA.
Anno de M. CC. XLVII.
Com licenças do Senhor Bispo.

Appendices

Luís de Albuquerque
Some Notes on Science in the Age of Discoveries

Charles R. Boxer
The Politics of the Discoveries

Francisco Contente Domingues
Chronology of Portuguese Discovery, 1415-1616

Selected Bibliography

Lenders to the Exhibition and Photographic Sources

Some Notes on Science in the Age of Discoveries

by Luís de Albuquerque

To speak of science in the Age of Portuguese Discoveries is, in a certain sense, an equivocation, since in our Exhibition we do not go beyond the middle of the sixteenth century. In effect, what we know of the activities of pilots and sailors up to that point encompasses various bodies of empirical data. But that body of empirical knowledge was by no means insignificant. With greater or lesser weight, it succeeded in nourishing various domains of science though it did not constitute in itself a scientific exercise.

And what kind of knowledge did the explorers accumulate? In the first place, it was only natural that they compiled data relating to geophysics: systems of winds and ocean currents, for instance. Without attending to those two factors, navigation would have been uncertain, and even more so as the ocean crossings became longer. Because of variations in the direction of prevailing winds, navigators had to find ways to circumvent them, although at the cost of spending long periods in the ocean's vastness, an adventure that at the time was without known precedents.

In the second place, voyages as early as the first half of the fifteenth century showed that the descriptive geography accepted up to then in Europe needed revision. People were found living in places that were formerly considered deserted and uninhabitable. Islands existed of which there had never been any knowledge, and others were never found which fanciful cartographers had recorded. Contacts with regions of Africa revealed the existence of unexpected forms of animal and vegetable life. In a word, the daily experience of navigators was an encounter with the unknown and the unexpected.

From the few descriptions we have of such matters, these adventurers were curious and astute observers of the customs, arts and practices of peoples whose lives were organized according to customs that almost always escaped the understanding of outsiders, people who manifested in their activities different forms of culture. The seamen of the early days of the voyages of discovery jotted down, in their contact with those people, data that today are of great interest to the vast domain called anthropology, in its physical, cultural and social ramifications.

Simultaneously, other elements of geographical interest were observed and registered. No doubt, errors were sometimes introduced that had their roots in very ancient traditions – as in the case of confusing the Senegal river with one of the branches of the Nile – but it is also true that on occasion totally new phenomena were revealed: for instance, the tidal bore observed in rivers of Guinea. With the passing of the years, it was recognized that the configuration of the West African coast did not conform to the geography then in vogue, that is, to the Ptolemaic maps that had begun to circulate throughout Europe at the beginning of the fifteenth century and were accepted as correct. Sometime in the fifteenth century, it was also recognized that the axis of the magnetic compass did not align itself in a geographically correct north-south direction, as appears to have been believed by sailors beginning in the thirteenth century or earlier. By comparing observations made in different places, it was concluded that the angle of the earth's axis with the line of the meridian, which came to be called the compass's *declinação* (declination) but at the beginning was called "variation", differed from place to place. Many years passed before sailors recognized that it also differed with time in a given place, this being the so-called "secular change".*

We could enumerate many other important bodies of data that were assembled as a result of the navigations. We shall end here and merely reflect a little more on some of those that have been singled out.

Toward a Geophysics of the Great Oceanic Masses

It is not possible to know with any certainty when, in the North Atlantic, a reconnaissance of the wind systems was begun. The arrival in the Azores, in 1427 or 1432, of at least one vessel under Diogo de Silves' command (as we read in a legend of the portolan chart made by Gabriel de Valseca) must have been by pure chance. But more than ten years after the first of those dates, when the Regent Dom Pedro became interested in populating the Azores in the name of his nephew King Afonso V, those islands were possibly the object of frequent visits, perhaps by vessels returning to Lisbon from the Guinea coast. True, this is pure conjecture; but by reading attentively the *Chronicle of Guinea* – to give its usual abbreviated title – we learn indirectly from Zurara that it had already become the norm to sail in an arc westward to speed up the return to the kingdom when coming from voyages of trade and exploration to Africa. We may thus surmise that the wind patterns which made this possible were at least partly understood.

There is other evidence as well. In 1447, Nuno Tristão imprudently went up an African river in small boats with most of his companions. They suffered a surprise attack by natives who, from their fast-moving dugouts, let loose on the adventurers a hail of arrows that were both poisoned and well-aimed. It was a catastrophe from which only some seven men escaped. There was only one sailor among them, who confessed immediately that he knew nothing about navigation. It was another of the group, a youth of seventeen or eighteen years, who guided the vessel back to Lisbon by the "arc sailing" route that became known as "the return from Guinea" (later, "the return from Mina"). He skirted the prevailing winds blowing from the northeast, a fact that stands as evidence of good awareness of these phenomena among those involved in high-seas voyaging.

On March 10, 1449, about two years after that wretched return trip, a letter was signed confirming the peopling of the Azores. It conferred certain privileges on Gonçalo Velho and anyone who might accompany him there. Consequently, there is no doubt that this nautical manoeuver was at that time well known and in use. However, we do not know the names of the pilots who, from personal experience, were involved in the important task of learning how to take advantage of the prevailing winds of the North Atlantic in a way suitable for navigation. What was done in that part of the ocean was later done in the South Atlantic, once the existence of great periods and areas of calms in the equatorial zone was recognized. Indeed, it would be impossible to suppose that Vasco da Gama's fleet, destined for Calicut on the Malabar Coast of India, would sail, after crossing the equator, on a course that was also in the form of an arc extending far to the west, unless the prevailing winds of that enormous ocean mass had already been reconnoitred.

No document mentions the names of the navigators involved in that mission. Nevertheless, we must recognize: (1) that Bartolomeu Dias passed through São Tomé before 1499, and possibly prior to 1497, as is known from a portion of the extensive testament of Álvaro de Caminha, the third captain of that island, written on April 24 of that year; (2) that in 1488 the same Bartolomeu Dias, on his return from the celebrated voyage in which he verified the link between the Atlantic and the Indian Oceans, brought back from the islands of São Tomé and Príncipe the great navigator Duarte Pacheco Pereira, whom he had found there in a very sick condition; and finally, (3) that Pacheco Pereira, in a passage that is much-cited yet quite unclear, mentions that he had sailed well out into the Atlantic. From this we can infer that Bartolomeu Dias and Duarte Pacheco Pereira were probably the principals responsible for the growing awareness of the prevailing winds of the South Atlantic and also, accordingly, for the tactic that Vasco da Gama and all the captains of the passage to India applied in order to go around those winds.

Revolution in Descriptive Geography

The events we have just related have generally been deemed of secondary importance. Nevertheless, they helped determine commercial sailing routes in the Atlantic for three centuries. It is therefore comprehensible that the revolution in descriptive geography that began during the fifteenth century must have made a much stronger impression on the people of that time – and also on us, who are more than four centuries further advanced in relation to them!

To understand what happened, let us bear in mind that in the first half of the fifteenth century various erroneous geographic ideas circulated among Europeans. Rooted in preconceptions that enjoyed great popularity in the Middle Ages, two principles contradicted one another. According to

one, all habitable lands were believed to be surrounded by a great ocean. According to the other, those lands were believed to envelop an interior sea into which all rivers emptied their waters. These contradictory ideas were enormously widespread.

As for the first, we have the evidence of various maps that show the surrounding sea/ocean; they perforce show Africa as navigable around its southern tip. This is the case of the planisphere known as Fra Mauro's, drawn around the middle of the fifteenth century. It has been argued that Fra Mauro worked with data sent to him from Portugal, the reason being that King Afonso V had placed an order with him for a planisphere that would be similar to the one by him that is still in existence today. And all of this has been argued in order to draw the conclusion that in the lifetime of Dom Henrique, the Portuguese already knew with certainty that the Atlantic and the Indian Oceans were a pair that communicated with each other.

Let us not forget, though, that an envoy from the Portuguese Court went to see Fra Mauro's work when it was in an advanced state and evaluated it in absolutely negative fashion. The work of the monk-cartographer was mediocre, according to the critic, yet the contract signed with him should not be cancelled, if for no other reason than that he had already been paid a large sum. It can be concluded from this that Mauro's geographical ideas were not shared by the Portuguese. We may also conclude that the surrounding sea depicted by him on the planisphere that is known to us does not represent empirically based knowledge, but merely the carry-over of a medieval idea that was unintentionally correct.

As for the second of the widespread notions, namely, the existence of an interior sea surrounded by land, there are fewer proofs. One of them is in a well-known Portuguese text. Duarte Pacheco Pereira, in a passage of his *Esmeraldo de Situ Orbis (Item 4)*, discusses the problem of the relative proportions of land and water. Though he had navigated the length and breadth of the Atlantic, he is inclined to accept the notion that land surrounds the sea. Not surprisingly, he wrote this in 1508 or slightly earlier. At the time, Ptolemy's authority still carried weight, though it was already shaken (as we shall see). After Ferdinand Magellan's circumnavigation of the globe, Duarte

Pacheco's claim would be less comprehensible!

Claudius Ptolemy, who lived in Alexandria in the second century A.D., was known in Europe as an astronomer; and his *Almagest* or *Great Syntax* was a book widely read in the Middle Ages. However, his work as a geographer (or "cosmographer", as they said at the time) only became known in the West when, at the beginning of the fifteenth century, a Greek exemplar of his *Geography* was brought to Italy and translated into Latin. Of that version, various copies were made and spread throughout Europe. The importance attached to the book was such that in 1475, with the art of movable-type printing having been barely invented, a printed edition appeared in Vicenza, followed by six more before 1490. All but the first included maps depicting the entire world known to the Alexandrian.

To raise, as many have, the question of whether Ptolemy had the maps drawn or drew them himself, or whether they were added to his text later, perhaps long after the sage's death, is insoluble and of no importance here. What is relevant is to call attention to these facts: (1) that on the map depicting all known lands the viewer is given clearly to understand that the Atlantic Ocean could well be a sea surrounded by land; and (2) that the Indian Ocean is depicted in like fashion, without the shadow of a doubt.

When Duarte Pacheco refers to a sea that is *medio terranum*, he was probably influenced by the image from Ptolemy's *Geography*, an image reinforced by the fact that the African continent is depicted as becoming so wide towards the south that it covers the entire width of the map from east to west. That enormous land mass remained traditional for some cartographers even in the sixteenth century, after the Ptolemaic conception had been superceded.

Take the example of the Lopo Homem planisphere, the first map in the so-called Miller atlas (in the Bibliothèque Nationale de Paris) of about 1519, which depicts the American continent and the connection between the Atlantic Ocean and the Indian Ocean. It depicts these two oceans as a pair of inner seas. To the south it limits them with a large unknown continent, which remained a fixture in various examples of the cartography of the 1500's and was called "Terra Austral Incognita",

("Unknown Southern Land") even after Magellan's voyage around the world. It appears on maps by Bartolomeu Velho and Luis Teixeira, to cite only two famous Portuguese cartographers.

In spite of these sporadic bows to the Ptolemaic configurations, the editions of Ptolemy stopped suddenly in 1490 and were only resumed seventeen years later, with the Strasbourg 1507 edition. Why?

One factor is the weight of the Portuguese discoveries, and Bartolomeu Dias' voyage in particular, which ended in December 1488. No doubt the results of this voyage were known at once in Europe, as evidenced by the map of Henricus Martellus Germanus, drawn about a year after Dias' return *(Item 28)*. On it the West African coast and the small part of the East African coast that extends to the Rio do Infante (River of Infante Dom Henrique) are presented in accordance with what the Portuguese navigators had observed. Beyond the limits of that river, the outline respects traditional configurations, with strong influence from Ptolemy.

In spite of this detail, the Henricus Martellus map casts serious doubt on the *Geography*; contrary to what was depicted in Ptolemy's book, Africa became ever narrower to the south, and thus it was possible to guide a vessel from Europe to the east coast of Africa and on to India. Conclusion: the known part of the world was *not Ptolemaic*, and there was need to review ideas that had their origin in a distant past. Therefore, as Armando Cortesão has concluded, the editions of the Alexandrian's geographical work were suspended in 1490. When they were resumed in the first quarter of the sixteenth century, and at a rate that suggested editorial success, they could no longer contain only the traditional maps. They included "new tables" *(tabulae novae)* depicting the outlines of Africa and Asia as eighty years' worth of maritime voyages had found them to be, and they reserved pages for maps of both Americas, the "New World".

Through direct contact with the world, humanity was compelled to produce a correct vision of its outlines and limits. Indeed, that investigation only reached completion in our own century, with the arrival of Amundsen at the south pole in 1911, and with the ascent of the highest mountain on the planet, an accomplishment of our own days.

Nevertheless, the impulse to reconnoitre our planet developed in the fifteenth and sixteenth centuries with an unprecedented strength that would not later be repeated. Men, in their greed, endeavoured to chase mirages into the least known and most distant places, and they gave an account of it all in reports and on maps. The fact is, they were at the threshold of a new age. It would take time to effect a scientific analysis of all the facts registered in the course of that superficial and hasty first survey.

The Emergence of Anthropology

Among those facts were the first indications of an emerging anthropology, though only recently were they recognized as significant aspects of an encounter not only between peoples and races but also between cultures. It was an encounter that was not always peaceful. Rather, it was one that brought strangers face to face, requiring them to learn to understand each other over the course of many years, until the barriers of preconceptions that separated them began to fall.

We shall select examples of this from the report of the voyage of Cadamosto (Alvise Cá da Mosto), an Italian navigator-merchant who in 1455 and 1456 undertook two expeditions, authorized by the Infante Dom Henrique, to the Guinea area. The narrative was first printed in Fracanzano da Montalboddo's *Paesi Nouamente retrouati* of 1507 *(Item 141)*. Although the "firsts" attributed to this navigator have been challenged by the scholar Avelino Teixeira da Mota, this does not negate the value of Cadamosto's testimony with respect to the contacts he established with the *regulos* or "chieftains" who ruled over more or less extensive zones within the Guinea region. Two are discussed in particular in the report: Budomel and Batimansa.

As for the first, Cadamosto explains: "This name Budomel is the title of a lord and not a proper name for a place, thus, 'the land of Budomel', as if one said 'country of such-and-such a person or count'." The Venetian lingered with him in order to learn about Portuguese who had been there before, for he was an open and serious man in his transactions. The least that can be said about this fraternization is that it was cordial. Cadamosto decided to journey into the interior with

Budomel in order to conduct his business, but also, he confesses, "in order to see and hear new things". And that is what he succeeded in doing, as we learn from his report, and he must have reported only a small part of what he was able to see, for he was in that land for more than a month.

Here, in summary fashion, is what he passed on to us:

a) The natives were extraordinary swimmers and incredibly brave.

b) The lords, and this aroused Cadamosto's admiration, did not rule from castles and cities nor did they issue coinage, a royal prerogative in Europe. Rather, they were lords merely by finding themselves surrounded by people who shared with them villages consisting of huts.

c) Budomel was a polygamist, as were some of his fellow countrymen; just in the village in which the Venetian stayed he had nine wives. Moreover, the slave women in the service of those wives could also join him in bed.

d) The report registers the lust that dominated these men and women, Cadamosto asserting that Budomel asked him, in exchange "for great favours", to explain the means, which he supposed was possessed by white men, whereby one would "be able to satisfy many women".

e) Positions within the domains of the lords were distributed among the officials of their retinues in accordance with the importance attributed to the functions carried out.

f) Budomel let himself be seen only twice a day; and he received in haughty fashion, subjecting visitors to all sorts of submissive practices, for example, having to appear naked and on bended knee, bowing at the waist until the head touched the ground, throwing handfuls of sand behind them and over their own heads, et cetera. (The part about total nudity for a man going into the presence of the lord is underlined in the text.)

Evidently, Budomel had been influenced by Islam, but what is clarified most in the description of this acquaintance is the nature of the encounter between the European and the Other, as it is common to say today. Scenes of this type would be repeated with Pero Vaz de Camina when he first came into contact with the Amerindians of Brazil *(Item 90)*; with Father Francisco Álvares regarding the Ethiopians, when he accompanied the first embassy sent by King Dom

Manuel to the Emperor of Abyssinia, as published in Portugal in 1540 under the title *Verdadera informacam das terras do Preste Joam (Item 81)*; with Fernão Veloso – discussed by Luis de Camões in *The Lusiads* – who did not fear risking his life in order to learn about the Africans who lived in the region that Vasco da Gama called St. Helena Bay; and with many, many others. Europeans thus learned, at their own cost, that humanity was not confined to their own Christian continent, nor to the Arab world, or the India of the East or China. At first, they reacted rather positively in accordance with that inherited "authority" of theirs, even though they also felt free to indulge at once in the traffic of slaves. Later they noted differences, or worse, they "dug in". Only with difficulty would Europeans learn that the differences have no profound significance in terms of the basic humanity of all peoples. Experience alone was able to teach us this. It was in those fifteenth and sixteenth centuries, however, that the first elements were assembled leading to reciprocal knowledge of the people who inhabit this planet. Though that knowledge is still incomplete, at least we have a huge fund of information, accumulated in bits and pieces since then, to help us study and explain the behaviour of different peoples.

Awareness of Terrestrial Magnetism

We should like to discuss one last subject because it takes us close to modern science: the matter of the magnetic phenomena of the earth, a topic that we partially discuss in connection with the problem of longitude in our essay in Section I of the Exhibition (see "The Art of Astronomical Navigation" in this catalogue).

It has been said that the properties of natural magnetism were taken advantage of in navigation as far back as the thirteenth century. It is further said that in the fifteenth century it came to be recognized – perhaps by German watchmakers, or by Christopher Columbus or Bartolomeu Dias – that a phenomenon existed, variable from place to place, that was called "magnetic declination". That recognition is beyond our discussion for several reasons. We shall say merely that the name of Cape Agulhas, not far from the Cape of Good Hope and pronounced in modern English "Uh-*gull*-us̆", confirms it as far back as the

fifteenth century: the name was selected because compasses (*agulhas*, literally "needles") in that place (34° 50' S, 20° 01' E) had zero variation.

Meanwhile, during the fifteenth century, Atlantic pilots carried certain instruments aboard ship in order to approximate their location, namely, the quadrant and the astrolabe. These altitude-measuring devices permitted them to obtain the latitude of their vessel's position by means of observations of meridian altitudes of stars, including principally the North Star and the sun. But to define the exact position of the vessel they also had to know how to determine the longitude for the same instant at which they measured latitude.

Various astronomical procedures for determining longitude were known, all of them theoretically correct but inapplicable in practice. Those based on lunar observations, for example, ran up against the deficient knowledge of the movement of the earth's satellite, a deficiency overcome only after Sir Isaac Newton discovered the law of universal gravitation. Moreover, all the procedures suffered from the inability to measure time with much accuracy, because the clocks manufactured were inadequate at that time. It was only in the eighteenth century that the Englishman John Harrison built the first chronometers, and they were quite large.

At the beginning of the sixteenth century, seamen groping in the unknown proposed various solutions to the problem of finding longitude. In a text dated 1514, the pilot João de Lisboa admits – but we do not know whether he might not have acquired the idea from someone else – that compass variation seemed to vary from place to place in direct proportion to longitude. It was an unfounded supposition, indeed it was bizarre, because in the same treatise the pilot conveyed data that flagrantly contradicted it. In any event, the hypothesis took hold and pilots accepted it as true; but since it was not true, many of the results obtained by applying it must have immediately begun to be viewed with skepticism. Suspicions grew to such an extent that in 1538, when Dom João de Castro left for Asia aboard the ship *Grifo*, as part of the fleet whose captain-major was Dom Garcia de Noronha, his brother-in-law and viceroy-designate of India, the king charged him with clarifying the doubts

that existed concerning the matter. For this purpose he was provided with a "shadow instrument" that facilitated measurements of magnetic variation. He states that the device had been conceived by Pedro Nunes, but in truth a description of it already existed in a book by Francisco Faleiro published in Seville in the Castilian language in 1535 *(Item 8)*. Pedro Nunes' exposition of the subject saw the light of day in 1537, in his *Tratado da Sphera (Item 9)*. Castro's intervention marks a first step in the accumulation of empirical data leading to a result that can properly be included within the domain of science. A few weeks after leaving Lisbon, his measurements of compass variation – which he made regularly and noted most scrupulously – seemed to lead him to the conclusion, written in no uncertain terms, that the phenomenon of variation had nothing directly to do with longitude. It must be related to something else, something certainly much more complicated (and indeed it was!), something that he did not dare to imagine.

That negative conclusion was doubtless valuable, but Dom João de Castro did not stop there. He continued to observe magnetic variation, and off the coast of Brazil he began to note anomalies among his results. By way of explanation, he admitted that the compass had been damaged by having been disassembled and adjusted the day before, so that it might have become "untempered". He would recognize the very next day that such an explanation was unfounded, since the observations carried out at that new time gave every indication of being "very much in line", as he puts it. These events took place on May 29 and 30, 1538, and Dom João de Castro continued to mix observations that merited his complete confidence with others that left him with justifiable doubts, without finding the cause of the anomalies in the latter cases.

He came upon the explanation on August 2, when his ship was anchored in the port of Mozambique and he began observing the variation of a number of compasses, all of them "out of order" internally, "because where one indicated east the other pointed to the north", he wrote. After attentively analyzing the instruments and the conditions in which they functioned, he found the explanation for the unusual phenomenon: "This held me in great suspense until I understood the cause.

It was a *berço* [small artillery piece] that was in the same place in which I wished to carry out the operations; the iron of the said *berço* attracted the compass needles and threw them off in this manner."

Dom João de Castro had just discovered the compass phenomenon later called "deviation". It was to a certain extent a truly notable discovery, for it took into account the scientific phenomenon of magnetism that underlay the purely practical matter of a compass-needle's ability to point north.

Let us add, in conclusion, that in spite of Castro's negative findings about compass variation based on a hypothetical but nonexistent meridian, equal to and in the same direction as longitude, pilots continued to measure that angle aboard their vessels. Still ignorant of secular changes in variation, they utilized such values as hints of their approximate position (or as *conhecenças*, the nautical term in use at the time). All of this was eventually useful for the development of an awareness of terrestrial magnetism. Such values, measured by pilots dozens and dozens of times, were taken advantage of by the physicists Gilbert and Stevin at the end of the sixteenth century, when they attempted to draw up the first explanations of the origin of the earth's magnetic phenomena. Thus, as we said at the beginning, the "science" of the Age of Discoveries may not truly merit that name, but it did contribute vitally to the development of the data, methods and theories upon which our present scientific knowledge is based.

* **Translator's Note.**
In U.S. nautical practice, declination is the angular distance of a heavenly body N or S of the celestial equator. Variation is the angle between the magnetic and geographical meridians, is expressed as E or W, and is obtained from charts. Deviation is the angle between the magnetic meridian and the axis of a compass card, is expressed as E or W, and is obtained from a magnetic compass table on the bridge (or in the cockpit of an aircraft) that in turn is based on swinging the ship periodically to various headings.

The Politics of the Discoveries
by C.R. Boxer

This topic has been taken to mean the political environment of Portugal and Europe at the time of the Discoveries (c.1415-1515), and the specific political forces which contributed to the Portuguese Crown's decision to pursue seaborne discovery as an instrument of policy. Portugal had attained its present boundaries, for practical purposes, with the expulsion of the Moors from their last stronghold at Silves in the Algarve, in 1249; this fact made it one of the earliest cohesive nation-states in Europe.

Few (if any) would dissent from the standpoint that Vitorino Magalhães Godinho is the most profound, lucid and innovative of the Portuguese historians dealing with the origins, development and progress of what are loosely but conveniently termed the Portuguese Discoveries. An economic historian with a keen eye for social and geopolitical factors, abreast with ongoing research and publication in many languages, his range and depth are evidenced by such works as *Estrutura da Antiga Sociedade Portuguesa* (3rd edition, Lisboa, 1977), *Os Descobrimentos e a Economia Mundial* (2 vols., Lisbon, 1963-1971). For those who cannot read Portuguese, an excellent synopsis of his views together with pertinent comments, is given by Malyn Newitt (ed.), *The First Portuguese Colonial Empire*, (University of Exeter, 1986, pp. 1-35).

One factor which perhaps has been insufficiently stressed in most accounts of Portuguese and Spanish maritime expansion is the lowly social position of sailors in the Iberian world of the Middle Ages and the Renaissance. In the religious processions participated in by working-class guilds, the sailors usually had to dispute over the bottom place with the cobblers, another despised if essential occupation. The soldier was always regarded as socially superior to the sailor, and the army officer superior to the naval officer, despite the sporadic efforts of the two

Iberian crowns to eradicate this invidious distinction, which lasted well into the 18th century. Portuguese accounts of voyages and shipwrecks, such as those included in the classic compilation edited by Bernardo Gomes de Brito, *História Trágica Marítima* (Lisboa, 2 vols., 1735-36), abound in pejorative remarks concerning sailors and their behaviour, or more frequently, their misbehaviour. Similar prejudices are evidenced in the writings of chroniclers, such as Diogo do Couto (1543-1616), who were experienced voyagers, as well as in land-based classical writers, such as Juan Luis Vives (1492-1540), who took care never to go to sea if they could help it. The word *marujo* was applied to 18th-century Luso-Brazilians as a pejorative term for the *reinois* or metropolitan Portuguese; and sensible women were strongly advised not to marry sailors.

The origins of the Portuguese Crown's policy of fomenting, patronizing or otherwise encouraging voyages of discovery have also been subjected to drastic revision in recent years, particularly through the works of Vitorino Magalhães Godinho and Luis de Albuquerque. The 19th-century idea, largely propagated by British writers, one of whom (R. H. Major) coined the term "Henry the Navigator", that the Infante Dom Henrique (1394-1460) with his nautical "School of Sagres" was the originator of this policy, has long been abandoned. The process was a long and complex one, but the Crown was involved, directly or indirectly, in all its stages. This involvement began with the contracting of the Genoese Admiral Manuel Pessanha (also spelled Pessagno or Pezagno), who entered the naval service of Portugal at the invitation of King Dom Diniz in 1317. The title of *Almirante* (Admiral) was borne by several members of this family down to 1397. Dom Henrique himself was more interested in crusading in Morocco (successfully at Ceuta in 1415, and disastrously at Tangier in 1437) than in organizing voyages of discovery in the Atlantic, although he did become involved in these as well, from a mixture of motives – religious, political, economic, and even astrological. Naturally enough, he never went on one of these voyages himself, which would have been *infra dignitatem* for a royal prince. But he encouraged and rewarded those members of his household who did, such as Gil Eanes, who rounded Cape Bojador in 1434. The voyages themselves were based primarily in the ports of Lagos and Faro, and not on the windswept promontory of Sagres. Lagos was the place where many of the best pilots and navigators were trained.

Overseas expansion was frequently hampered by rivalry between Portugal and Castile in the Iberian Peninsula itself. Both Portuguese and Castilian rulers were prone to intervene in each other's internal disputes, since the Portuguese were tempted by the idea of hegemony under the Portuguese Crown, whereas the Castilians naturally opted for the reverse. Frequent marriages between the two royal houses were also undertaken for this purpose; but the results seldom turned out as expected, since death intervened and prevented such projects from coming to fruition, as happened in 1497-1500, for example. The decisive stage came in 1479-1495.

The Treaty of Alcáçovas in the first-named year established peace between the two Crowns, on the basis of the King of Portugal renouncing all his rights to the Castilian Crown, and receiving in exchange several important concessions in Africa, with the Castilians withdrawing from some disputed areas.

King Dom João II (ruled 1481-1495) was an outstandingly successful Renaissance ruler, termed "the man" (el hombre) by his cousin Isabella of Castile. His own subjects called him Príncipe Perfeito, the "Perfect Prince". Three years after ascending the throne, Dom João had tamed the high feudal nobility by killing or banishing those of them who looked as if they might challenge his position, including his cousin and brother-in-law, the Duke of Viseu, whom the King stabbed to death with his own hand on August 28, 1484. There is no doubt that Dom João was influenced by events which happened elsewhere in Europe during this period, when King Louis XI in France and the Catholic Monarchs, Ferdinand and Isabella, in Castile reinforced the centralizing powers of the monarchy by abrogating long-standing feudal privileges and organizing an efficient bureaucracy. Professor A.H. de Oliveira Marques has argued (History of Portugal Vol. I, From Lusitania to Empire, Columbia University Press, 1972, p. 210) that

Dom João's policy probably sought its greatest support, not among the people, but rather among the lower ranks of the nobility. At the same time, he promoted many lawyers and civil servants to top positions until then reserved for the upper strata of the aristocracy. It is to King Dom João II rather than to Infante Dom Henrique or to anyone else that the creation of a comprehensive plan of discovery and overseas expansion should be credited. He, perhaps in consultation with his advisors, conceived the idea of reaching India by sea and concentrated his resources on this end, after Castilian rivalry had been fended off by the Treaty of Alcáçovas.

In 1482 John sent his first voyage of discovery to West Africa under the command of his squire Diogo Cão. The results were of great importance. In the time of a year and a half, Cão discovered most of the West African coast from Gabon to about 15 degrees south of the Equator. On a second voyage he went as far as 22° 10' S, almost reaching the Tropic of Capricorn (1485-86). He also explored the mouth of the Congo (Zaire), following the course of the river for a hundred miles as far as the Ielala waterfalls, where he left some inscriptions which are still preserved. This was an astonishing feat of navigation apart from anything else. On these and other voyages of discovery, the practice was begun of bringing from Portugal some stone pillars (padrões), surmounted by a cross and sculptured with the royal arms, leaving them at prominent landmarks, to mark Portuguese priority. Some have survived, and one of those relating to Diogo Cão's first expedition reads: "In the era of the World's creation 6681 years, of the Birth of Our Lord Jesus Christ 1482 years, the very high, excellent and powerful prince King João II of Portugal ordered this land to be discovered and these padrões to be erected by Diogo Cão, squire of his household" (A.H. de Oliveira Marques, History of Portugal, Vol. I, 1972, pp. 219-220). At the same period, Portuguese voyages of discovery were made westward into the Atlantic as far as Newfoundland, Labrador and perhaps Greenland. The first-named was called Terra de Bacalhau from the cod fisheries which were exploited there by the Portuguese until the French and English aggression drove them out.

In 1485 the King sent an ambassador, Vasco Fernandes de Lucena, to pronounce an "Oration of Obedience" to Pope Innocent VIII, which he did on December 11, 1485, and which was printed in Rome in Latin before the end of that year (Item 32). In the course of this oration, Lucena stated that the Portuguese had reached the Promontorium Prassum, which was stated by Ptolemy to be the southernmost part of Africa, "where the Arabian gulf begins". "Quippe cum emerso iam multo maximo Affricae ambitu prope prassum promontorium unde Arabicus incipit sinus superiori anno nostri appulerunt". (cf. the monograph by A. Fontoura da Costa, As Portas da India em 1484; Lisboa, Imprensa da Armada, 1936, p. 80, where the oration of Lucena is published in full, together with a Portuguese translation). However, the second voyage of Diogo Cão in 1485-86, when he sailed much further south down the West African coast, showed him that he still had not reached the southern extremity of Africa, with the result that he fell into disgrace and oblivion after his return to Portugal. Immediately on the return of Diogo Cão in 1486, King Dom João II ordered the preparation of three vessels to continue the discovery of the sea-route to Indian waters. Two of these vessels were caravels and the third a still smaller one designed to do service as a storeship. Command of the expedition was entrusted to Bartolomeu Dias, superintendent of the royal warehouse and a knight of the royal household. The expedition set sail at the end of July or early in August, 1487, and its progress has been studied in great detail by Eric Axelson (Southeast Africa, 1488-1530; London, 1940, pp. 12-22). After rounding the Cape of Good Hope, but well out of sight of it, the ships sailed up the coast as far as the Rio do Infante, probably identical with either the Keiskama or the Kowio River. Here the crew, exhausted and mutinous, compelled Dias to turn back, and on the homeward way discovered the cape that had recently been passed, where the southern trend of the continent changed to eastward. They sighted the Cape probably in April, 1488, when Dias gave it the name of Cabo de Boa Esperança. Pacheco Pereira, who accompanied Dias during the latter portion of the trip home, commented: "Nam sem muita rezam se pos nome a este promontorio Cabo de

Boa Esperança, porque Bartolomeu Dias, vendo que esta costa e ribeira do mar voltava a'ly em diante ao norte a ao nordeste – onde se mostrava e se esperava aver-se de descobrir-ha India por esta causa lhe pos nome Cabo de Boa Esperanca" ("It is not without reason that this promontory is named the Cape of Good Hope, because Bartolomeu Dias could see that this coast and shoreline turned thereafter towards the north and northeast – which showed, as they hoped, that they would have to discover India, and for this reason it received the name Cape of Good Hope").

It is true that the chronicler João de Barros stated that Dias had originally called this cape the Stormy Cape, but that King Dom João II, after receiving Dias' report, changed it to the Cape of Good Hope ". . . o grande e natural cabo ao qual Bartholomeu Diaz e os da sua companhia por causa dos perigos e tormentas que em dobrar delle passaram, lhe poseram nome Tormentosa; mas el Rey Dom Joam vindo elles ao Reyno lhe deu outro nome mais illustre, chamando-lhe Cabo de Boa Esperança, polla que elle prometia deste descubrimento da Índia tam esperada e por tantos annos requerida. O qual nome foy dado por el rey." (". . . the large natural cape to which Bartholomeu Dias and those of his company, because of the perils and storms they passed through in the course of rounding it, gave it the name Stormy Cape, but King Dom João, upon their return to the kingdom, gave it a different, more illustrious name, calling it the Cape of Good Hope, because its discovery promised to lead to the discovery of India, so hoped-for and demanded for so many years. That name was given by the king . . . .")

But the evidence of Pacheco Pereira on this point would seem to be better than that of Barros. In any event, what is certain is that it was mainly due to the persistence and energy of Dom João II in organizing these voyages that the seaway to India was finally opened; although the full achievement had to wait for Vasco da Gama's celebrated voyage in 1497-98.

Dom João II had a veritable passion for Africa and its products, whether these were human, animal, vegetable or mineral. He took a keen personal interest in the direction of the trade, reserving for the Crown the monopoly of importing gold, slaves, spices and ivory, and of exporting horses, carpets, English and Irish textiles, copper, lead, brass utensils, beads and bracelets. Private traders were allowed to import on payment of a licence, such less valuable articles as parrots, seals, monkeys, cotton and raffia textiles, etc. Subsequently the Crown leased the rights to import slaves and ivory to certain favoured individuals, but it always retained a strict monopoly of the gold. In reality, of course, this monopoly was not nearly as rigid and effective as it appeared to be on paper. It was impossible to prevent the crews of the ships from trading privately on their own account, to say nothing of the royal officials and agents themselves, and the inhabitants of the Cape Verde Islands. This West African trade had originally been driven mainly by ships equipped at Lagos and other ports of the Algarve. But by the end of the 16th century it was concentrated at Lisbon, where it was channelled through the *Casa da Mina* (House of the Mine). This establishment was a Crown office and warehouse situated on the ground floor of the royal palace by the waterfront on the river Tagus, where the King could personally watch the loading and unloading of the ships. Dom João II ordered the construction of a castle on the Gold Coast of Lower Guinea at a site called *A Mina* (The Mine), of which the foundation-stone was laid by Diogo de Azambuja in January, 1482. This favoured the development of fascinating cross-cultural artistic influences between both parties, a good idea of which can be obtained from the lavish catalogue, *Africa and the Renaissance: Art in Ivory* (edited by Ezio Bassani, William B. Fagg, Susan Vogel, Carol Thompson and Peter Mark) published by the Center for African Art, New York, 1988.

Dom João II also dispatched two emissaries to reach Ethiopia (the kingdom of the medieval "Prester John") by land. Disguised as merchants and speaking Arabic, Pero de Covilhã and Afonso de Paiva left Lisbon in May, 1487, travelling together until they reached Aden, via Alexandria, Cairo and Suez. Afonso de Paiva's fate is uncertain, but Pero de Covilhã reached India, where he visited several cities on the West Coast, then proceeding to Persia and East Africa. Back in Cairo again, he sent João II a detailed report of what he had seen and heard. He finally reached Ethiopia, where he settled down, married and died after 1526 (A.H. de Oliveira Marques, *History of Portugal*, I, pp. 220-221).

It is uncertain whether Covilhã's report ever reached Dom João II, for the evidence on this point is conflicting. If it did, then Dom João II had at his disposal a first-hand report about the spice trade in the Indian Ocean, and this would help to explain why Vasco da Gama was ordered to make for Calicut, then the most important Indian *entrepot* of the spice trade, on his voyage to India seven years later. On the other hand, Da Gama and his men were very surprised at the high degree of civilization attained by the Swahili city states of Mozambique, Mombasa and Malindi, which they visited on their epic voyage; whereas if Covilhã's report had reached Lisbon, the Portuguese should have been well-informed about these places, since Covilhã had visited them. Similarly, Da Gama on his arrival at Calicut was unable to distinguish properly between Hindu temples and Christian churches, something which Covilhã must surely have done and reported on after his lengthy visits to the trading-ports of Malabar. Finally, Da Gama was provided with the most trumpery presents for the ruler of Calicut, and the most unsuitable trade-goods – cloth, brass utensils and the like – to barter for the pepper and other spices which he sought; whereas Covilhã would certainly have reported that these could only be purchased with gold and silver specie.

Nine years elapsed after the return of Bartolomeu Dias from his voyage round the Cape of Good Hope until the departure of Vasco da Gama on his epic voyage of fulfillment. Many reasons have been advanced for this, all of them more or less speculative, as we do not know what the King and his councillors discussed confidentially. Among them may be cited the following:

a) The Crown was still awaiting news from Pero de Covilhã. There is no proof that this arrived (if it ever did) before the departure of Vasco da Gama.

b) The war in Morocco was going through a difficult phase, which obliged the Crown to send costly relief expeditions to the Portuguese coastal strongholds.

c) The ill-health of the King, which deteriorated after 1490, was further aggravated by the tragic death of his only son in a riding accident.

d) The discontent of sailors to endure such long voyages at such enormous distances from Portugal. There were incipient mutinies in the fleets of both Dias and Da Gama.

e) The opposition of some of the King's councillors, who were disquieted by such expensive voyages without any immediately profitable returns.

f) The Crown might have decided to delay the final voyage until after the conclusion of the Treaty of Tordesillas in June, 1494 (Item 63). This Treaty regulated the awkward situation which had arisen after the voyage of Christopher Columbus in 1492-93, in which he claimed that he had discovered the East Indies. The terms of this Treaty defined the respective spheres of influence of the Portuguese and Castilian Crowns, and the line of demarcation between them in the Atlantic Ocean.

g) This nine-year interval might also have been used by the Portuguese to make secret voyages in the South Atlantic, which led to the discovery of the "great arc". This meant utilizing the prevailing winds to avoid hugging the Southwest African coast and moving within sight of Brazil. This route was employed by Vasco da Gama on his pioneer voyage to India. The last explanation is the most plausible, but some or all of the other factors may have been involved as well. See the documented discussion in W. G. L. Randles, L'Image du Sud-Est Africain dans la littérature Européenne au XVIème Siècle (Centro de Estudos Históricos Ultramarinos, Lisboa, 1959, pp. 22-24).

When João II died in 1495, he had already appointed Vasco da Gama as the supreme commander of the decisive voyage. His successor, Dom Manuel, had tactfully kept a low profile during the reign of João II, and showed no resentment at the murder of his brother, the Duke of Viseu, or at the disgrace of the Braganzas. After ascending the throne, Dom Manuel continued his predecessor's policies in colonial expansion, but reversed his internal policies by pardoning and recalling the Braganzas to favour. Dom Manuel was rightly termed "The Fortunate" (o Venturoso), but although he was favoured by good luck, he skillfully made the most of his chances and further strengthened the authority of the Crown. This he did through extensive fiscal and administrative reforms, the details of which do not concern us here, but which had the effect of transforming Portugal into a bureaucratic and mercantilist state, controlled by an authoritarian ruler. Under pressure from the "Reyes Catholicos", Ferdinand and Isabella, Dom Manuel decreed the expulsion or the possible conversion of the Jews, but he modified this decree in practice by issuing another, prohibiting the genuineness of their conversion from being judicially investigated. He extensively revised and codified the existing laws, which were promulgated in the Ordenações Manuelinas (1512-1513-1521). Last, but by no means least, a couple of days after the return of the first of Da Gama's ships to the Tagus in July, 1499, King Manuel wrote a jubilant letter to Ferdinand and Isabella (Item 85), announcing that his discoverers had reached their goal in India, and had found great quantities of cloves, cinammon, pepper and other spices, besides "rubies and all kinds of precious stones".

The King also stated "that they also found lands in which there were mines of gold", probably an allusion to Southeast Africa. He further announced his intention of following up this voyage of discovery and wresting the control of the spice trade in the Indian Ocean from the Muslims by force of arms, with the aid of the newly-discovered Indian "Christians" (actually, Hindus). In this way, the existing Venetian-Muslim monopoly of the Levant trade in spices and in other Oriental luxury goods would be replaced by a Portuguese monopoly exercised via the sea route around the Cape of Good Hope.

Writing a few weeks later to the Cardinal-Protector of Portugal in Rome, the King urged him to obtain from the Pope confirmation of all the existing Bulls and Briefs by which the suzerainty and dominion over all these new-found lands had been granted to the Crown of Portugal in perpetuity. In this letter to Rome, dated August 28, 1499, the King entitled himself as follows: "Our King Dom Manuel, by the grace of God, King of Portugal and of the Algarves on this side of and beyond the sea in Africa, and Lord of Guinea and of the conquest of the navigation and commerce of Ethiopia, Arabia, Persia and India." A note of triumph which was perfectly excusable and understandable in the circumstances.

Chronology of Portuguese Discoveries 1415-1616

by Francisco Contente Domingues

1415: Conquest of Ceuta

1424: Expedition to the Canaries by Dom Fernando de Castro

1425: Beginning of the "peopling" of Madeira

1425/8 : Travels of the Infante Dom Pedro through Europe

1427: Discovery of the Azores by Diogo de Silves

1434: Gil Eanes rounds Cape Bojador

1436: Afonso Gonçalves Baldaia arrives at the Gold River and Galley Rock in Africa

c. 1441: Special type of Latin caravel comes into use in the Portuguese discoveries

1444: Dias Dinis reaches Cape Verde and the island of Bezeguiche in Africa

c. 1445: probable beginnings of Portuguese cartography, according to Charles Verlinden

1453: Gomes Eanes de Zurara, *Crónica da Guiné*

1460: Death of the Infante Dom Henrique "The Navigator", promoter and organizer of the first Portuguese voyages of discovery and colonization
- discovery of the Cape Verde archipelago, near African cape of the same name

1469: Portuguese Crown makes contract with Fernão Gomes, who promises to explore the West African coast in exchange for private commercial rights

1471: Discovery of the islands of São Tomé and Príncipe

1474: Infante Dom João (future D. João II) assumes direction of the exploration of Africa

1479: Treaty of Alcáçovas

1481/2 : First voyage of Diogo Cão down the African coast

1482: Construction of the castle of São Jorge da Mina (coast of Ghana): permanent Portuguese trading post

1483/4 : Second voyage of Diogo Cão (?)

1485: In an *Obedience Oration* proferred before the new Pope, Innocent VIII, in the name of the King of Portugal, Vasco Fernandes de Lucena announces that Portuguese navigators are on the verge of reaching India

c. 1485: First known Portuguese map with maker's signature (Pedro Reinel)

1485/6 : Third voyage of Diogo Cão (?)

1487: Two agents of Dom João II, Pero da Covilhã and Afonso de Paiva, depart by land for Asia, in search of information about the commerce and maritime route to India

1487/8 : Voyage of Bartolomeu Dias, who for the first time rounds the extreme southern tip of Africa

1489: Pêro da Covilhã arrives in Goa

1492: João Fernandes and Pêro de Barcelos discover the peninsula of Labrador
- Martim Behaim's World Globe
- First Portuguese map with maker's signature and date: Jorge de Aguiar

1493: Bull *Inter Caetera* of Pope Alexander VI, dividing the Atlantic between Portugal and Castile

1494: Treaty of Tordesillas: Portugal and Castile re-divide the Atlantic world between themselves

1496: Abraão Zacuto, *Perpetual Almanac*, first edition (two printings), Leiria (Portugal)

1497/9: Voyage of Vasco da Gama, establishing for the first time the maritime connection between Europe and India

1500: Discovery of Brazil by Pedro Álvares Cabral
- Letter of Pêro Vaz de Caminha to the King of Portugal, Dom Manuel I, giving an account of the finding of Brazil

1500/1: Navigation to the New World by Gaspar Corte Real

1501/2 : First voyage of Gonçalo Coelho to reconnoitre the coast of Brazil, with participation of Amerigo Vespucci

1502: World map commissioned by Alberto Cantino, the first Portuguese map to show Brazil; also the first to show the Equator and the tropics.

1503/4: Second voyage of Gonçalo Coelho to Brazil

1504: Nautical chart of Pedro Reinel which introduces, for the first time, a scale of latitudes

1505/8: Duarte Pacheco Pereira, *Esmeraldo de situ orbis*

1507: Fracanzano da Montalboddo publishes a collection of voyages under the title *Paesi nuovamente retrovati*

c. 1509: "Munich" *Nautical Guide* published

1513: Arrival of the Portuguese in China

1514: *Book of Seamanship* of João de Lisboa

c. 1516: "Évora" *Nautical Guide* published

1519: Departure of the armada of Fernão de Magalhães, Portuguese navigator in the service of Spain; one of its ships, the "Victória", returns in 1522, having made the first ocean voyage around the world

1530: Departure of the first colonizing expedition to Brazil, under the command of Martim Afonso de Sousa

1530/2 : Pero Lopes de Sousa, *Diary of the Navigation of the Coast of Brazil*

1531: Founding of São Vicente, first Portuguese municipality in Brazil

1534: Brazil is divided into Captaincies

1536 (?): Dom João de Castro, *Treatise on the Globe*

1537: Pedro Nunes, *Treatise on the Globe*

1538/41: *Rutters* of D. João de Castro

1540 : Francisco Álvares, *Truthful Information on the Lands of Prester John of the Indies*

1542 : João Rodrigues Cabrilho, Portuguese navigator in the service of Spain, explores the coast of California

1543: Arrival of the Portuguese in Japan

1549: Arrival of the first Governor-General in Brazil
- Manuel da Nóbrega, *Information on the lands of Brazil*

1550: Publication of Giovanni Battista Ramusio's compendium of accounts of voyages, *Delle navigatione et viaggi*

1551: Fernão Lopes de Castanheda, *History of the discovery and conquest of India by the Portuguese*

1552: João de Barros, *Ásia - Década I*

1566: Works of the Portuguese mathematician, Pedro Nunes, published in Basel

c. 1570: Fernando Oliveira, *Ars nautica*, first European encyclopedia of naval matters

1570: Law prohibiting the enslavement of Brazilian Indians (dated March 20)

c. 1580: Fernando Oliveira, *Book of the construction of naus*, first text written in Portuguese on shipbuilding

1587: Gabriel Soares de Sousa, *News of Brazil and truthful description of the coast of that state*

1614: Publication of the *Peregrinations* of Fernão Mendes Pinto, the best-known account of voyages and adventures of the epoch of the Portuguese discoveries

1616: Manuel Fernandes, *Book of carpentry drawings*

Selected Bibliography
by Francisco Contente Domingues

Ackerlind, Sheila R., *King Dinis of Portugal and the Alfonsine heritage*. New York: Peter Lang, 1990.

Albuquerque, Luís de, *Curso de História da Náutica*. Coimbra: Livraria Almedina, 1972.

Idem, *Os guias náuticos de Munique e Évora*. Lisboa: Junta de Investigações do Ultramar, 1965.

Idem, *Introdução à história dos descobrimentos*, 3ª ed. Mem-Martins: Publicações Europa-América, 1983.

Idem, *Navegadores, viajantes e aventureiros portugueses. Séculos XV e XVI*, 2 vols. Lisboa: Círculo de Leitores, 1987/Lisboa: Caminho, 1987.

Idem, *Portuguese books on nautical science from Pedro Nunes to 1650*. Lisboa: Instituto de Investigação Científica Tropical, 1984.

Anselmo, António Joaquim, *Bibliografia das obras impressas em Portugal no século XVI*. Lisboa: Biblioteca Nacional, 1926. Re-edition, Lisboa: Telles da Silva, 1977.

Bacon, Leonard (translation, introduction and notes), *The Lusiads of Luiz de Camões*. New York: The Hispanic Society of America, 1950.

Boorstin, Daniel J., *The discoverers*. New York: Random House, 1983.

Bowditch, Nathaniel, *American pratical navigator: an epitome of navigation*, 2 vols. Washington D.C.: Defense Mapping Agency Hydrographic Center, 1975-1977. Pub. Nº 9.

Boxer, Charles R., *The Portuguese seaborne empire 1415-1825*. New York: Alfred A. Knopf, 1969. Portuguese translation: *O império colonial português*. Lisboa: Edições 70, 1981.

Brown, Lloyd A., *The story of maps*. Boston: Little, Brown, 1949.

Calahan, Harold Augustin, *The sky and the sailor: a history of celestial navigation*. New York: Harper & Brothers, 1952.

Chiappelli, Fredi (ed.), *First images of America: the impact of the New World on the Old*, 2 vols. Berkeley: University of California Press, 1976.

Cortesão, Armando/Albuquerque, Luís (eds.), *Obras completas de D. João de Castro*, 4 vols. Coimbra: Academia Internacional de Cultura Portuguesa, 1968-1982.

Cotter, Charles H., *A history of nautical astronomy*. New York: American Elsevier Publishing Company, 1968.

Davenport, Frances Gardiner, *European treaties bearing on the history of the United States and its dependencies to 1648*. Reprint, Gloucester MA: Peter Smith, 1967.

Dias, José Sebastião da Silva, *Os descobrimentos e a problemática cultural do século XVI*, 2ª ed. Lisboa: Presença, 1982.

Idem, *Camões no Portugal de Quinhentos*. Lisboa: Instituto de Cultura e Língua Portuguesa, 1981.

Diffie, Bailey W./Winius, George D., *Foundations of the Portuguese empire 1415-1580*. Minneapolis: University of Minnesota Press, 1977. Portuguese translation: *A fundação do império português 1415-1580*, 1º vol., Lisboa: Vega, 1989 (2º vol. in press).

Domingues, Francisco Contente/Guerreiro, Inácio, *A vida a bordo na Carreira da Índia (século XVI)*. Lisboa: Instituto de Investigação Científica Tropical, 1988.

Esparteiro, António Marques, *Dictionary of naval terms, English-Portuguese*. Lisboa: Centro de Estudos de Marinha, 1974.

Idem, *Dicionário de marinha português-inglês*. Lisboa: Centro de Estudos de Marinha, 1975.

Faria, Francisco Leite de, *Estudos bibliográficos sobre Damião de Góis e a sua época*. Lisboa: Secretaria de Estado da Cultura, 1977.

Guedes, Max Justo, *O descobrimento do Brasil*, 2ª ed. Lisboa: Vega, 1989.

Idem (dir.), *História naval brasileira*, vol. I em 2 tomos. Rio de Janeiro: Ministério da Marinha-Serviço de Documentação Geral da Marinha, 1975.

Harley, J. B./Woodward, David, *The history of cartography, vol. 1: Cartography in prehistoric, ancient and medieval Europe and Mediterranean*. Chicago: The University of Chicago Press, 1987.

Hewson, J. B., *A history of the practice of navigation*, rev. ed. Glasgow: Brown, Son & Ferguson, 1963.

Lucena, Vasco Fernandes de, *The obedience of a king of Portugal*, translated with a commentary by Francis M. Rogers. Minneapolis: University of Minnesota Press, 1958.

Mauro, Frédéric, *Le Portugal, le Brésil et l'Atlantique au XVIIème. siècle (1570-1670)*, 2ème ed. Paris: Fondation Calouste Gulbenkian-Centre Culturel Portugais, 1983. Portuguese translation: *Portugal, o Brasil e o Atlântico 1570-1670*, 2 vols., Lisboa: Estampa, 1989.

Morison, Samuel Eliot, *The European discovery of America: the northern voyages A.D. 500-1600*. New York: Oxford University Press, 1971.

Idem, *The European discovery of America: the southern voyages A.D. 1492-1616*. New York: Oxford University Press, 1974.

Idem, *Portuguese voyages to America in the fifteenth century*. Cambridge MA: Harvard University Press, 1974.

Mota, Avelino Teixeira da, *Portuguese navigations in the north Atlantic in the fifteenth and sixteenth centuries*. St. John's (Newfoundland): Memorial University of Newfoundland, 1965.

Parry, John H., *The age of reconnaissance*. Cleveland: World Publishing Company, 1963/ New York: Mentor Books, 1963.

Idem, *The discovery of the sea*. New York: Dial Press, 1974.

Penrose, Boies, *Travel and discovery in the Renaissance 1420-1620*. Cambridge MA: Harvard University Press, 1952.

Reis, A. Estácio dos, *O quadrante náutico*. Lisboa: Instituto de Investigação Científica Tropical, 1988.

Rogers, Francis M., *Atlantic islanders of the Azores and Madeira*. Cambridge MA: Harvard University Press, 1952.

Idem, *The quest for Eastern Christians: travels and rumor in the Age of Discovery*. Minneapolis: University of Minnesota Press, 1962.

Idem, *The travels of the Infante Dom Pedro of Portugal*. Cambridge MA: Harvard University Press, 1961.

Taylor, E. G. R., *The haven-finding art: a history of navigation from Odysseus to Captain Cook*, new enlarged edition. New York: American Elsevier Publishing Company, 1971.

Warner, Deborah J., *The sky explored: celestial cartography 1500-1800*. New York: Alan R. Liss / Amsterdam: Theatrum Orbis Terrarum, 1979.

Washburn, Wilcomb, *The first European contacts with the American Indians*. Lisboa: Instituto de Investigação Científica Tropical, 1988.

Idem, *Representation of unknown lands in XIV-, XV- and XVI-century cartography*. Lisboa: Junta de Investigações do Ultramar, 1969.

Waters, David W., *The art of navigation in England in Elizabethan and early Stuart times*, 2nd ed. rev., Greenwich (UK): National Maritime Museum, 1978.

Lenders to the Exhibition and Photographic Sources

Belgium
Musées Royaux des Beaux-Arts de Belgique: 101

Brazil
Biblioteca Nacional, Rio de Janeiro: 107, 140, 159
Instituto Histórico e Geográfico Brasileiro, Rio de Janeiro: 134, 135, 136
Mapoteca, Ministério das Relações Exteriores, Rio de Janeiro: 137
Museu de Arte Sacra de Santos: 108
Museu Nacional de Belas Artes, Fundaçao Nacional Pro-Memória: 138
Serviço de Documentação Geral da Marinha, Rio de Janeiro: page 114

Denmark
National Museum, Copenhagen: 47

England
The National Maritime Museum, Greenwich: 11
The British Library: 16, 24, 25, 26, 28, 36
Whipple Museum of the History of Science, University of Cambridge: 13

Federal Republic of Germany
Bayerische Staatsgemäldesammlungen, Munich: 139
Herzog August Bibliothek Wolfenbüttel: 64
Staatliche Museen Preussischer Kulturbesitz, Kupferstichkabinett, Berlin: 133
Württembergische Landesbibliothek, Stuttgart: 112

France
Archives Départementaux de la Gironde, Bordeaux: 27
Bibliothèque de l'Assemblée Nationale, Paris: 6
Bibliothèque Nationale, Paris: 2, 10, 30, 77, 119, 125, 154, 155
Musées Départementaux de la Seine Maritime, Rouen: 130

Holland
Royal Library, The Hague: 120

Portugal
Academia de Ciências de Lisboa: 44
Arquivo Histórico Ultramarino, Lisbon: 102, 132
Arquivo Nacional da Torre do Tombo, Lisbon: 45, 57, 58, 60, 61, 62, 63, 65, 66, 67, 69, 71, 75, 76, 82, 88, 90, 91, 94, 99, 100, 103, 109, 121
Biblioteca da Ajuda, Lisbon: 20, 97, 127

Biblioteca Geral da Universidade de Coimbra: 17
Biblioteca Nacional, Lisbon: 9, 18, 19, 105, 110, 123, 150
Biblioteca Pública e Arquivo Distrital de Évora: 4, 5, 104, 111, 126
Comissão Nacional para as Comemoraçõs dos Descobrimentos Portugueses, Lisbon: 15, 21, 152
Museu Nacional de Etnologia, Lisbon: 84
Museu Grão Vasco, Viseu: 129
Museu Nacional de Arte Antiga, Lisbon: 42
Palácio Nacional da Ajuda, Lisbon: 83
Sociedade de Geografia de Lisboa: 87
Superior Geral da Sociedade Missionaria de Cucujaes: 85, 86

Scotland
Dundee Art Galleries and Museums: 12

Spain
Archivo General de Indias, Seville: 59, 72, 73
Biblioteca Nacional, Madrid: 2, 7, 74, 149

United States
Anonymous Lender: 1, 68, 80
Cleveland Public Library: 31
Houghton Library, Harvard University: 33, 35, 37, 79, 153
James Ford Bell Library, University of Minnesota: 23, 29, 32, 34, 46
John Carter Brown Library at Brown University: 8, 38, 39, 95, 106, 148, 161
Lilly Library, Indiana University: 151
The Peabody Museum of Salem: 14
Smithsonian Institution, Washington DC: 22
The Beineke Rare Book and Manuscript Library, Yale University: 96
The New York Public Library (photographs by Robert D. Rubic): 3, 40, 41, 48, 49, 50, 51 (exhibition item loaned by John Carter Brown Library), 52, 53, 54, 55, 56, 70, 78, 81 (exhibition item courtesy of James Ford Bell Library), 92, 93, 113, 115, 116, 117, 118, 124, 128, 131, 141, 142, 143, 144, 147, 156, 157, 160
The Newberry Library, Chicago: 122, 145, 146
Courtesy of The Pierpont Morgan Library, New York (photographs by David Loggie): 43, 89, 98, 158

Unexhibited Items that Appear in the Catalogue

Denmark
National Museum, Copenhagen: pages 216, 217, 218

France:
Bibliothèque Nationale, Paris: pages 35-35

Italy:
Biblioteca Apostolica Vaticana: pages 156-158
Biblioteca Estense, Modena: pages 147-149
Biblioteca Marciana, Venice: pages 36-37
Biblioteca Nazionale Centrale, Florence: pages 56-57

Portugal:
Biblioteca Nacional, Lisbon: pages 150-151

United States:
The Beinecke Rare Book and Manuscript Library, Yale University: pages 38-39
The New York Public Library: pages 238, 239